ESSENTIALS OF THE INTERNET

ESSENTIALS OF THE INTERNET

Gretchen Marx / *Robert T. Grauer*

Saint Joseph College   University of Miami

Prentice Hall, Upper Saddle River, New Jersey 07458

Acquisitions editor: Carolyn Henderson
Editorial/production supervisor: Greg Hubit Bookworks
Interior and cover design: Suzanne Behnke
Senior manufacturing supervisor: Paul Smolenski
Editorial assistant: Audrey Regan

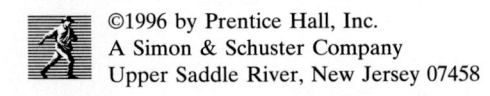

©1996 by Prentice Hall, Inc.
A Simon & Schuster Company
Upper Saddle River, New Jersey 07458

All rights reserved. No part of this book may be
reproduced, in any form or by any means,
without permission in writing from the publisher.

Printed in the United States of America
10 9 8 7 6 5 4 3 2 1

ISBN 0-13-588971-5

Prentice Hall International (UK) Limited, *London*
Prentice Hall of Australia Pty. Limited, *Sydney*
Prentice Hall of Canada Inc., *Toronto*
Prentice Hall Hispanoamericano, S.A., *Mexico*
Prentice Hall of India Private Limited, *New Delhi*
Prentice Hall of Japan, Inc., *Tokyo*
Simon & Schuster Asia Pte. Ltd., *Singapore*
Editora Prentice Hall do Brasil, Ltda., *Rio de Janeiro*

Contents

1

Introduction to the Internet: Welcome to Cyberspace 1

CHAPTER OBJECTIVES 1
OVERVIEW 1
The Internet 2
What You Will Find on the Internet 3
    Sending and Receiving E-Mail 3   Using a Web Browser 5   Gopher and FTP 7   Conversing on the Internet 12   Netiquette, Safe Surfing, and Other Issues 14   Web Publishing with HTML 16
Connecting to the Internet 17
How the Internet Works 20
    The TCP/IP Protocol 21   Internet Architecture Layers 22
    The Domain Name System 24   Internet Addresses 24
Learning by Doing 25
HANDS-ON EXERCISE 1: WELCOME TO CYBERSPACE 26
Summary 30
Key Words and Concepts 31
Multiple Choice 31
Exploring the Internet 33
Practice with the Internet 36
Case Studies 36

2

Global Communication on the Internet: Using E-mail 39

CHAPTER OBJECTIVES 39
OVERVIEW 39

E-mail 40
    The Structure of an E-Mail Message 40   Logins and Security 42
    Mailboxes 42

Sending and Receiving E-Mail 44
    E-Mail Using a POP Mail Client 44

Learning by Doing 46
HANDS-ON EXERCISE 1: WELCOME TO E-MAIL WITH PC EUDORA 46
E-Mail with a Unix Mail Program 55
HANDS-ON EXERCISE 2: E-MAIL USING PINE 56
Additional E-Mail Capabilities 60
    Distribution Lists 60   Customizing Your Signature 60   Personal Mail
    Folders 61

Mailing Lists 62
    Finding Mailing Lists 63   Subscribing to a List 63   Subscription
    Options 64

HANDS-ON EXERCISE 3: CUSTOMIZING E-MAIL
AND SUBSCRIBING TO MAILING LISTS USING A PC MAIL CLIENT 64
HANDS-ON EXERCISE 4: CUSTOMIZING E-MAIL
AND SUBSCRIBING TO MAILING LISTS USING PINE 71

Summary 77
Key Words and Concepts 77
Multiple Choice 78
Exploring the Internet 80
Practice with E-Mail 82
Case Studies 84

3

Finding Things on the World Wide Web: Netscape and Lynx 85

CHAPTER OBJECTIVES 85
OVERVIEW 85

The World Wide Web 86
Netscape 88
    The Uniform Resource Locator (URL) 88   Hypertext Transport Protocol
    (HTTP) 89   Hypertext Markup Language (HTML) 91   Saving and
    Printing Web Documents 92   Bookmarks 93

Learning by Doing 94
HANDS-ON EXERCISE 1: SURFING THE NET 94
Web Search Engines 100
    Search Rules and Techniques 103   And, Or, and Not 106
Other Browser Capabilities 106
    To Load or Not to Load Images 106   Using E-Mail in Netscape 107
HANDS-ON EXERCISE 2: SEARCHING THE WEB AND USING ADDITIONAL NETSCAPE FEATURES 108
Lynx 114
HANDS-ON EXERCISE 3: USING LYNX ON THE WORLD WIDE WEB 115
Summary 122
Key Words and Concepts 122
Multiple Choice 123
Exploring the Internet 125
Practice with the World Wide Web 127
Case Studies 128

INDEX

INTRODUCTION TO THE INTERNET: WELCOME TO CYBERSPACE

OBJECTIVES

After reading this chapter you will be able to:

1. Describe the Internet and its history.
2. Describe some of the services and resources available on the Internet, and identify which of these are available at your college or university.
3. Define the TCP/IP protocol; explain in general terms how data is sent across the Internet.
4. Define the domain name system of Internet addresses; show how your Internet address adheres to the conventions within the domain name system.
5. Explain how to access the Internet in your campus computing environment.

OVERVIEW

The Internet. You see the word on the cover of half the magazines on the newsstand. The media make continual reference to the Information Highway. Movie ads provide Internet addresses so you can download and view movie clips. Your friends at other colleges want to know your Internet e-mail address. But what exactly is the Internet, and how do you use it? In this chapter we answer both of these questions.

After a brief discussion of how the Internet came to be, we describe the many services and resources available on the Net. Most of what you will want to do on the Internet can be done using Windows-based PC software applications, which handle the complicated task of connecting to the computer network on your campus, and from there to the Internet. We discuss how this is done, and how the Internet itself works. From there you will start your journey into cyberspace by learning how to connect to the Internet in your campus computing environment.

THE INTERNET

The Internet is a network of networks that connects computers across the country and around the world. It grew out of a U.S. Department of Defense (DOD) experimental project begun in 1969 to test the feasibility of a wide area (long distance) computer network over which scientists and military personnel could share messages and data. The network had to work regardless of where the users were or the type of computer they were using. The DOD imposed the additional requirement that the network be able to function with partial outages in times of national emergency, when one or more computers in the network might be down.

The proposed solution was to create a network with no central authority. Each *node* (computer attached to the network) would be equal to all other nodes, with the ability to originate, pass, and receive messages. The path that a particular message took in getting to its destination would be insignificant. Only the final result was important, as the message would be passed from node to node until it arrived at its destination.

The experiment was (to say the least) successful. Known originally as the ***ARPAnet (Advanced Research Projects Agency),*** the original network of four computers has grown exponentially to include millions of computers at virtually every major U.S. university and government agency, and an ever increasing number of private corporations and international sites. To say that the Internet is large is a gross understatement, but by its very nature, it's impossible to determine just how large it really is. At the time this book went to press, a commonly accepted estimate was 36 million users worldwide. Recent figures indicate it is growing at 15% per month, which means it is doubling every seven months!

The Internet, as described, is a network of networks. However, if that was all it were, there would hardly be so much commotion over it. It's what the user can *do* on the Internet that makes it so exciting, rather than the hardware and software of which it is composed. No longer confined to the Pentagon and DOD, the Internet brings a worldwide library of on-line information resources on a seemingly limitless number of topics to anyone connected to it. All you need to access data anywhere on the Internet is a computer connected to it, and a username and password, which you will get from your college or university data center or LAN administrator. (If you are dialing into your campus network or a commercial service provider from a remote computer, you will need special hardware and software, which is described in Appendix A: Remote Access to the Internet.)

What can you do on the Internet? The primary capabilities are information retrieval and worldwide communication, two functions already provided by postal systems, libraries, print media, telephones, television, and other types of long distance media. Three characteristics, when taken together, set the Internet apart from these other information and communication technologies. The first two are the immediacy and global nature of the medium. When you request a document or send an e-mail message, the transmission begins almost instantly. And it doesn't matter if the document or message is coming from across the world or two blocks away.

The other defining characteristic of the Internet is the personal, two-way nature of much of the communication. Television has the capability to send information globally in real time (while events are unfolding). Yet you don't control the content or the timing of the message sent by the television studio. On the Internet users control the services and the content of the messages. You can search for resources of interest to you and request them whenever you want. You can create your own documents to put on the Internet. You can determine what is

EXPLORING THE INTERNET

newsworthy and create information that can be accessed by any other authorized user, anywhere on the globe.

Writing and sending a message to thousands of people around the world at the same time instantly—that's heady stuff. Being able to request a picture of 5th century B.C. antiquities from a museum in Sardinia, and getting it instantly without leaving your chair—that's amazing. Retrieving satellite images of a meteor crashing into Jupiter, *while it is actually happening*—that's awe inspiring!

WHAT YOU WILL FIND ON THE INTERNET

At the time the Internet was created, the primary objective of its developers was to be able to send and receive files from any computer to any other computer on the Net. A second desirable objective was the ability to log into a remote computer as though the user were actually physically attached to it. From there the use of the Internet expanded to *e-mail,* which is the passing of electronic messages through a network. These services required the user to know and understand the sometimes complex syntax of computer commands. The services were generally limited to forwarding files, which meant that graphics, sound, and video resources could not be viewed on the Net. Accounts were available only to government employees and scientists and researchers at major universities. The legislation creating the Internet prohibited the use of the network for commercial purposes.

In the 1970s and '80s membership in the Internet community was expanded to include smaller colleges, international sites, and commercial organizations that were involved in the computer and networking industries. Services were expanded to include the ability to search for documents by using menu-driven programs instead of commands. Eventually graphics files became accessible, and easy-to-use Windows interfaces, which provided point-and-click access, were designed. These resources and programs attracted a flood of new users, so that by the early 1990s the Internet was no longer the exclusive province of computer scientists, physicists, and mathematicians. In addition, commercial access was expanded to include any company that wanted to pay for a site on the Internet.

Anyone with a PC and an Internet connection can travel through **cyberspace,** the term coined to describe the invisible realm of the Internet universe. College students, families, employees of businesses and nonprofit organizations—all are now **surfing** the Net, sending messages, retrieving files, and visiting remote sites to find information. To become an accomplished **Internaut,** or Internet explorer, you will want to try using as many of these services as you have available at your college or university.

Sending and Receiving E-mail

Electronic mail is available in many forms, some of which are limited to internal mail on your campus network. The focus of our discussion will be the tools that let you send and receive e-mail using the Internet. As with many other Internet applications, there are menu-based e-mail services that require the user to know a series of commands to use e-mail. Other e-mail programs run in a Windows environment and provide the user a **graphical user interface (GUI).** (GUIs provide pull-down menus and icons that allow the user to invoke commands by using a mouse and/or keyboard shortcuts.) Figure 1.1 shows the same e-mail message using (a) a menu-based system called Pine, and (b) a Windows-based mail program, PC Eudora.

Message —

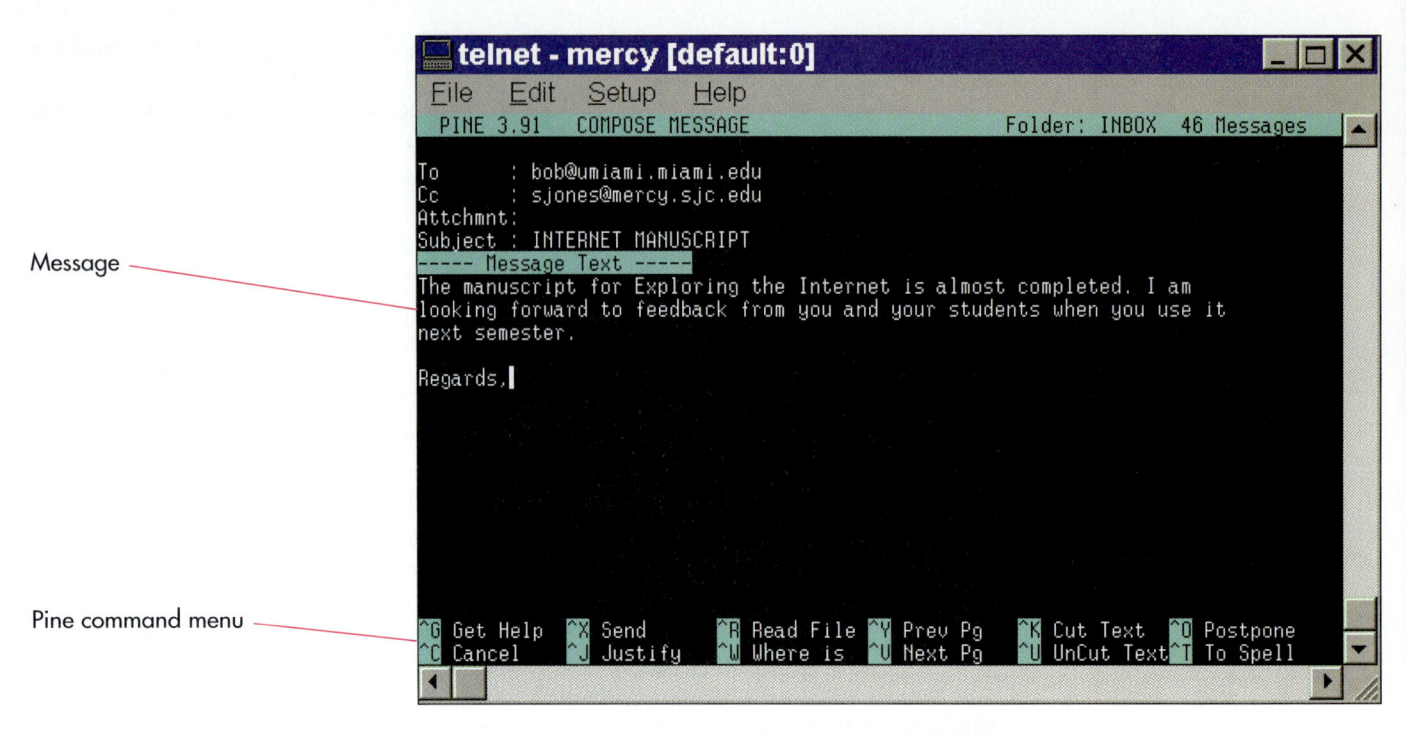

Pine command menu —

(a) An E-mail Message in Pine

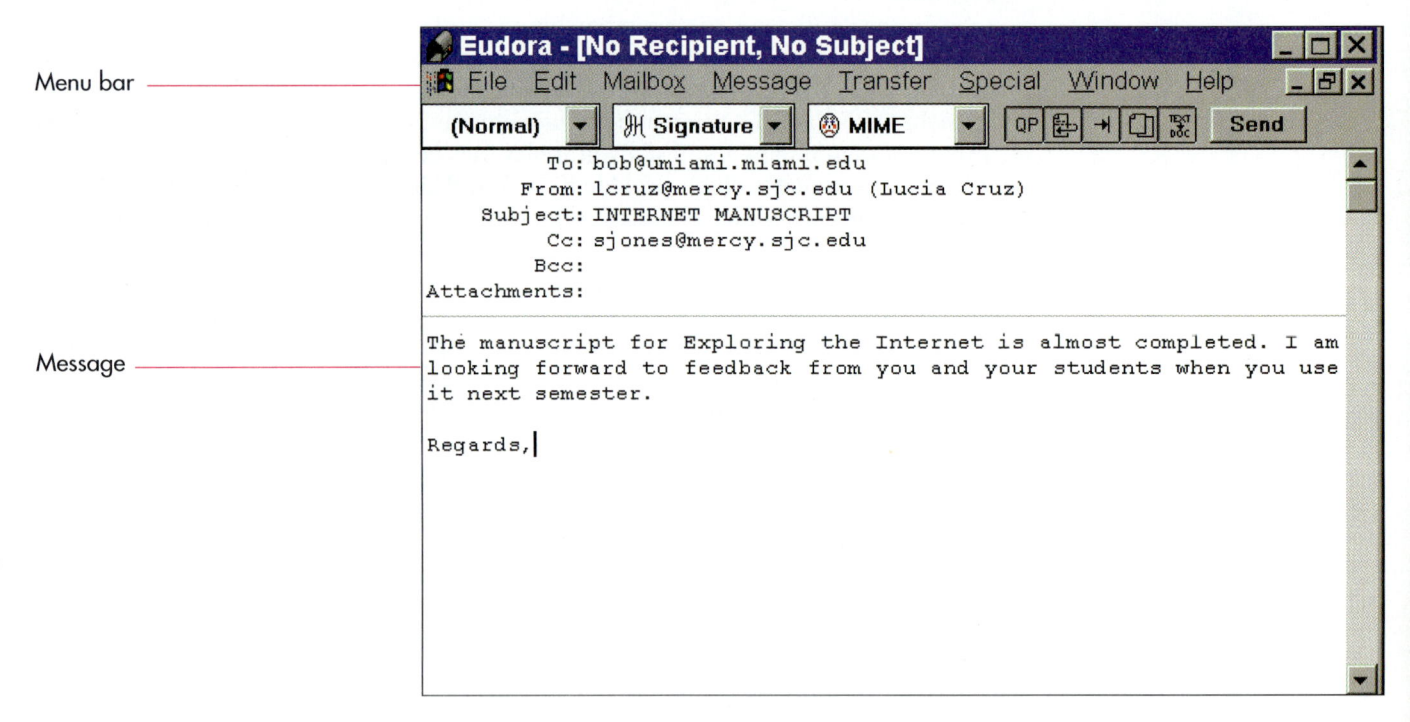

Menu bar —

Message —

(b) An E-mail Message in Eudora

FIGURE 1.1 E-mail

You will experience both types of e-mail interfaces in Chapter 2, and will perform special e-mail functions such as replying to a message and creating a distribution list to send mail to more than one person. Internet e-mail also lets you sign up to an electronic mailing list on a specific topic, so you can participate in ongoing discussions on that subject with other subscribers around the world. You will learn how to retrieve the global list of the mailing lists so you can choose one, to which you will then subscribe. After subscribing, you can expect to receive lots of mail!

Using a Web Browser

The resources on the Internet are vast and fascinating. You will find yourself wanting to browse through these resources just as you might browse through your local library or bookstore reading a page from a book or magazine here, a chapter there. In the beginning you had to know the correct commands in many different programs to access the resources you wanted. Furthermore, those resources were not cataloged or indexed globally, so you had to search through many different archives to locate the information for which you were looking. In 1991 a new way of organizing Internet resources, called the **World Wide Web,** was developed. The Web, as it is often called, provides a way to locate a file on the Internet, regardless of where it is stored, or what type of resource it is.

You can meander through the Web using a GUI interface called, aptly enough, a **browser.** Two of the most widely used Web browsers, **Mosaic** and **Netscape,** are shown in Figures 1.2a and 1.2b, respectively. Since many users do not have access to GUI browsers (primarily because of the extensive hardware requirements), the University of Kansas developed a text-based browser called **Lynx.** Lynx provides much of the functionality of the GUI browsers, but lacks the ability to display graphics. Figure 1.2c shows the Web document found in Figure 1.2b as it appears using Lynx.

(a) A Mosaic Document

FIGURE 1.2   Web Browsers

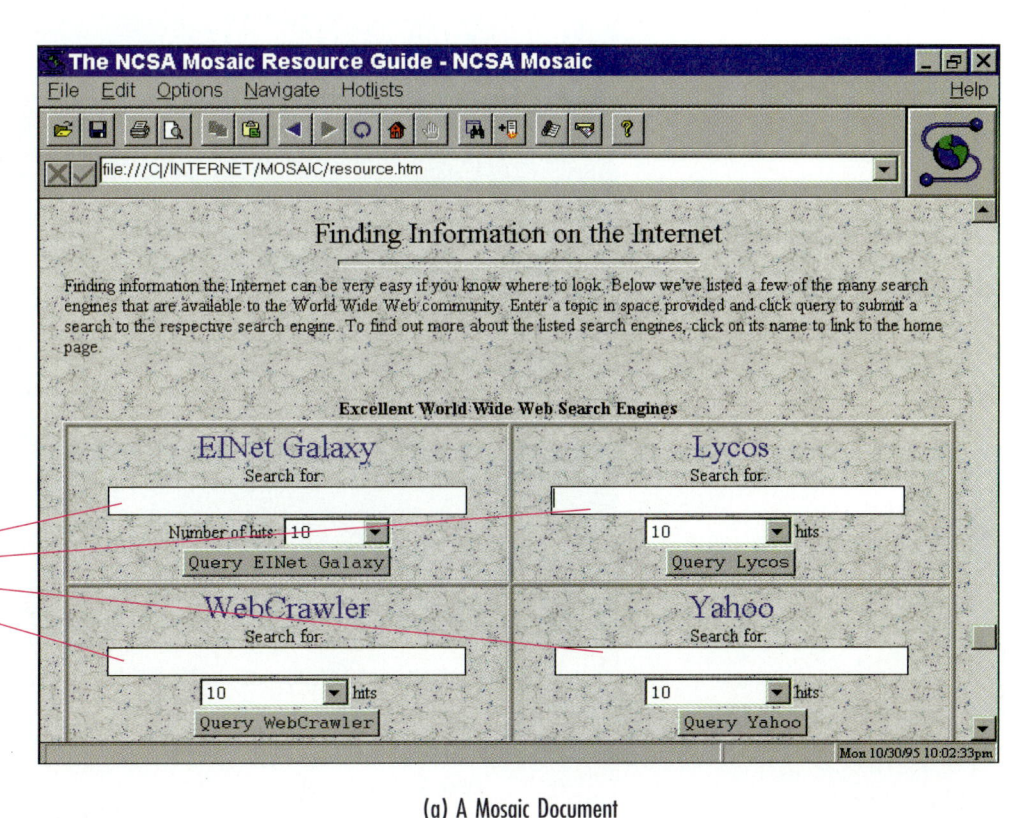

Graphic images

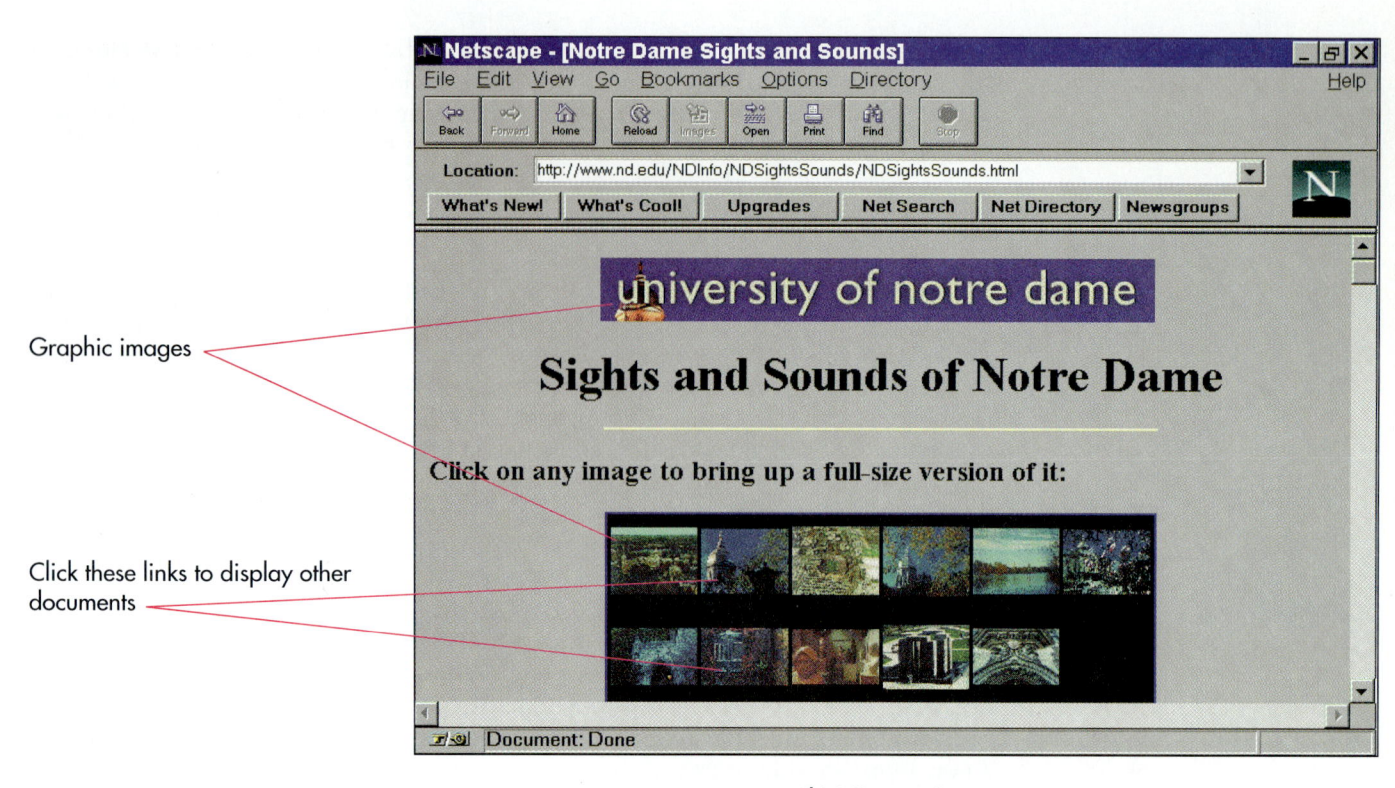

Click these links to display other documents

(b) A Netscape Screen

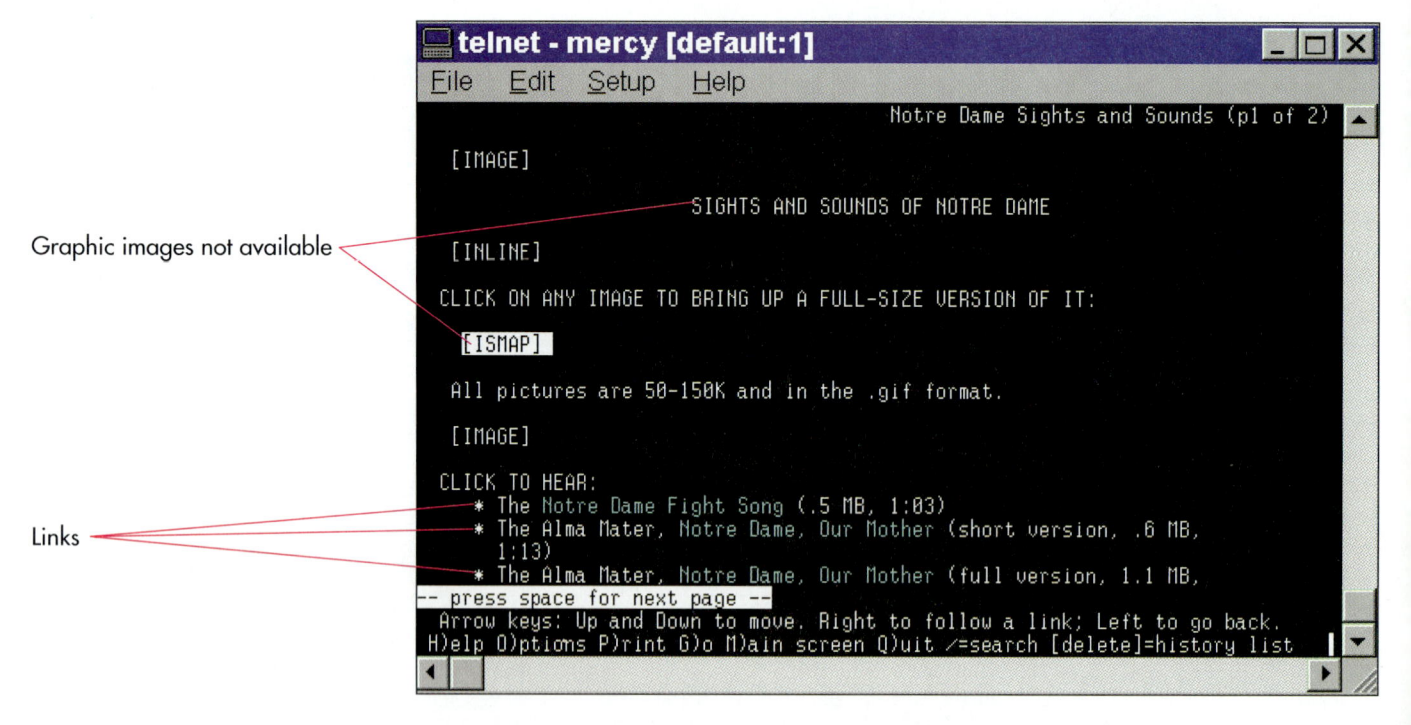

Graphic images not available

Links

(c) A Lynx Document

FIGURE 1.2 Web Browsers (continued)

6 EXPLORING THE INTERNET

Documents created for the World Wide Web contain embedded *links* to other documents. You simply select (click) a link, and your browser will automatically display the associated document, no matter where it is on the Internet. You can browse indefinitely, clicking on link after link. You will find many fascinating tidbits of information and visit many interesting **Web sites** (computers that have a connection to the portion of the Internet that is the World Wide Web).

You will also find that, while fun and interesting, browsing is not a very efficient way of locating specific information. If you are writing a paper on the architecture of European churches for an art history class, for instance, you would probably not do your research by browsing through all of the stacks in the campus library. In similar fashion you would not want to browse the Web at random until you found the pictures of Notre Dame shown in Figure 1.2b.

It is much more efficient to use your browser to link to a special Web search tool called a *search engine*. Using the search engine you can conduct a keyword search of the Web, much as you search a card catalog or online database in the library. The search engine will return abstracts of documents it finds that match the keywords. The abstracts will contain links to the documents themselves, so you can quickly locate the sources you want to read. You will learn to browse and search the World Wide Web using Netscape (or the browser you have at your college or university) and Lynx in Chapter 3.

Gopher and FTP

You can also find interesting resources on the Internet using a menu-based service called **gopher** (as in, if you want something, go "pher" it!). Figure 1.3 shows a gopher menu as it appears in Netscape. In Figure 1.3a you see the highest menu

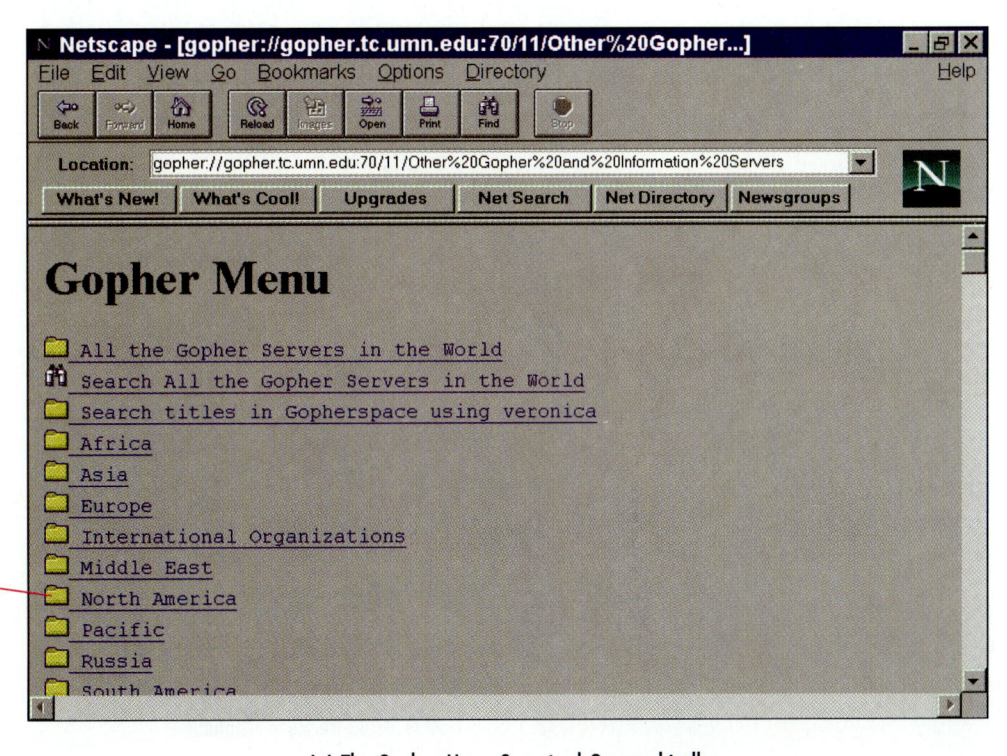

(a) The Gopher Menu Organized Geographically

FIGURE 1.3 Gopher Using Netscape

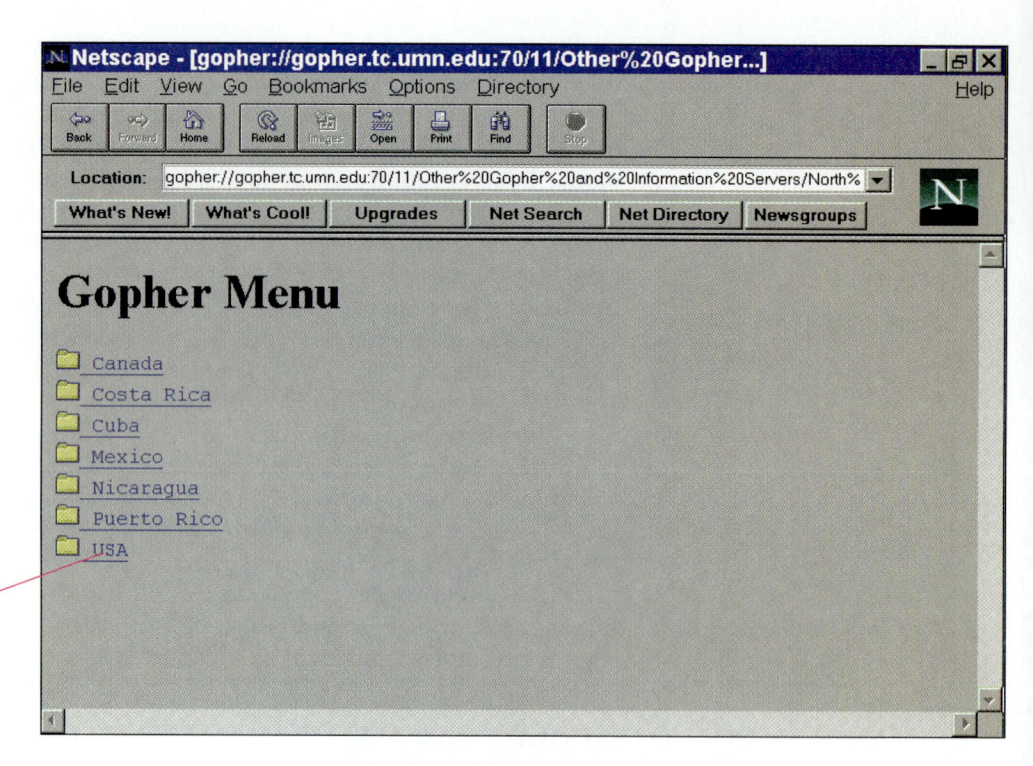

Click here to jump to USA menu

(b) The North America Gopher Menu

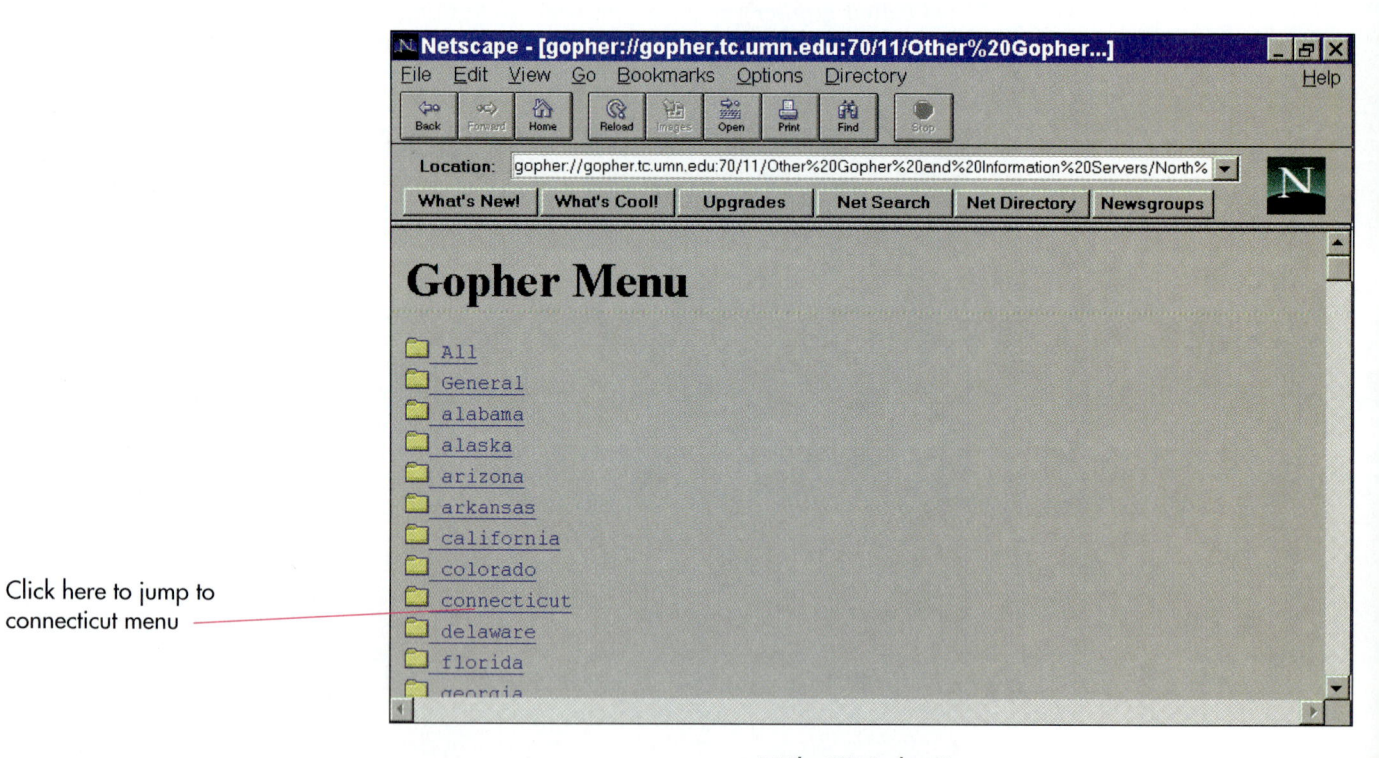

Click here to jump to connecticut menu

(c) The USA Gopher Menu

FIGURE 1.3   Gopher Using Netscape (continued)

EXPLORING THE INTERNET

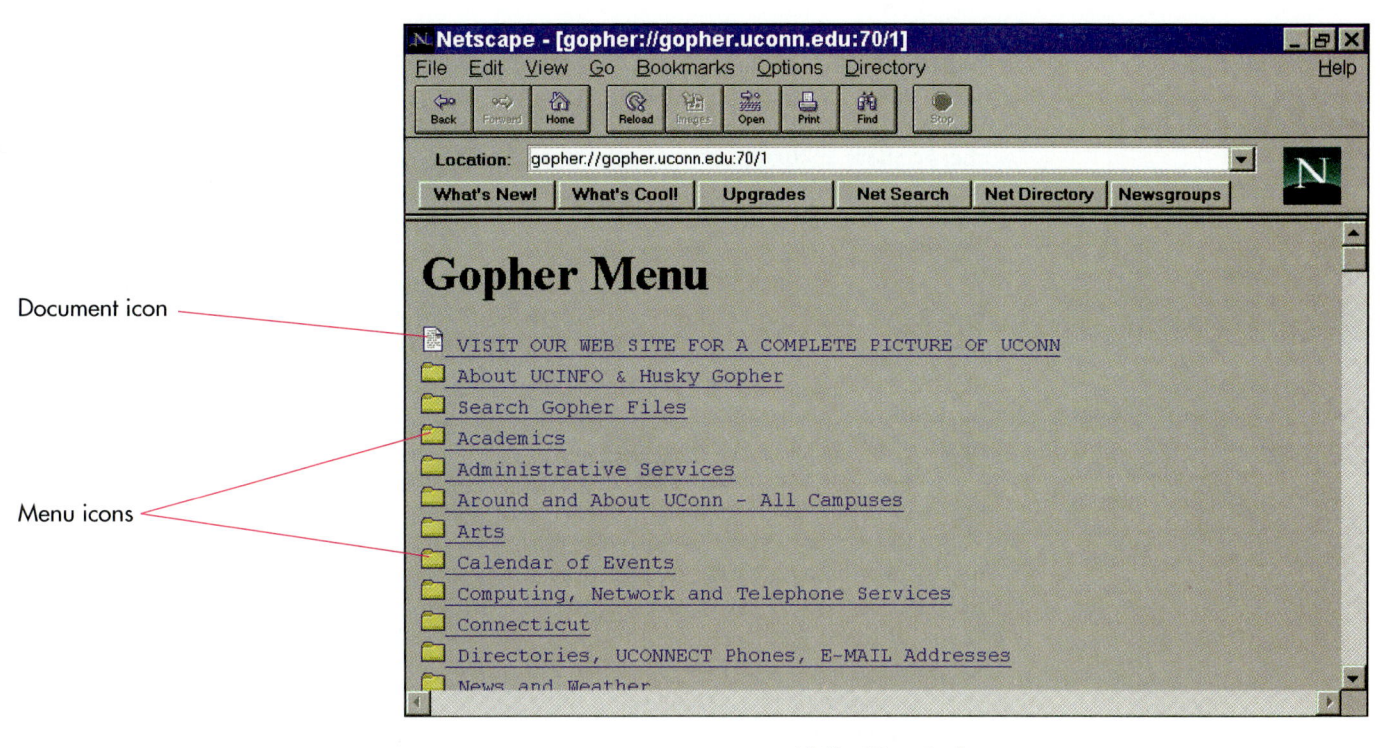

Document icon

Menu icons

Gopher Menu

- VISIT OUR WEB SITE FOR A COMPLETE PICTURE OF UCONN
- About UCINFO & Husky Gopher
- Search Gopher Files
- Academics
- Administrative Services
- Around and About UConn – All Campuses
- Arts
- Calendar of Events
- Computing, Network and Telephone Services
- Connecticut
- Directories, UCONNECT Phones, E-MAIL Addresses
- News and Weather

(d) The UConn Gopher

Gopher Jewels

Gopher Jewels is a list of gopher sites by category. Gopher sites are placed in particular categories as a result of finding related information buried somewhere in their hole.

Contents of the Gopher Jewels list:

Gopher menus by subject

1. About Gopher Jewels
2. Gophers with Subject Trees
3. Agriculture
4. Arts, Music, Sound and Humanities
5. Astronomy and Astrophysics
6. Biology and Biosciences
7. Books, Journals, Magazines, Newsletters, Technical Reports & Publications
8. Botany
9. Chemistry

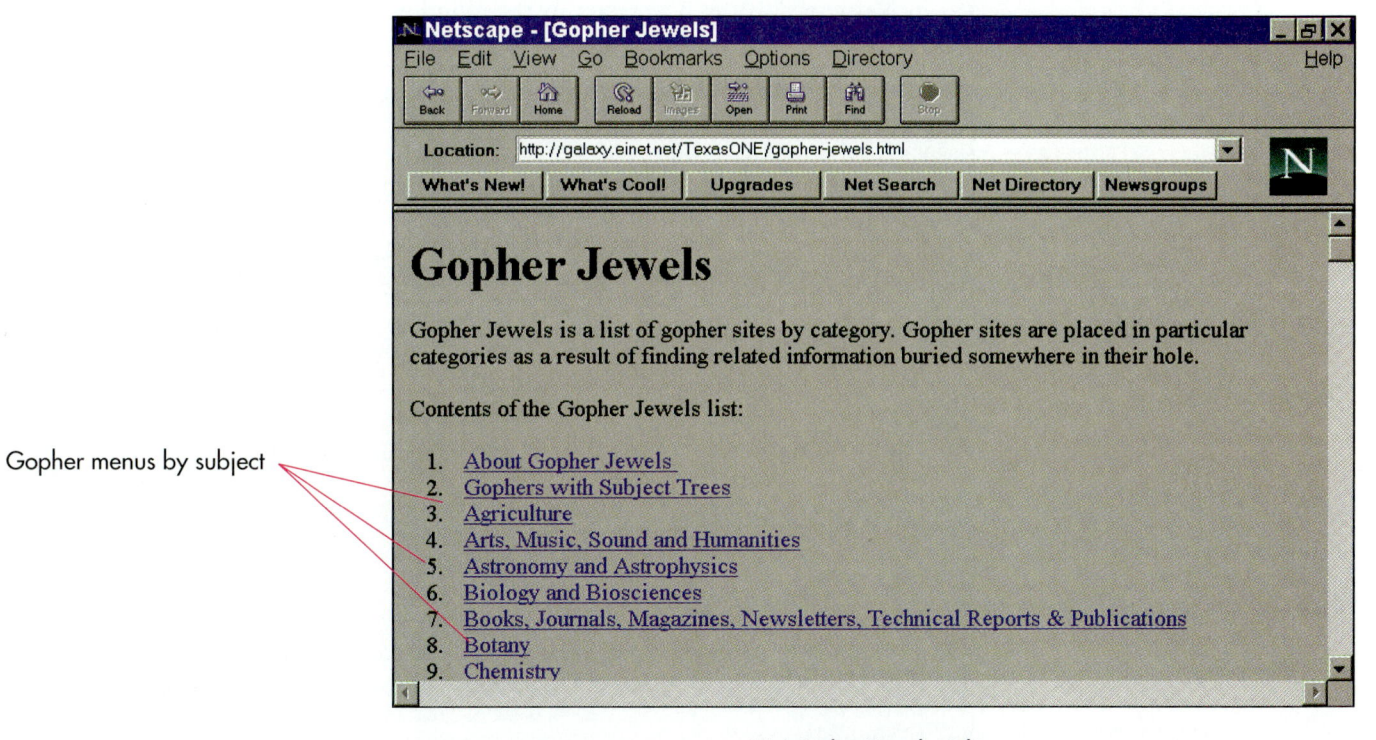

(e) A Gopher Menu by Subject

FIGURE 1.3 Gopher Using Netscape (continued)

on the particular gopher shown, which is organized geographically. If you select North America gophers from this menu, you will see the menu shown in Figure 1.3b, which lists regions in North America. Figure 1.3c shows the USA menu, from which you could select the state of Connecticut, for instance. From the list of all the gophers in Connecticut, selecting the University of Connecticut gopher displays a menu that the computing staff at UConn created and has stored on a computer at their site, shown in Figure 1.3d. You can continue to select menus until you find the information you want.

This method of searching is, of course, quite time consuming, and assumes you know where you want to look for the information. To avoid this problem, other gopher menus are organized by subject, as shown in Figure 1.3e. Fortunately, as you will discover in Chapter 4, almost all gopher resources are indexed and can be found by using the search engines in your browser. You will find this much more efficient than starting at the top of the gopher menu structure.

Some of the documents you find while browsing, searching, and gophering you will simply read on your PC and then go on to something else. At other times you will find files such as software programs and graphic images, which you will not display using a browser, but instead will want to retrieve to use locally on your PC. The browser you use can also perform this function, called ***downloading.*** Many of these files are actually transferred over the Internet by the browser using something called the ***File Transfer Protocol (FTP).***

A ***protocol*** is a set of rules by which computers interact; FTP is a protocol that governs how computers exchange files. In Chapter 4 you will retrieve files from an ***FTP site,*** a computer that archives files, using both your browser and special FTP software. Figure 1.4 shows a list of ***FTP files*** (files stored at an FTP site), (a) in Netscape, (b) as it appears in the Windows-based FTP program WS_FTP,

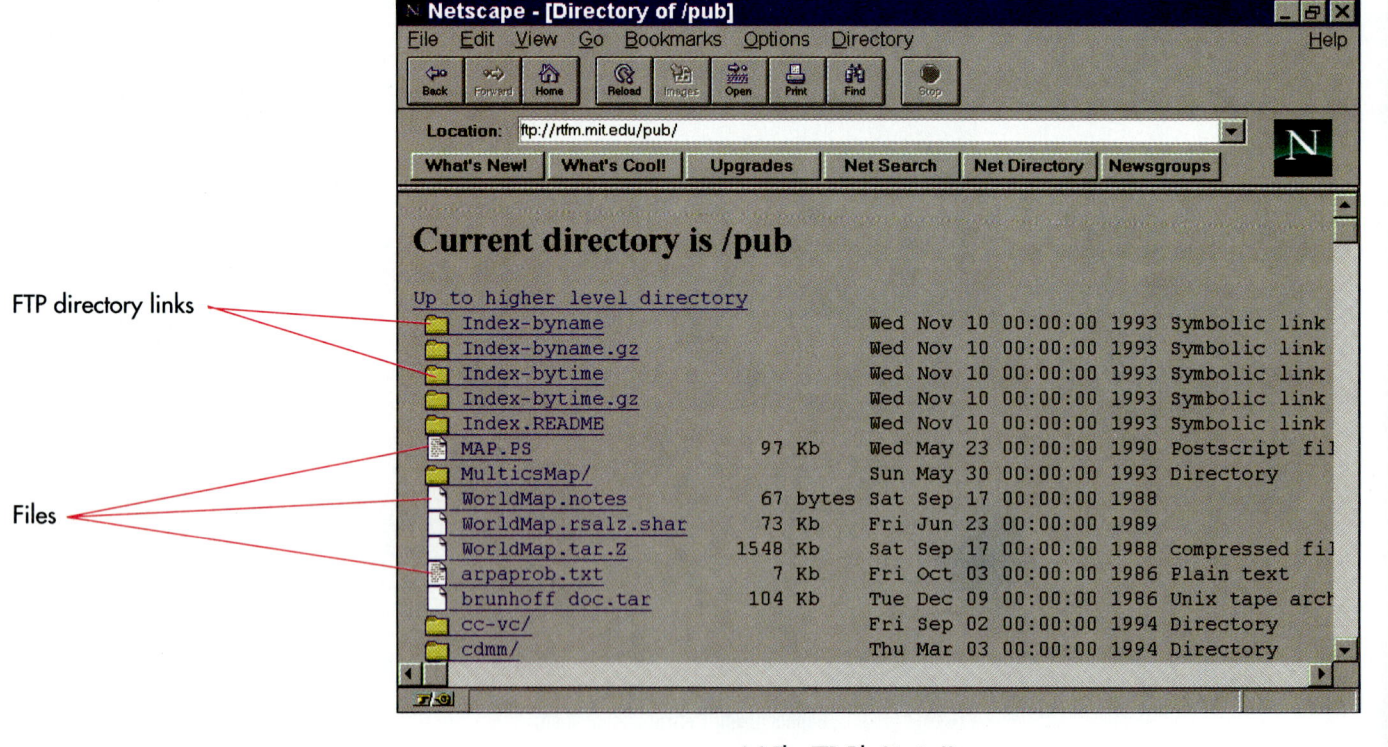

(a) The FTP File List in Netscape

FIGURE 1.4   FTP

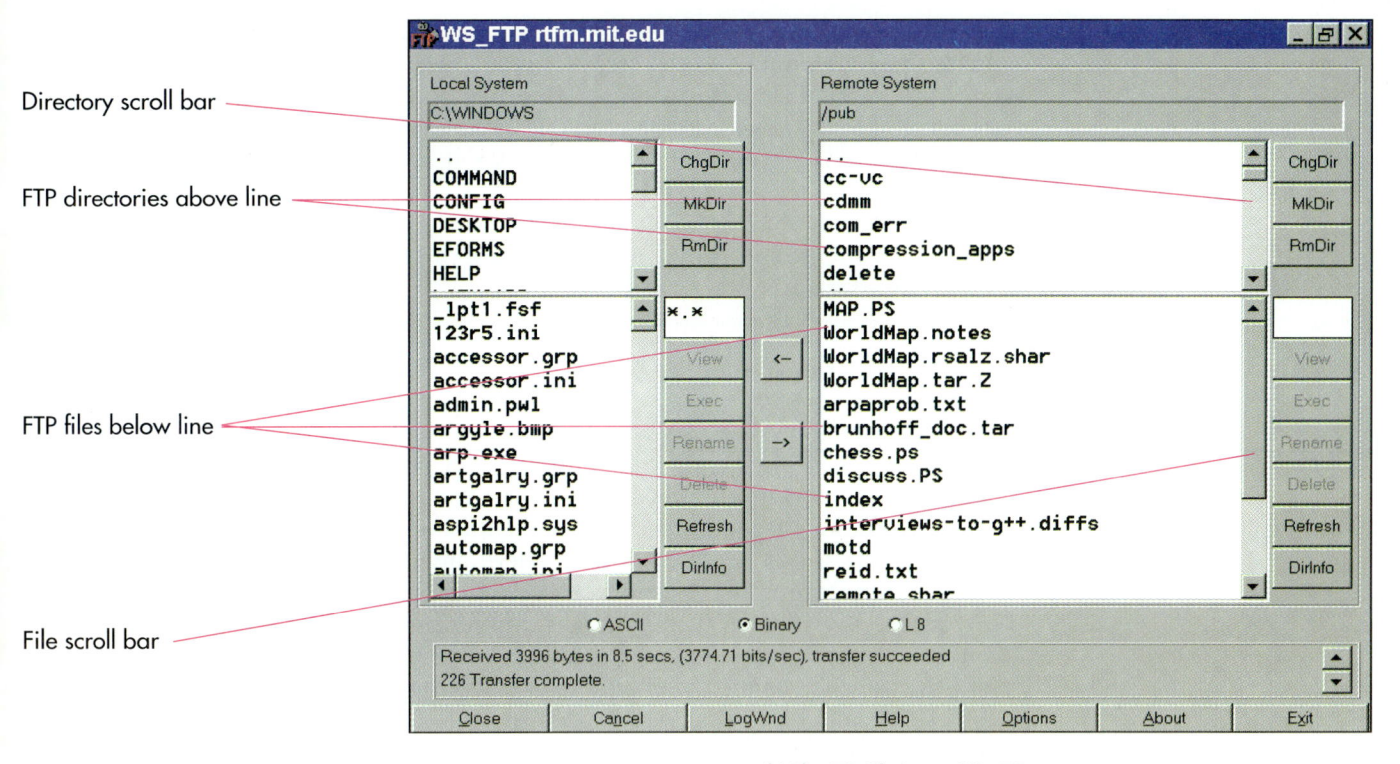

(b) The FTP File List in WS_FTP

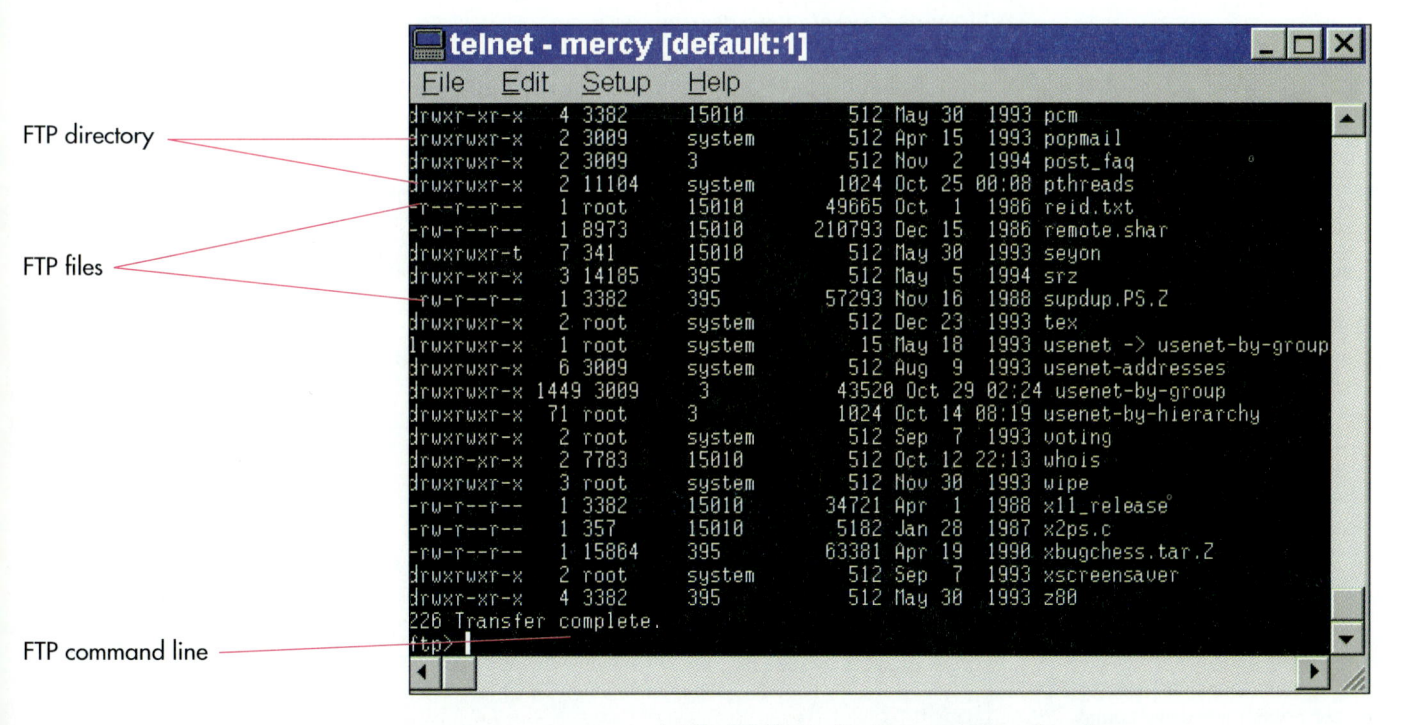

(c) The FTP File List Using a Command-based Interface

FIGURE 1.4 FTP (continued)

INTRODUCTION TO THE INTERNET 11

and (c) as it appears using a command-based FTP program on the computer that connects your campus to the Internet, your **Internet host.**

As with other services on the Internet, you will find it very time consuming to locate files to download simply by browsing. You can use a Web search engine to locate gopher menus and FTP sites. We also discuss in Chapter 4 how to find these resources by using the special search tools, **Veronica** to search **gopherspace,** and **Archie** to search FTP archives. Figure 1.5 shows a Veronica search using Netscape; Figure 1.6 shows an Archie search using a Windows-based program called WSArchie.

Conversing on the Internet

You already know you can send mail and subscribe to mailing lists on the Internet. You can also instantly communicate with people all over the world by using what are called *chat* programs. They allow you to send a typed message to everyone else who is logged in to the same channel at the same time you are. A **channel** is like a global conference call, where anyone who picks up the phone and dials a certain number can join an ongoing conversation and hear everything everyone else is saying. The messages everyone is sending are displayed on everyone's monitor as they are received, as shown in Figure 1.7. As long as you are attached to the channel, you will continue to see the messages.

Participating in chat sessions can be fun and interesting, but it can also be an addicting waste of time. Many people prefer to subscribe to mailing lists and get their mail **offline,** that is, at a different time than it was sent, when it is convenient for them. Another kind of offline subscription service is provided by Usenet. **Usenet, newsgroups,** or **news,** as it is also called, allows you to subscribe to one or many discussion groups, which are organized by topic. Subscribers can read and submit, or **post,** messages to the group by using a program called a **newsreader.**

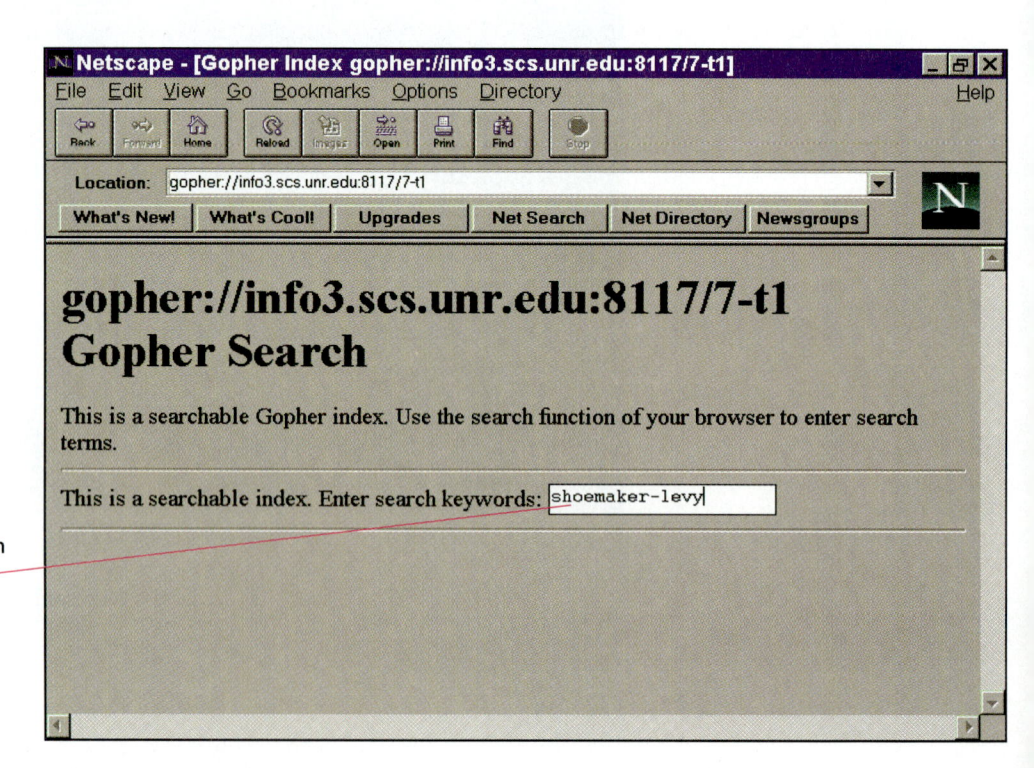

A Veronica search for information about Shoemaker-Levy comet

FIGURE 1.5 A Veronica Search

An Archie search for FTP archives about Shoemaker-Levy comet

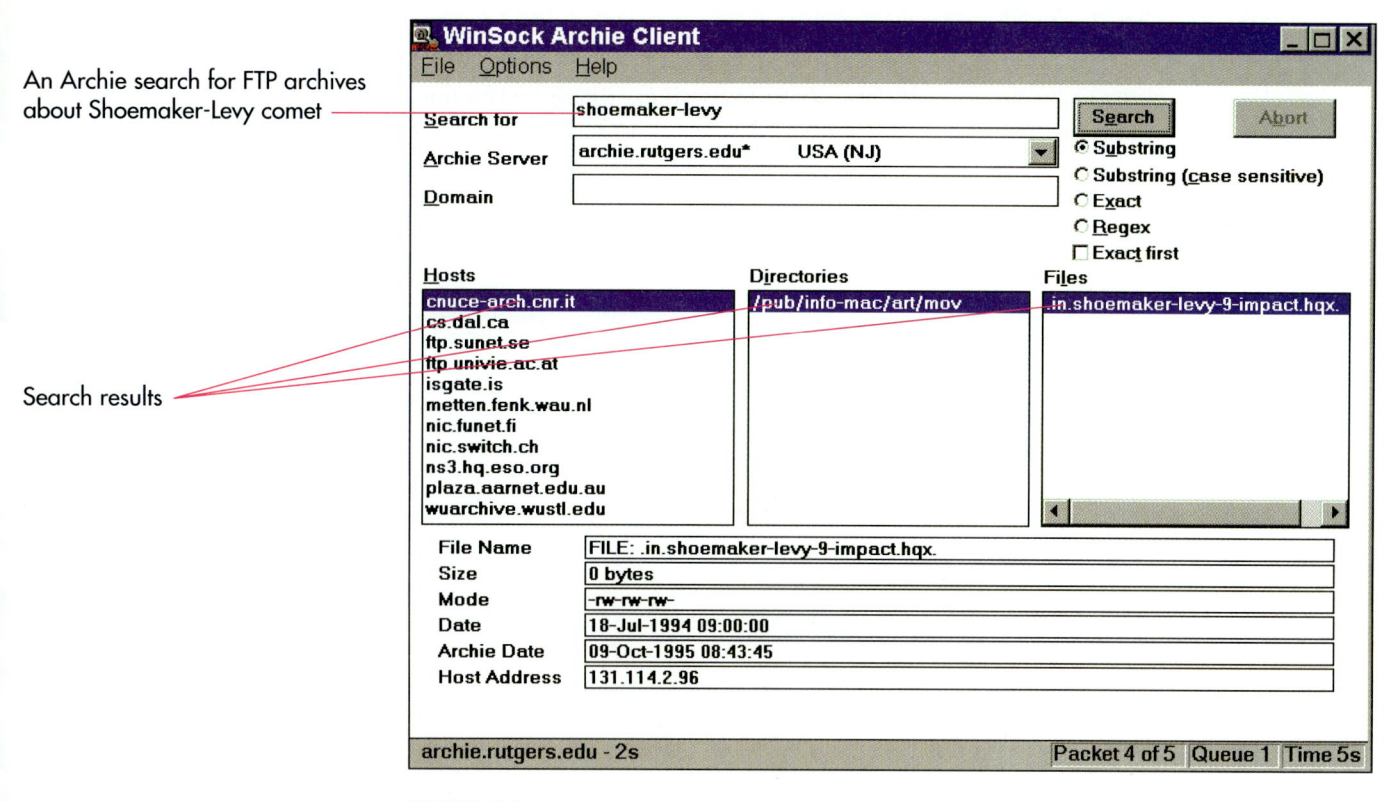

Search results

FIGURE 1.6 Using Archie to Search for Files

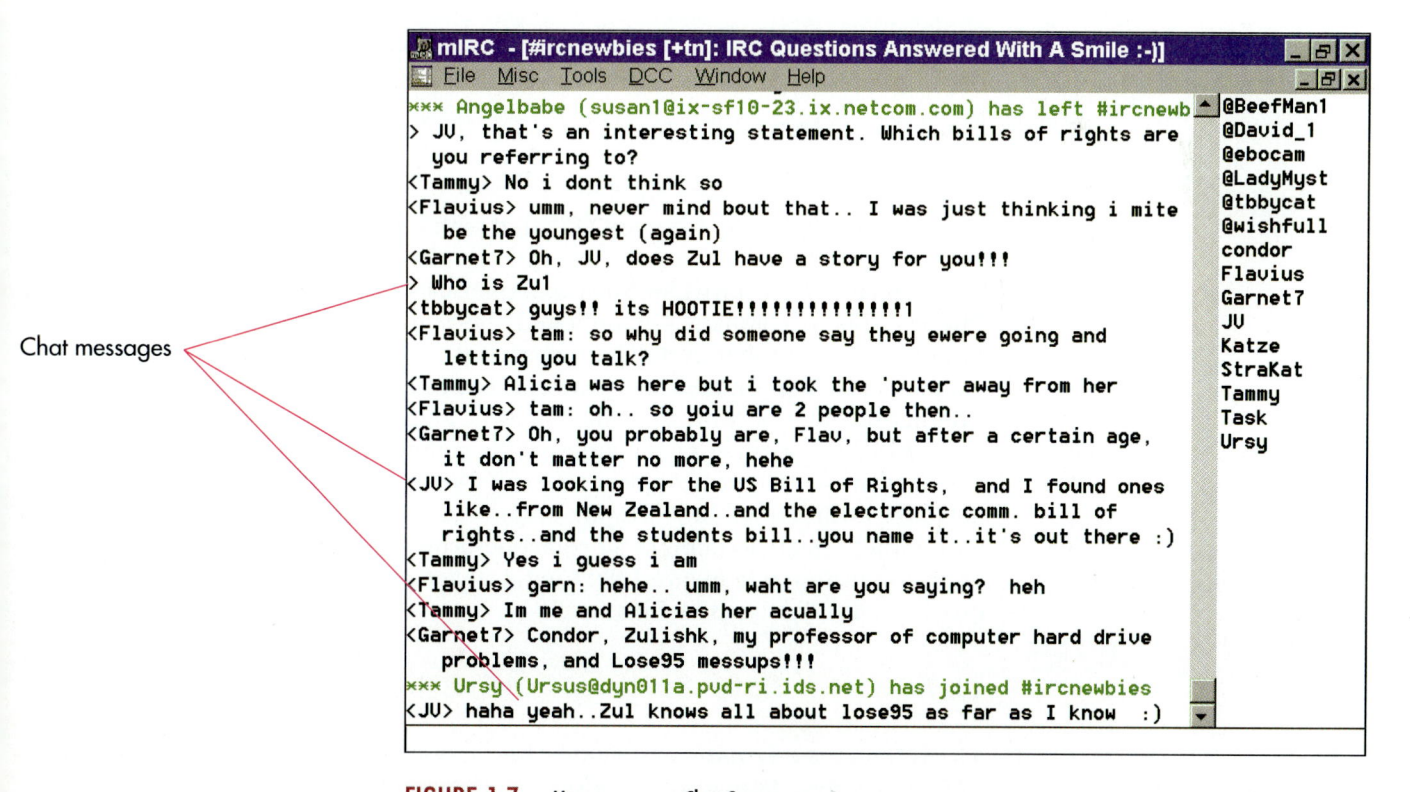

Chat messages

FIGURE 1.7 Messages on a Chat Screen

INTRODUCTION TO THE INTERNET

The postings are collected and then periodically mailed in batches with all the other newsgroup messages submitted since the last mailing. Since there are over 7,000 newsgroups, you can imagine the number of messages that arrive from all over the world with each mailing! Your computer center may elect to receive all, some, or none of the newsgroups. Figure 1.8 shows a message about Netscape being sent to a newsgroup. You can see that it looks very similar to an e-mail message.

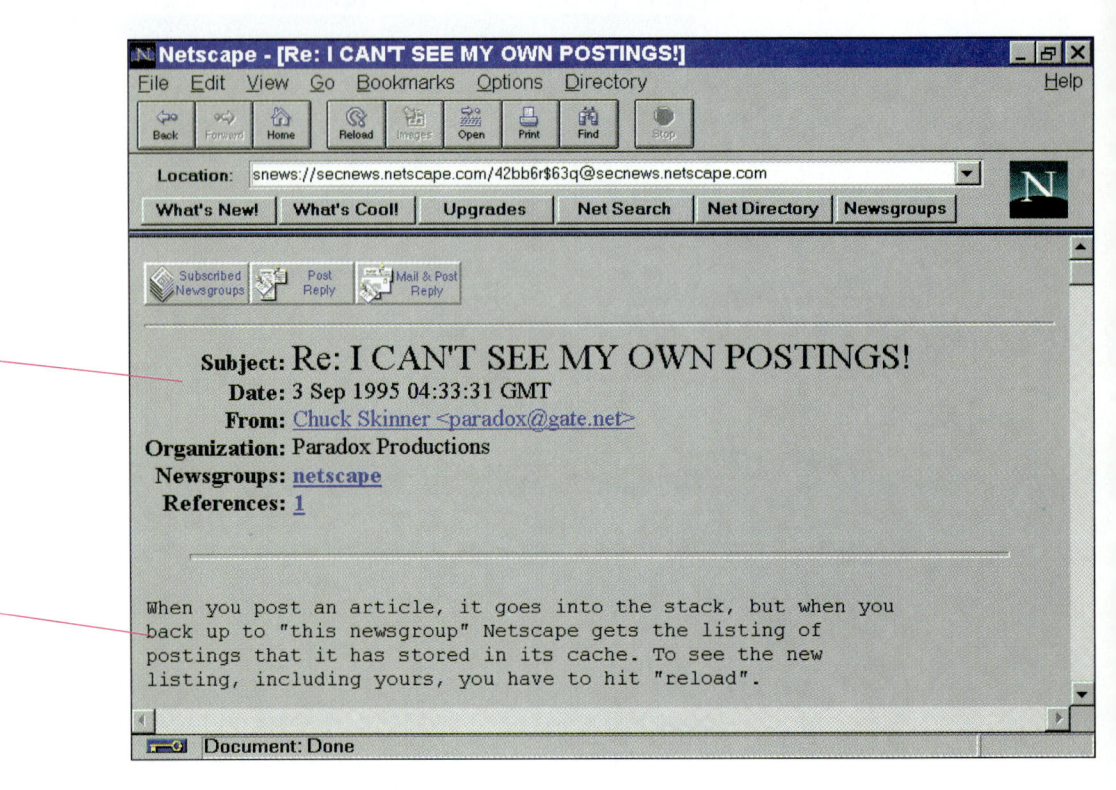

FIGURE 1.8 A Newsgroup Message

Many people who were not affiliated with a college or university were unable until recently to gain access to the Internet. Instead they often subscribed to a commercial service provider such as America Online (AOL), CompuServe, or Prodigy. These companies maintained their own networks, separate from the Internet. A subscriber could participate in a discussion group or send mail to another subscriber on the same network, but could not access the resources of the Internet or other networks, as illustrated in Figure 1.9a.

With the opening of the Internet to commercial providers, the online services have rushed to provide browsing and e-mail capabilities that access the Internet. Now a subscriber on AOL, for example, can send a message to someone with an Internet e-mail account, or to someone using the newly formed Microsoft network, as illustrated in Figure 1.9b. Chat, Usenet, and the services offered by online providers are discussed in Chapter 5.

Netiquette, Safe Surfing, and Other Issues

The Internet is a *virtual* community, that is, one that exists outside the bounds of time and space. People the world over communicate, carry on commerce and research, fall in love, and otherwise conduct the same kinds of human interactions

(a) Before Internet Access

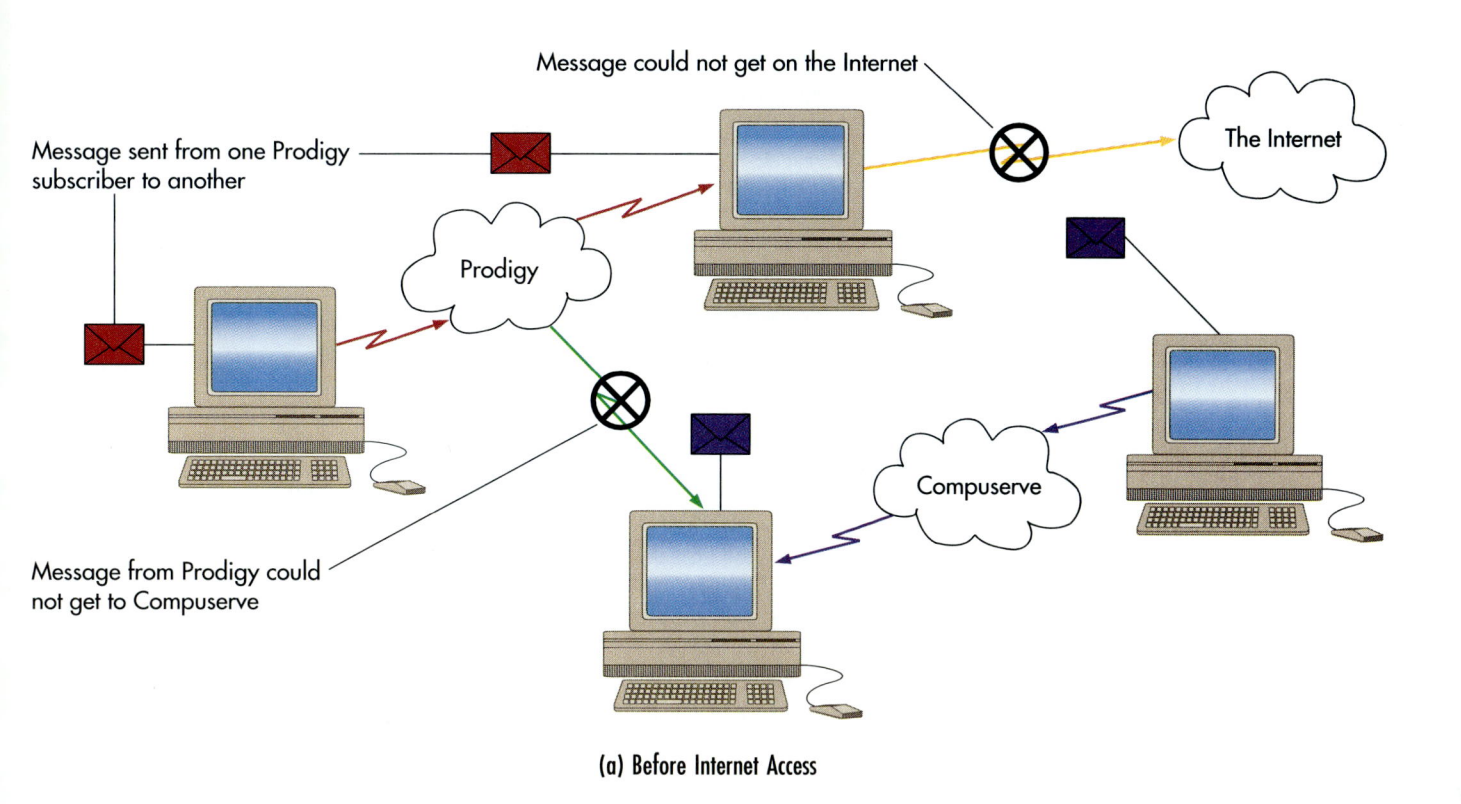

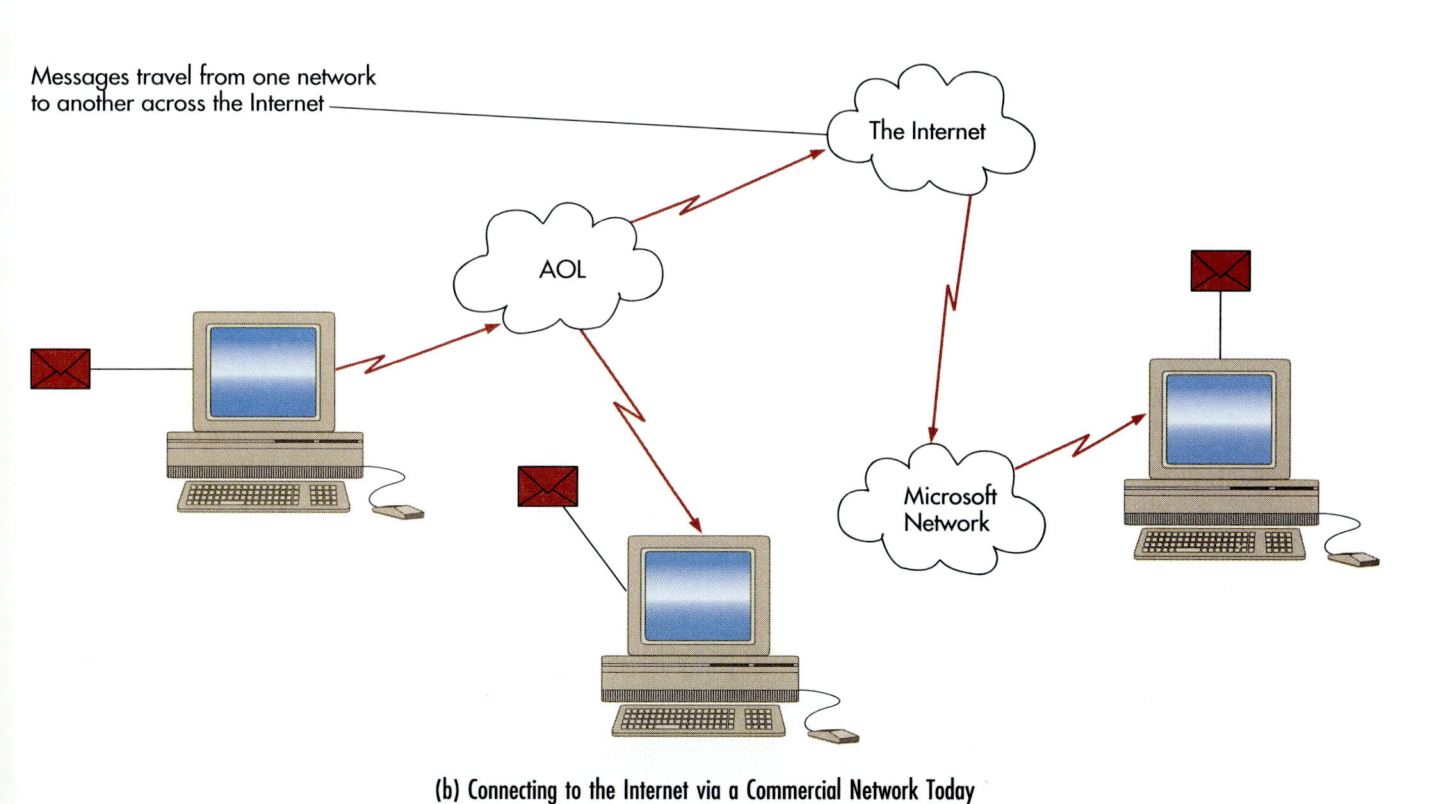

(b) Connecting to the Internet via a Commercial Network Today

FIGURE 1.9 Commercial Online Networks

over the Net as they would via the telephone or postal systems. Just as in any other community, there are well-intentioned people and those who are con artists and crooks. The overwhelming majority are pleasant and helpful, but you will occasionally come across someone who is downright nasty.

Chapter 6 discusses some of the rules of the road for traveling the ***Information Superhighway.*** We strongly urge you to read it before you find yourself running afoul of the unwritten laws governing its use. While you probably won't get a speeding ticket on the Net, that might be less painful than getting 6,000 pieces of unwanted e-mail in response to your violating some taboo. Ignorance on the Net, as in life, is no excuse.

Web Publishing with HTML

Web documents, as you have seen in the figures in this chapter, contain both text and graphic images. Some contain audio and video clips as well. Web documents are produced using a special language called **Hypertext Markup Language (HTML),** which we discuss in Chapter 7. ***Hypertext*** refers to the embedded links we described earlier, which allow you to jump from document to document on the Web. HTML is composed of special ***tags,*** or codes, which you insert in a standard word processing document. A sample HTML page is shown in Figure 1.10. The tags, the codes surrounded by angled brackets (< >), control how the document will appear to a Web browser. You will create your own Web document in Chapter 7.

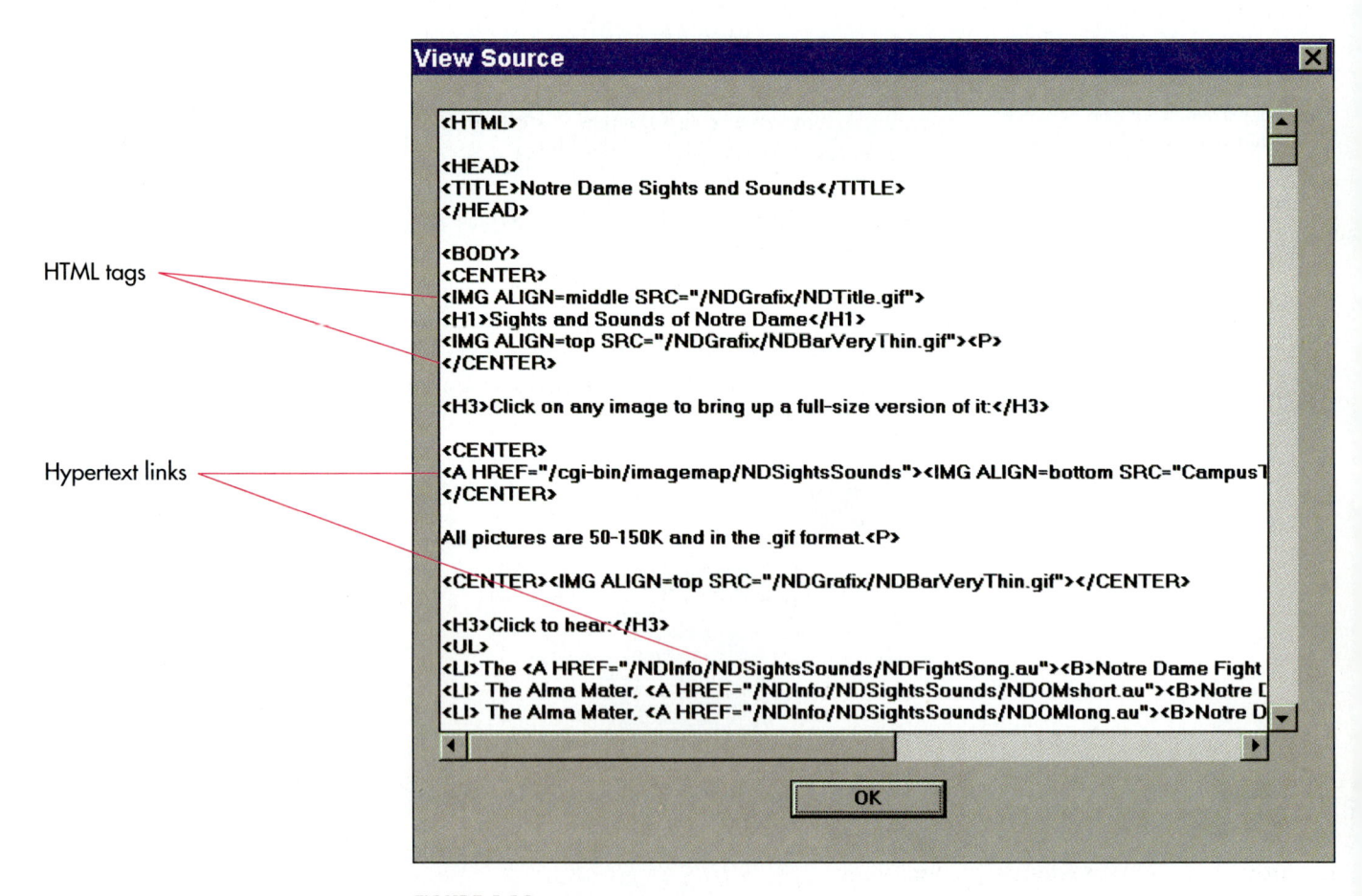

```
<HTML>

<HEAD>
<TITLE>Notre Dame Sights and Sounds</TITLE>
</HEAD>

<BODY>
<CENTER>
<IMG ALIGN=middle SRC="/NDGrafix/NDTitle.gif">
<H1>Sights and Sounds of Notre Dame</H1>
<IMG ALIGN=top SRC="/NDGrafix/NDBarVeryThin.gif"><P>
</CENTER>

<H3>Click on any image to bring up a full-size version of it:</H3>

<CENTER>
<A HREF="/cgi-bin/imagemap/NDSightsSounds"><IMG ALIGN=bottom SRC="CampusT
</CENTER>

All pictures are 50-150K and in the .gif format.<P>

<CENTER><IMG ALIGN=top SRC="/NDGrafix/NDBarVeryThin.gif"></CENTER>

<H3>Click to hear:</H3>
<UL>
<LI>The <A HREF="/NDInfo/NDSightsSounds/NDFightSong.au"><B>Notre Dame Fight
<LI> The Alma Mater, <A HREF="/NDInfo/NDSightsSounds/NDOMshort.au"><B>Notre D
<LI> The Alma Mater, <A HREF="/NDInfo/NDSightsSounds/NDOMlong.au"><B>Notre D
```

(HTML tags and Hypertext links are labeled with arrows pointing into the source code.)

FIGURE 1.10 A Sample HTML Page

CONNECTING TO THE INTERNET

There are several ways of gaining access to the Internet, depending on whether you are using a computer in your campus computer lab or dialing in from home. If you are connecting from your computer center, the PC you use in the lab is most likely connected to a *local area network (LAN)*. A LAN is a group of computers within close physical proximity to one another, which are connected via special cable to a powerful PC called a *file server*. The file server provides a common place to store data and programs, and provides rapid access to those files. The PCs on the network can share the disk storage on the server and can share print resources on the network. Figure 1.11 represents a conceptual view of a LAN consisting of multiple workstations and a laser printer connected to a file server. A *workstation* (also known as a client or node) is any PC on which an individual works. Different types of workstations (PCs and Macs, for instance) can be connected to the same network.

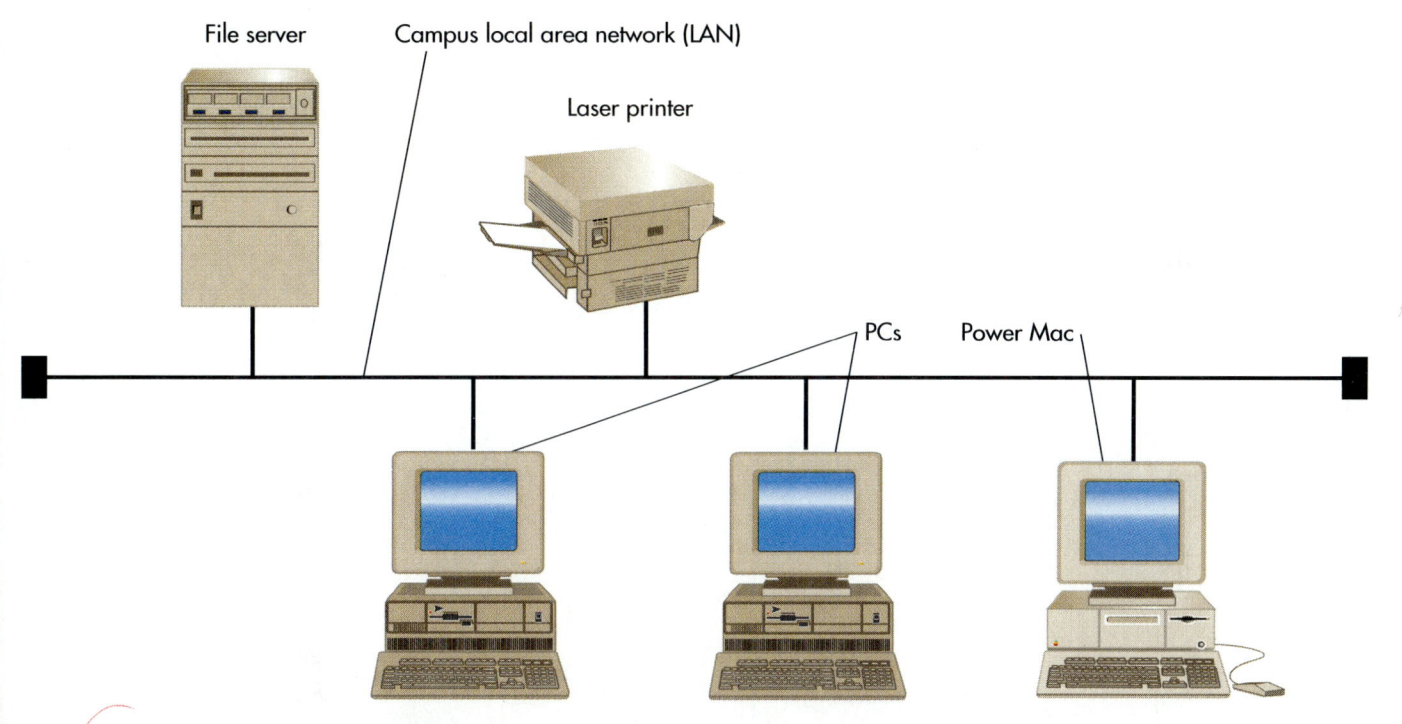

FIGURE 1.11 A Conceptual View of a LAN

The memory and processing requirements for file services and Internet services may compete and degrade performance if they are both on the same computer. It is, therefore, common for the Internet services to reside on a separate file server running a version of the Unix operating system, as shown in Figure 1.12. When you select a link in a Web document, send an e-mail message, or select some other Internet resource, the message sent from your PC includes instructions indicating that it should be handled by the Internet server. Figure 1.12 shows the Internet server being on the same LAN as your computer lab. However, in a computing environment that includes more than one LAN, the Internet server may be in an entirely different location. You may connect to it via a high-speed fiber optic cable, generically called a campus backbone, as shown in Figure 1.13.

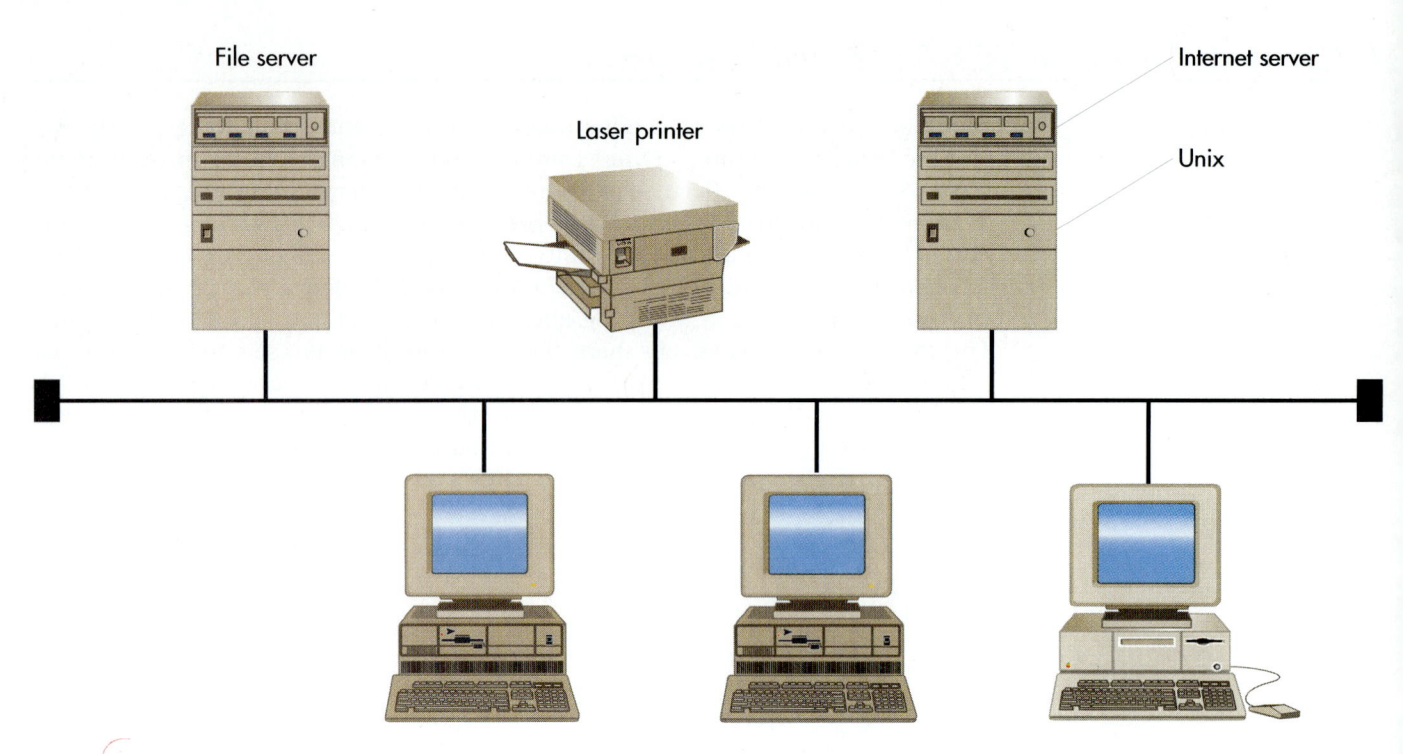

FIGURE 1.12 The Internet Server on the LAN

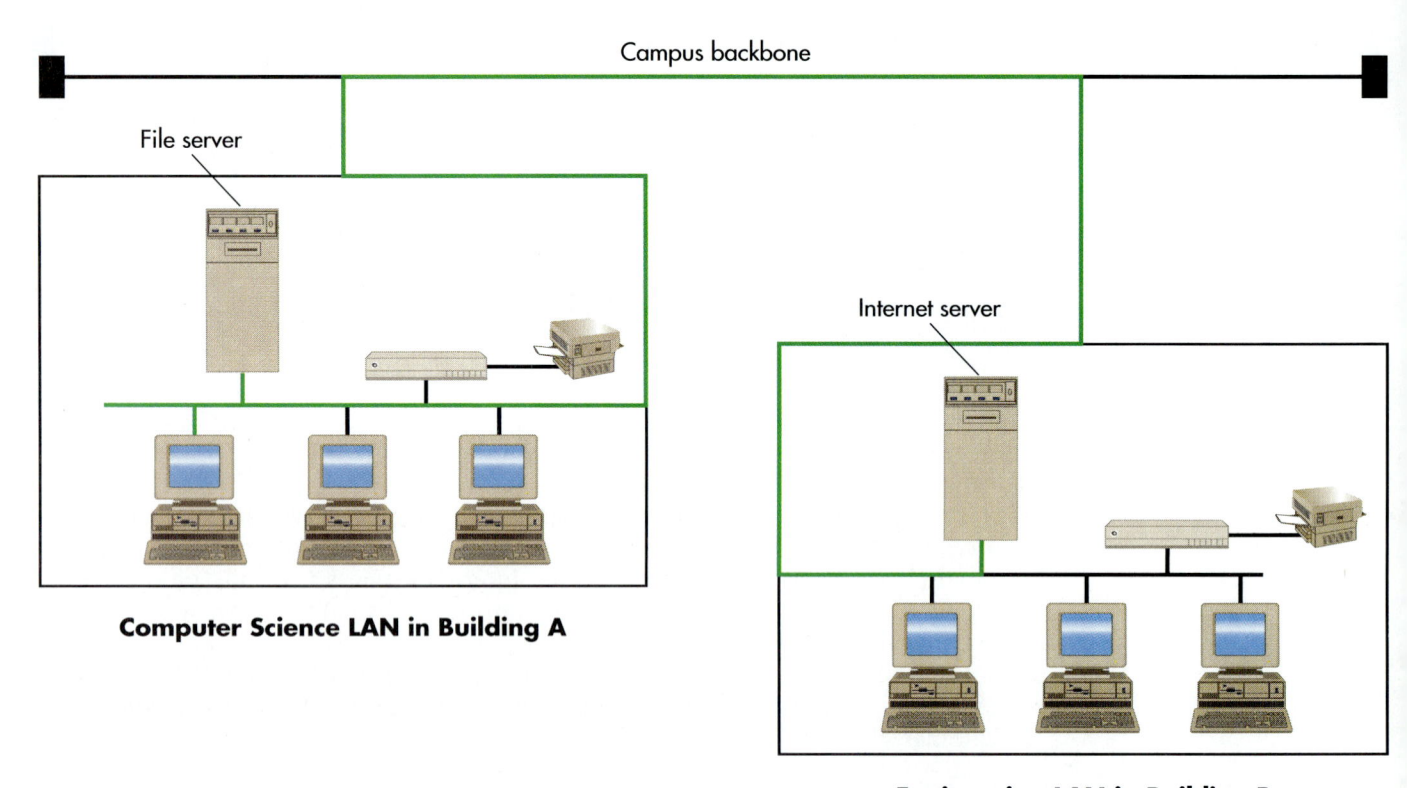

Computer Science LAN in Building A

Engineering LAN in Building B

FIGURE 1.13 The Internet Server at Another Location

TWO FORMS OF ID REQUIRED

If your campus computing environment uses a local area network with both a file server and a Unix Internet server, chances are good that you will have a login ID and password on both machines. This seems a bit confusing; however, it helps ensure system security. When you use word processing, a spreadsheet program, or other general academic software, you will log on to the file server. When you want to send e-mail, you will log on again to the Internet server with your Internet username and password. Check with your LAN administrator, lab assistant, help desk, or instructor for more information about user IDs, usernames, and passwords in your environment.

When you start up an Internet program such as e-mail, you may be using a Windows-based program that runs on your PC. Such a program, called a *client,* passes your request on to the network, where it is picked up by the Internet server and acted upon. On the other hand, particularly if you are dialing into the campus from home, you may run a program on your PC that sets up a terminal session with your Internet server. A *terminal session* is a connection to the Internet server that emulates, or mimics, a terminal directly attached to the computer. (A *terminal* is a device without memory or disk storage that can communicate with a computer via a keyboard and display.) If you are using a terminal session, you will log on to the Internet server with your Internet username, which is generally a different login ID than you used to access the file server. A typical login screen for a terminal session is shown in Figure 1.14. The Unix $ prompt (or % prompt on some systems), indicates that you are communicating with the Internet server and have successfully logged in.

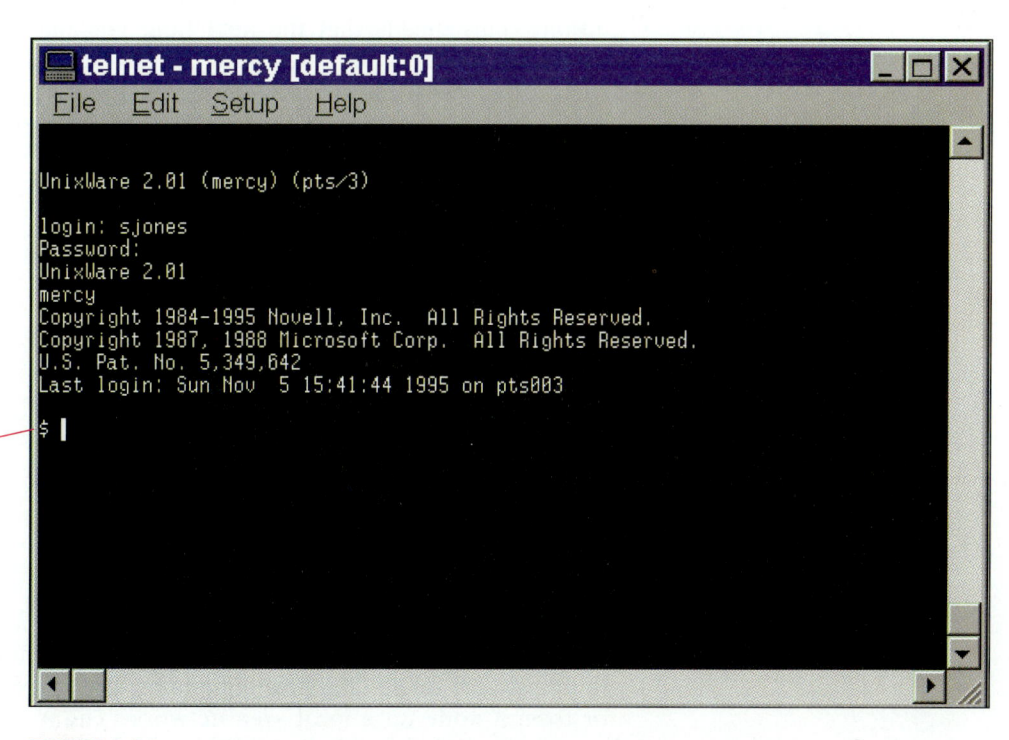

FIGURE 1.14   The Login Prompt for a Telnet Session

When using a terminal session to log on to a computer on the Internet, called a *telnet session,* or *telnetting,* you will use commands instead of a GUI interface to browse, search, and retrieve Internet resources. You will not be able to use pull-down menus or view the graphics incorporated into most Web documents. For these reasons most people prefer to access the Internet via a GUI interface on their PC. We will return to the topic of telnetting several times, and you will retrieve various Internet resources using the appropriate commands as you complete hands-on exercises in other chapters.

HOW THE INTERNET WORKS

The postal system provides a good analogy of how (but certainly not how fast) information travels across the Internet.[1] (E-mail travels at the speed of light, which is infinitely faster than the air- and land-based transportation to which the post office is limited.) When you mail a letter, you drop it in a mailbox where it is picked up with a lot of other letters and delivered to the local post office. The letters are sorted and sent on their way to a larger post office or substation where the letters are sorted again, until eventually each letter reaches the post office closest to its destination. The local mail carrier at the receiving post office then delivers each letter to its final destination.

There is no direct connection between the origin and destination because it is impossible to connect every pair of cities within the United States. If you were to send a letter from Coral Springs, Florida, to Englewood Cliffs, New Jersey, the letter would not travel directly from Coral Springs to Englewood Cliffs. Instead the postal service would route the letter from one substation to the next, making a new decision at each substation—for example, from Coral Springs, to Miami, to Newark, to Englewood Cliffs.

Each postal substation considers all of the routes it has available to the next substation and makes the best possible decision according to the prevailing conditions. This means that the next time you mail a letter from Coral Springs to Englewood Cliffs, the letter may travel a completely different path. If the mail truck from Coral Springs to Miami has already left or is full to capacity, the letter can be routed through Fort Lauderdale to New York City and then to Englewood Cliffs. It really doesn't matter because your only concern is that the letter arrive at its final destination.

THE INTERNET IS NOT FREE

The fact that there is no "Internet Incorporated" to collect a usage fee has given many people the mistaken idea that the Internet is free. The computers and networks that make up the Internet cost money, and each node (e.g., your college or university) must fund its own network connection through grants, user fees, or tuition.

The Internet works the same way, as data travels across the Internet through several levels of networks until it gets to its destination. E-mail messages arrive at the local post office (the host computer) from a remote PC connected by modem, or from a node on a local area network. The messages then leave the local post

---

[1] Krol, Ed, *The Whole Internet,* O'Reilly and Associates, Inc., Sebastopol, CA, 1992, pp. 24, 26.

office and pass through a special-purpose computer known as a ***router*** that connects the networks on the Internet to one another.

A message may pass through several networks to get to its destination. Each network has its own router that determines how best to move the message closer to its destination, taking into account the traffic on the network. A message passes from one network to the next, until it arrives at the local area network on the other end, from where it can be sent to its final destination. The process is depicted graphically in Figure 1.15.

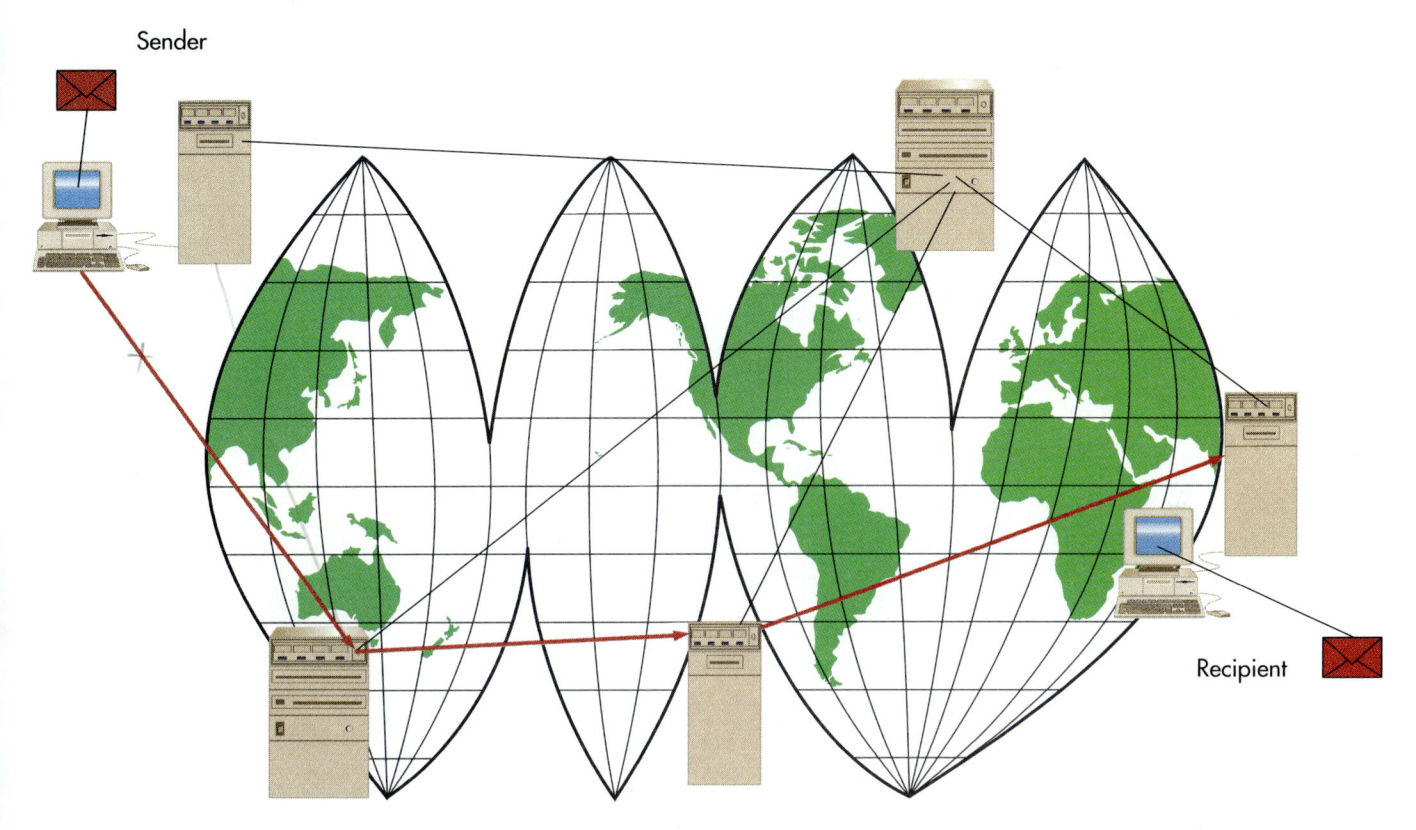

FIGURE 1.15   A Message Travels the Internet

The TCP/IP Protocol

Let's assume that you are working on a research project with a professor at another campus, and that you have several reports the professor must see tomorrow morning. The entire bundle is a stack six inches high. Now, let's pretend that the post office no longer accepts large packages for overnight delivery. One alternative would be to mail the pages individually by placing each page into its own envelope, then trust that all the envelopes would arrive on time, and finally that the professor would be able to reassemble the individual pages. That may sound awkward, but it is a truer picture of how the Internet works.

Information is sent across the Internet in ***packets,*** with each packet limited in size. The rules for creating, addressing, and sending the packets are specified by the ***TCP/IP protocol (Transmission Control Protocol/Internet Protocol)*** that governs the flow of data across the Internet. The TCP portion divides the file that you want to send into pieces, then numbers each piece so that the message can be reconstructed at the other end. The IP portion sends each packet on its way by specifying the address of the sending and receiving computer so that the routers will be able to do their job.

Why, you might ask, are files divided into packets rather than sent in their entirety? When the messages are divided into packets, many different messages may be flowing over the network at the same time. The packets may be routed to best utilize network resources, avoiding busy lines and allowing better load balancing across the network. If one part of the network is down, the packets can still get through on multiple other routes.

A second reason has to do with ensuring that the file arrives correctly. Static or noise on a telephone line is merely annoying to people having a conversation, but devastating when a file (especially a computer program) is transmitted and a byte or two is garbled. The larger the file being sent, the greater the chance that noise will be introduced and that the file will be corrupted. Sending the data in smaller pieces (packets), and verifying that the packets were received correctly, helps ensure the integrity of the data. If one packet is received incorrectly, the entire message does not have to be sent again.

Internet Architecture Layers

The Internet is built in layers that revolve around the TCP/IP protocols, as shown in Figure 1.16. At the sending computer, the **application layer** (with which you interact) creates the message and passes it to the **transport layer** on your computer, where the message is divided into packets. The packets are addressed at the **Internet layer,** then sent across the Internet using the **network access layer,** which interacts with the various levels of networks through which the data must travel to get to its destination. The process is reversed at the receiving computer. The Internet layer receives the individual packets from the network access layer, then passes the packets up to the transport layer where they are reassembled and sent to the application layer to display the message.

Each computer communicating with the Internet, whether dialing in or attached on a local area network (LAN), must have the software necessary to accomplish the task of the four layers. TCP/IP protocol drivers, or **stacks** as they are called, must be installed on each computer. Each computer must also have an **IP address,** a unique Internet address that identifies the computer as a node on the Internet.

The IP address is like a street address on a letter. Each computer on the Internet has a unique numeric address composed of four numbers, each less than 256, and each separated by a period: 192.25.13.01, for example. Each site on the Internet must apply for a specific block of IP addresses from its Internet provider. Each PC, Mac, router, server, and other device on the network must be assigned an IP address by the network administrator, just as someone in your town has designated a number for every house or building on your street.

The protocols in the lowest level in the architecture, the network access layer, control the sending of messages to devices physically attached to the local

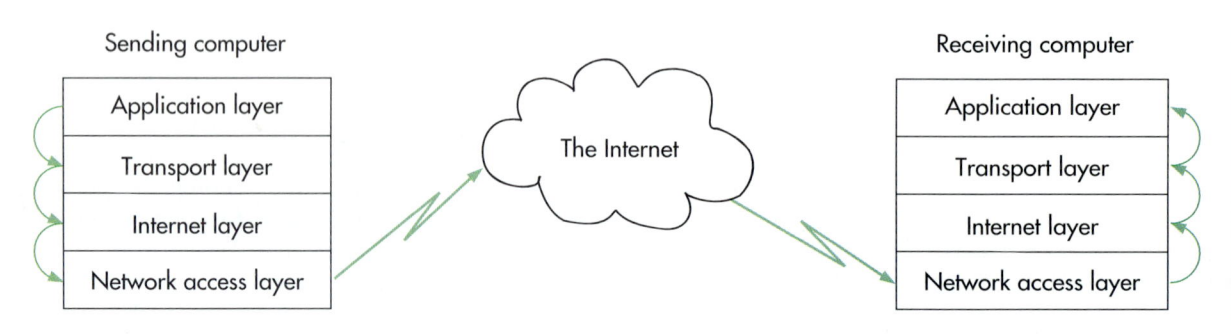

FIGURE 1.16 The Internet Architecture

network. They map the IP address of inbound messages to the actual hardware address of each local workstation on the LAN.

Let's use the more specific example shown in Figure 1.17. Bob, at the University of Miami, composes and sends an e-mail message. The transport layer divides the message into packets and delivers the packets to the Internet layer. The transport layer also keeps track of how many bytes have been sent, and waits to hear back from the receiving end whether the data was transmitted. Since the destination address is not on the local network to which Bob is attached, the Internet layer attaches a **header** (address information) to it and forwards it to the network access layer.

The network access layer, in turn, adds additional header information and sends the message out through the router onto the Internet. From there it is passed to another router, which examines the header and passes the packet on to another router. Each router contains a routing table that determines where (to what network router) to send the message next, based on the IP address of the message. This process continues until the destination router is reached, and the TCP/IP stacks on the receiving host deliver the message. They then send an acknowledgment of receipt to the sending computer. All of this happens in a matter of seconds, in a network that spans the globe!

The protocols that govern each layer are hardware independent, enabling the sender and recipient to use two different types of computers, yet receive the messages without problems. In our diagram we show Bob working on a Windows 95 PC and Gretchen on a Mac. In addition, the networks themselves may be different—that is, use different types of wiring—in which case the Internet layer will change the size of the packets to those required for the specific network.

Think of the post office analogy. Some mail routes are handled by mail truck, others on foot. If the mail carrier is on a walking route, he or she must remove the mail from the plastic mail tub and place it in the mail shoulder bag. Not all of the mail will fit, so some pieces will wait for the carrier to return and load

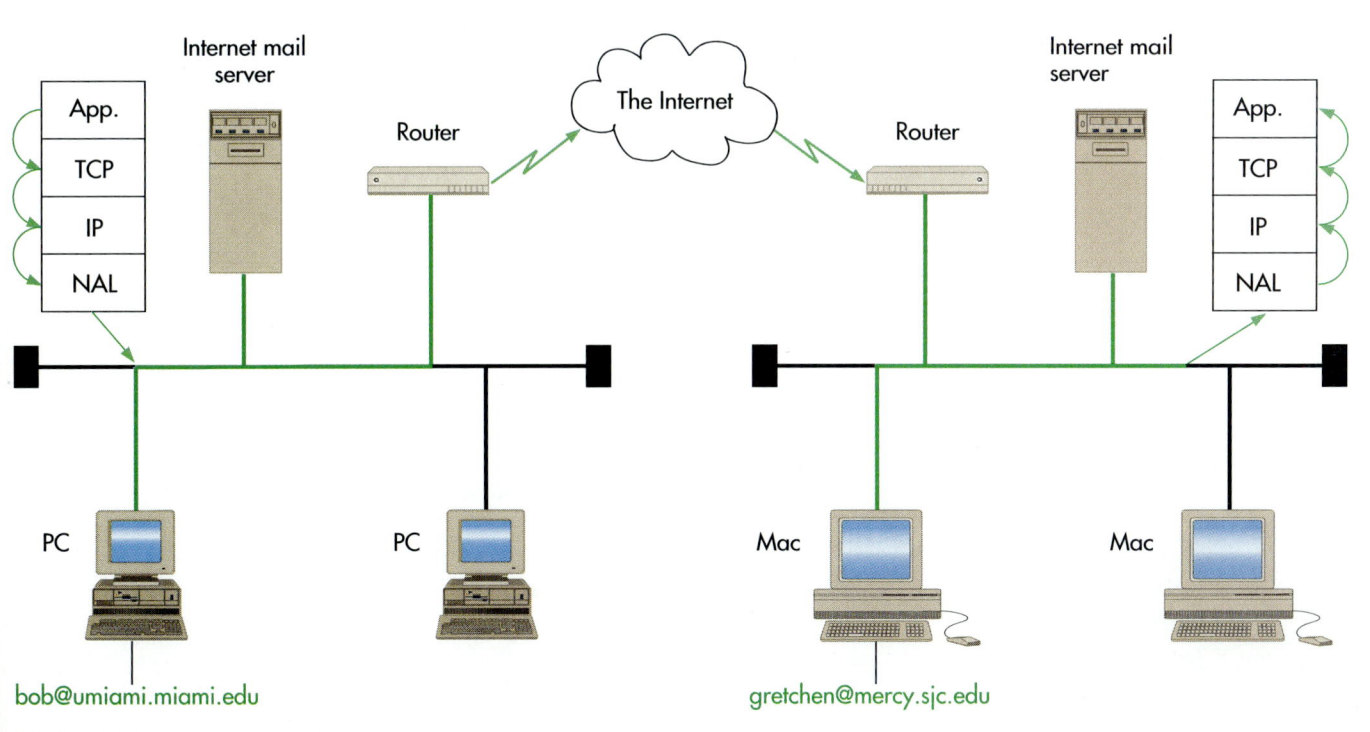

FIGURE 1.17 A Message Is Routed over the Internet

up for the second round. In a similar way, some Internet messages must be broken into different size packets for different parts of the physical network. The information about the type of protocols used is contained in the header attached to the packets.

The Internet layer performs additional important functions in the transmission of messages:

- Requesting routers to slow down the traffic when too many messages are being received (flow control)
- Returning error messages to the sender if a message is undeliverable
- Checking remote hosts to determine if they are operational

Similarly, the transport layer has additional responsibilities:

- Notifying the remote host that data is coming
- Keeping track of how many bytes of data have been sent
- Receiving acknowledgments from the receiving host
- Retransmitting the message if no acknowledgment is received
- Delivering data from the Internet layer to the correct application

Fortunately, most, if not all of these functions are transparent to the user. You simply type your message, click Send, and off it goes, aided by all the protocol stacks installed on your system.

The Domain Name System

The **Domain Name System (DNS)** was created to ensure a unique Internet address for every site. The Internet is divided into a series of component networks called **domains** that enable e-mail (and other files) to be sent across the entire network. Each site attached to the Internet belongs to one of the domains. Universities, for example, belong to the EDU domain. Government agencies are in the GOV domain. Commercial organizations (companies) are in the COM domain. Large domains are in turn divided into smaller domains, with each domain responsible for maintaining unique addresses in the next lower-level domain, or subdomain. Table 1.1 lists the six major Internet domains.

Internet Addresses

An **Internet address** or **Fully Qualified Domain Name (FQDN)** consists of the username, the host computer, and the domain (or domains) by which the com-

TABLE 1.1 Internet Domains

Domain	Description	Example Subdomain
edu	Educational institutions	Your college or university
gov	Federal, state, and local government entities	NASA, the CIA, the U.S. Senate, the Library of Congress, the National Archives
mil	Military organizations	U.S. Navy
com	Commercial nodes	Microsoft, Prentice Hall, Prodigy
net	Network service providers	The National Science Foundation's Internet Network Information Center
org	Nonprofit organizations	The Internet Town Hall

puter is connected to the Internet. The domains are listed in importance from right to left; that is, the highest-level domain appears on the end (the extreme right) of the Internet address. (You may find additional information following the highest-level domain. This is the country code, used if the host computer is located outside the U.S.) The @ sign separates the username from the host computer. For example:

```
gmarx@mercy.sjc.edu
  │      │     │   └─ Highest-level domain
  │      │     └───── Next-level domain (subdomain)
  │      └─────────── Host computer
  └────────────────── Username
```

Each Internet address has an underlying numeric IP address, which the software uses to establish connections between machines. Fortunately, we are generally able to use a name instead of the numeric IP address to send messages.

Since messages are sent from all over the world to all over the world, these names must be translated to IP addresses constantly. That is the purpose of a special program called Domain Name Service (DNS), which runs on your Unix host. If your message contains an Internet address that is unknown to your host, it can look up the numeric IP address by querying the nearest **domain root server,** a special site on the Internet that keeps information about IP addresses in its domain. This is similar to your going to the post office to look up a zip code for a letter you wish to send. You can keep the zip code handy in case you want to send a letter to that address again. In a similar fashion the Internet host can keep in memory the numeric IP address found in any query so it will not have to look it up again the next time a message is sent to that Internet address.

AN ADDRESS TO REMEMBER

An Internet address is easier to remember when you realize that the address consists of the username, the host computer, and the domain (or domains) by which the computer is connected to the Internet. For example, President Clinton's e-mail address is president@whitehouse.gov, where president is the username, whitehouse is the host computer, and gov is the domain. Vice President Gore may be reached at vice-president@whitehouse.gov. (Use lowercase only—addresses are usually case sensitive.)

LEARNING BY DOING

Learning is best accomplished by doing, and so we come to the first of the many hands-on exercises that appear throughout the book. The exercises enable you to apply the concepts you have learned, then extend those concepts to further exploration on your own.

In contrast to subsequent exercises in the book, our first exercise is up to you to complete largely on your own. You will find out about the computing environment on your campus, learn how to apply for and get a user account and password for your LAN, and another for your Internet server, if required. You will log on to your LAN and investigate what Internet tools are available. If possible, you will set up a telnet session to your Unix host, log on, then log out. These simple activities will help you verify the validity of your username or password. There is nothing more frustrating than being several weeks into the semester and still not being able to log on. If you are unable to log on, please seek immediate assistance from your instructor, lab assistant, and/or LAN administrator.

THERE'S ALWAYS A REASON

We would love to tell you that everything will go perfectly, that you will never be frustrated, and that the computer will always perform exactly as you expect. Unfortunately, that is not going to happen, because a computer does what you tell it to do, which is not necessarily what you want it to do. There can be a tremendous difference! There is, however, a logical reason for everything the computer does or does not do; sooner or later you will discover that reason, at which point everything will fall into place.

HANDS-ON EXERCISE 1

Welcome to Cyberspace

Objective: Log on to your campus network. Determine what Windows-based Internet programs you can access on your PC. Open a telnet session with the campus Unix host. Use Figure 1.18 as a guide in the exercise.

STEP 1: Get Your Username and Password

➤ While it may seem self-evident, the first thing you must do before you can proceed with any other exercises in the book is get a username and password. Take some time to familiarize yourself with your campus computing environment. It is much better to answer these questions before you start than the night before a big assignment is due!

- What are the lab hours?
- Is there a help desk? What are its hours?
- Will you need to have your student ID with you to get in?
- How do you get a username and password?
- Do you need two different accounts (one for your academic LAN, one for the Internet)?

➤ Apply for your username(s) and password(s).

STEP 2: Start Netscape (or Another Browser)

➤ If you received more than one user account and password, check with your lab assistant or help desk to determine which one to use to log on to the campus network. Log on now. (Our example uses Windows 95, but it works equally well in Windows 3.1.)

- Check the Windows 95 desktop for any shortcuts to Internet programs, such as the Netscape icon shown in Figure 1.18a, then double click the icon, *or*
- Click **Start** on the taskbar, then click **Programs.** Search the program list for any Internet programs or program groups such as the Internet program group shown in Figure 1.18b. Start Netscape (or another browser) by selecting it from the list of programs.

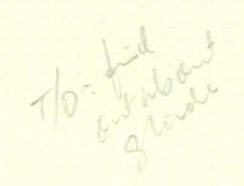

26 EXPLORING THE INTERNET

Double click here to
start Netscape

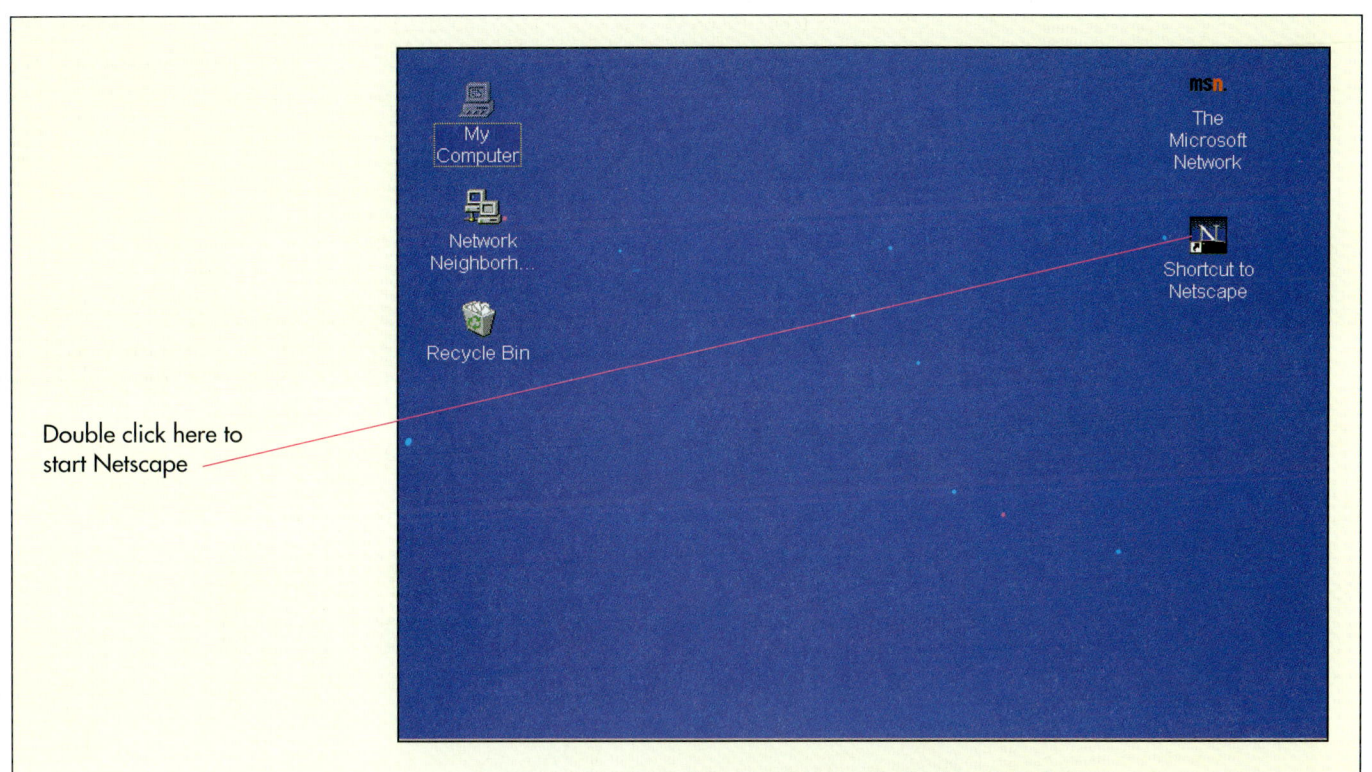

(a) The Netscape Icon on the Windows 95 Desktop

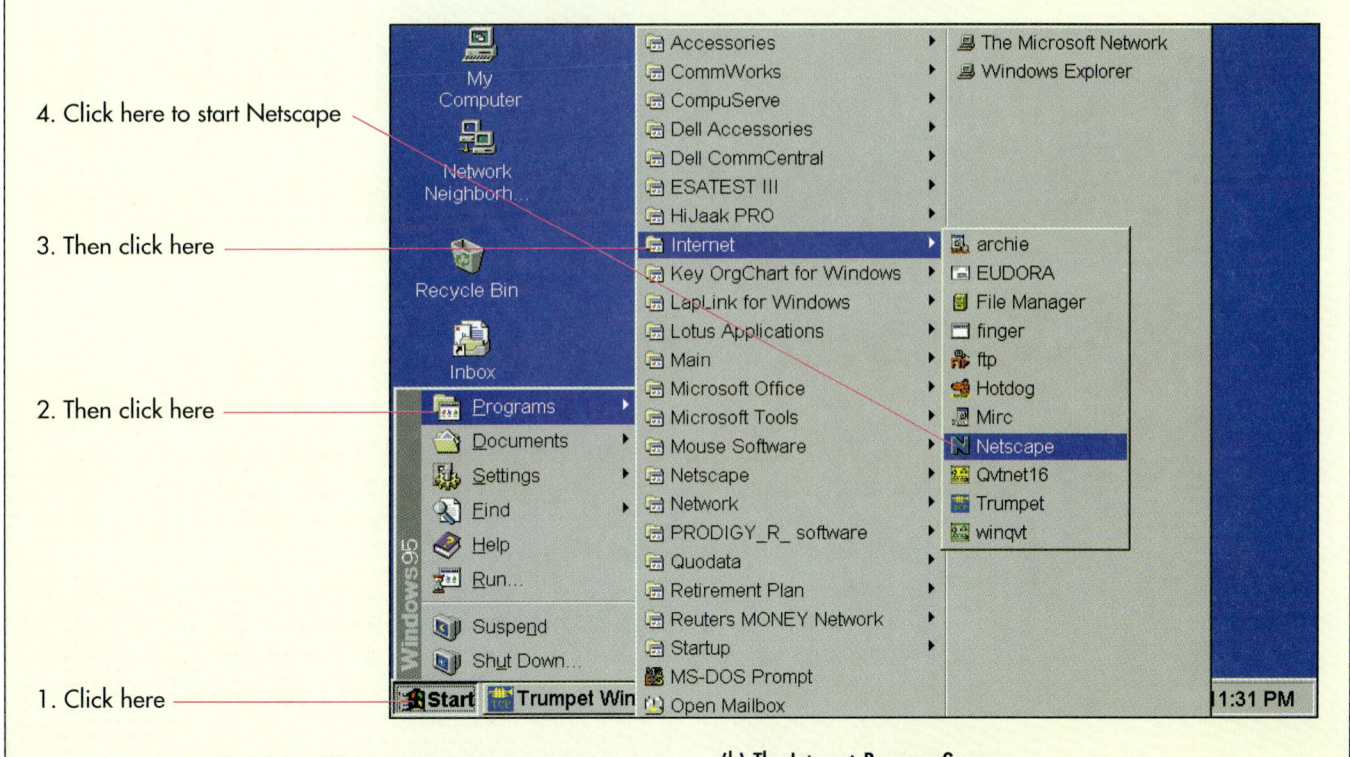

4. Click here to start Netscape

3. Then click here

2. Then click here

1. Click here

(b) The Internet Program Group

FIGURE 1.18   Hands-on Exercise 1

INTRODUCTION TO THE INTERNET

- Exit Netscape the same way you exit any other Windows 95 program. Select **Exit** from the **File** menu or double click the **program icon** in the upper-left corner of the screen.

STEP 3: Find Out How to Start a Telnet Session

➤ You will need to get to the Unix prompt for a number of subsequent hands-on exercises. Therefore you will need to know how to start a telnet session and log on to your Unix Internet host.

➤ Check with your instructor, lab assistant, or help desk to determine how to set up a telnet session in your campus computing environment. (WinQVT is a widely used Windows program that provides telnet access. Check to see whether it is available.)

- Select **WinQVT** or other appropriate icon or program from the program list. If you are using WinQVT, you should see a window similar to the one shown in Figure 1.18c. Select **Terminal** from the **Services** pull-down menu.

- Enter the name of the site to which you want to telnet (your campus Inter-

Click here

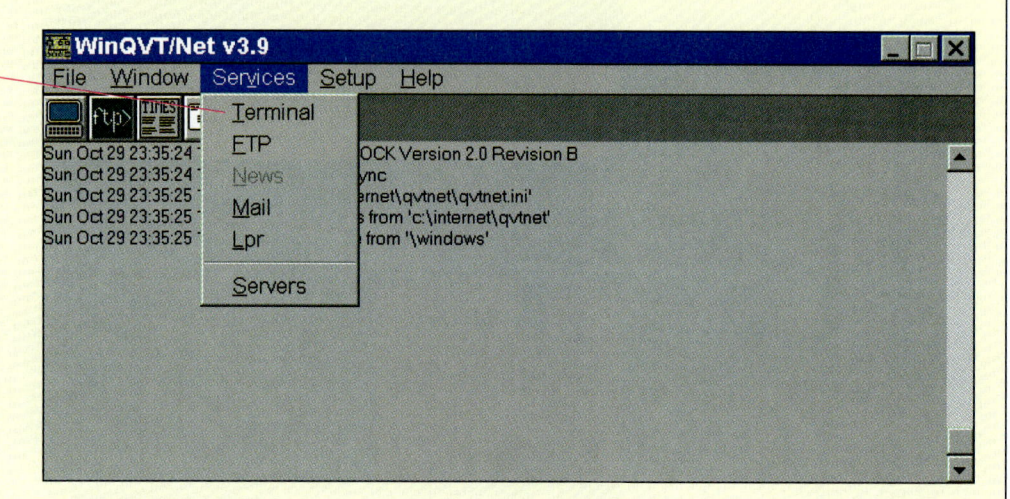

(c) The WinQVT Window

FIGURE 1.18 Hands-on Exercise 1 (continued)

net host). Depending on your environment, you may be able to enter the host name only, instead of the Fully Qualified Domain Name (FQDN) (the complete Internet address), as shown in Figure 1.18d. If that doesn't work, try the entire FQDN, as shown in Figure 1.18e, substituting the address of your Internet host. Click **OK**.

- If successful, you will see a window similar to the one shown in Figure 1.18f, which shows the Unix Login: prompt. Type your **login ID** (your username) and press **Enter.** Type your password and press **Enter.** You should see the Unix $ prompt (you may see a % or other symbol). Congratulations! You made it to your Unix account!

➤ Type the command to exit your Unix account. It may be **exit, logoff, log,** or some other command. (See your lab assistant or help desk for assistance.)

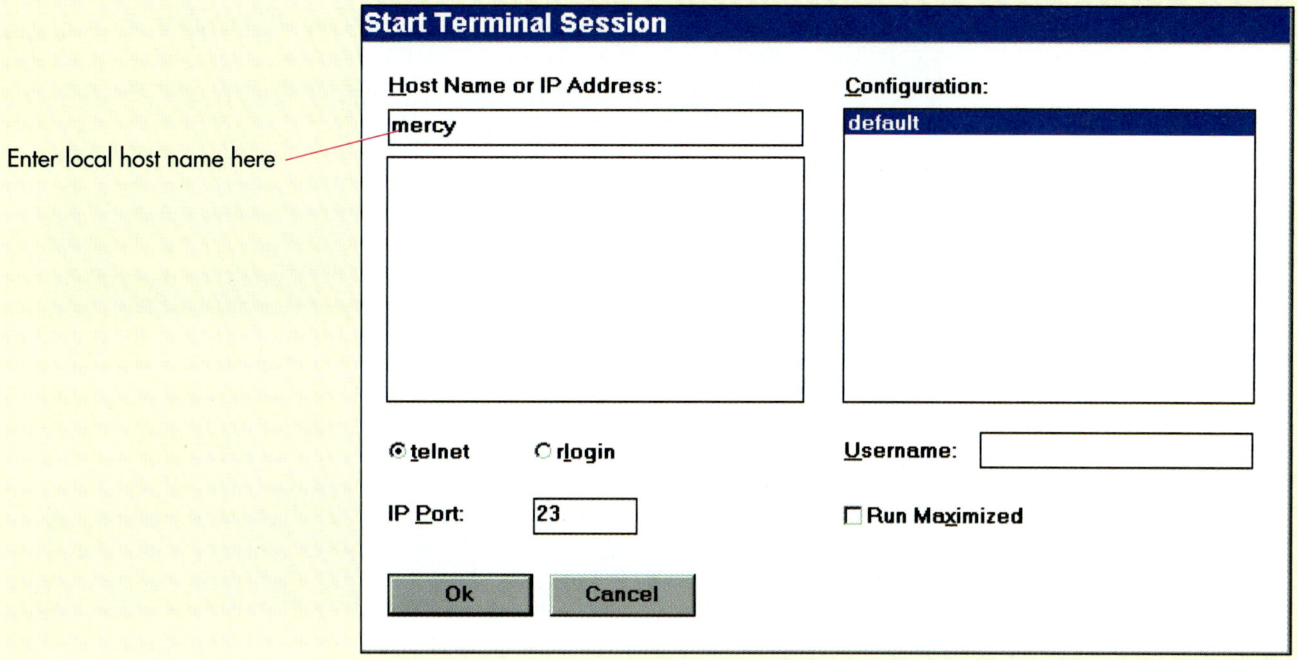

Enter local host name here

(d) Setting Up a Connection Using the Host Name

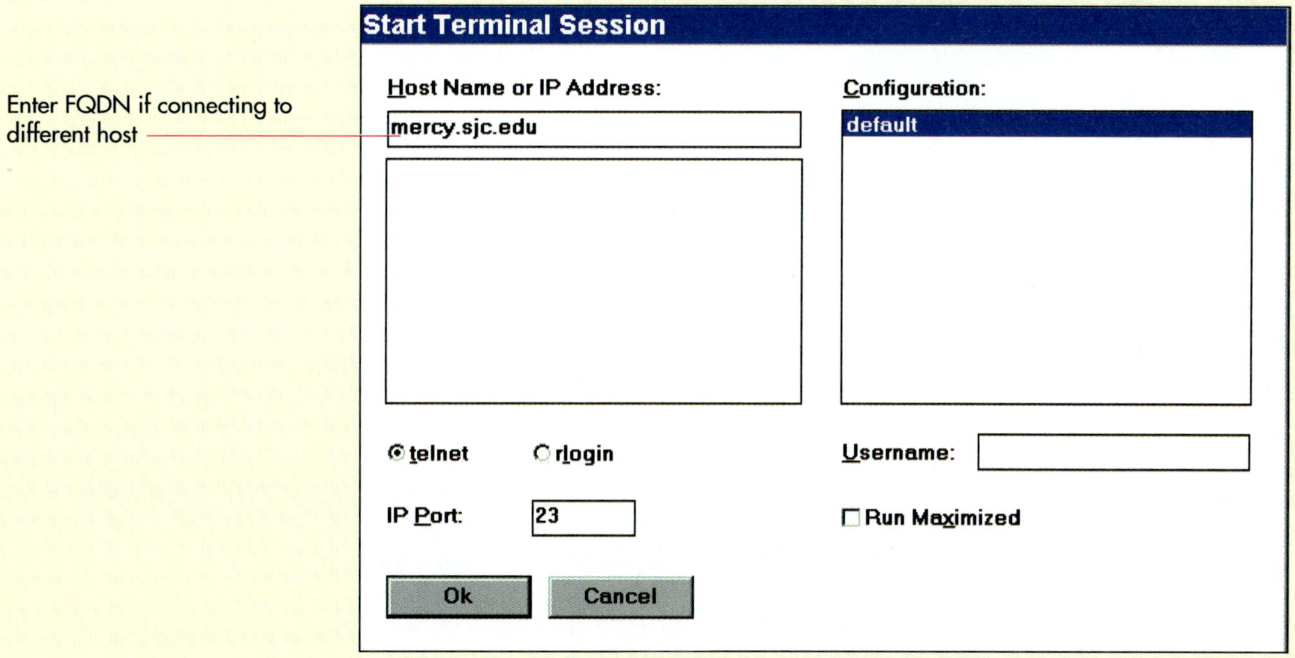

Enter FQDN if connecting to different host

(e) Setting Up a Session Using the Fully Qualified Domain Name

FIGURE 1.18   Hands-on Exercise 1 (continued)

INTRODUCTION TO THE INTERNET   29

Unix login prompt ⟶

(f) The Unix Login Prompt

FIGURE 1.18   Hands-on Exercise 1 (continued)

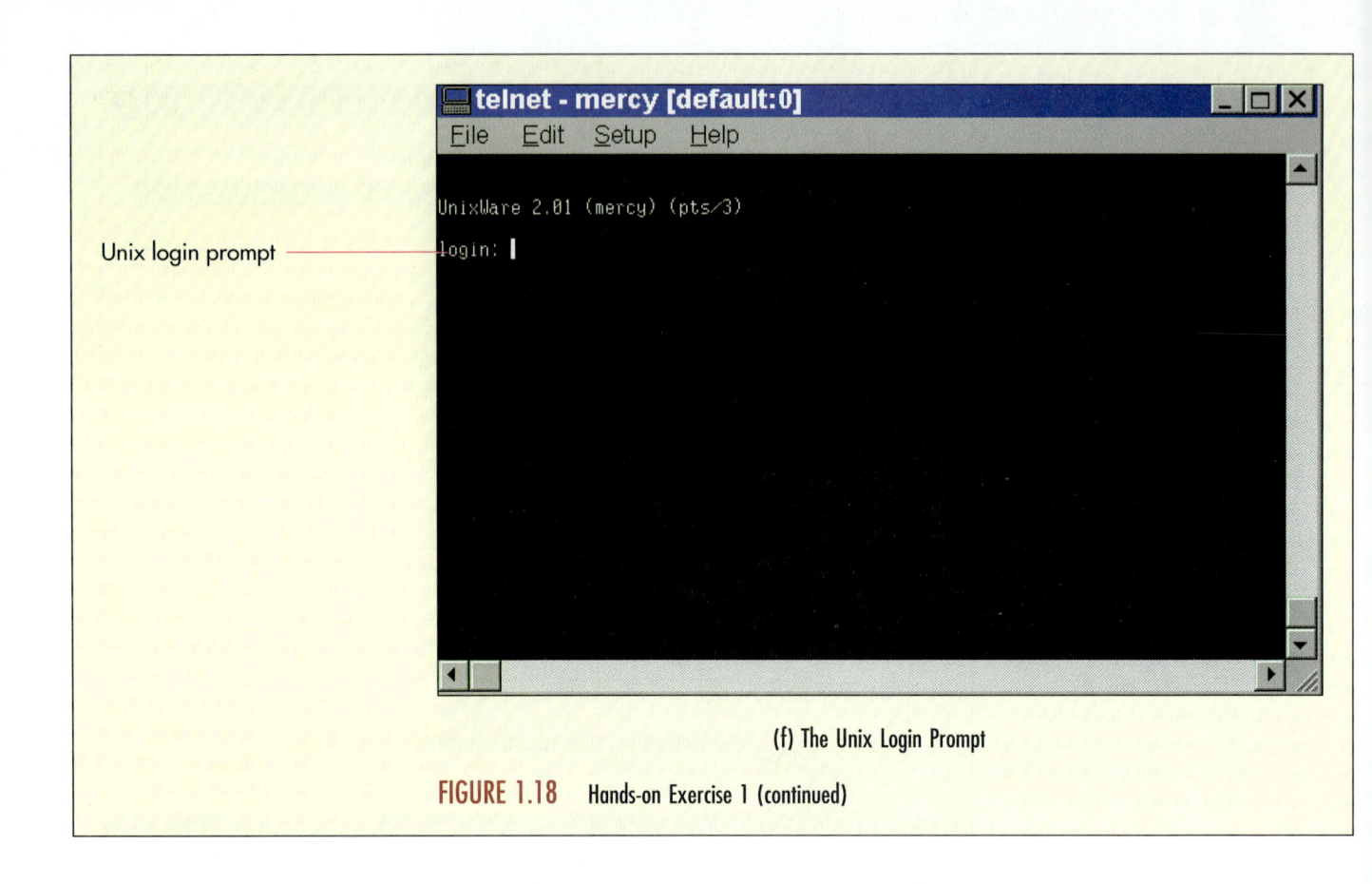

SUMMARY

The Internet is a network of networks that connects computers across the country and around the world. It began as an experimental project in 1969 to test the possibility of creating a network over which scientists and military personnel could share messages and data no matter where they were. Today the Internet includes virtually every major U.S. university, various government agencies, and an ever increasing number of commercial networks around the world.

You can access many resources and services on the Internet. E-mail users send electronic messages instantly around the world. World Wide Web documents let you link from one document to another by using a Web browser. Search engines help you locate Web resources, including HTML documents, gopher menus, and FTP sites. Chat and Usenet are additional resources for online and offline Internet communication, respectively. Some of these resources will be available using Windows-based GUI programs. Others will be accessed from the Unix prompt on your campus Internet host. You will need a username and password to get started.

Each institution that maintains a node on the Internet is responsible for supporting and administering that node. Each individual node pays its own way, and is responsible for providing services such as e-mail to its users.

The Internet works by sending all files and messages in packets. Packets are routed using TCP/IP, the software protocols that govern the flow of data across the Internet. Each computer using the Net must have a TCP/IP stack installed, and must have an IP address. Users generally prefer to use Internet addresses that consist of names as opposed to numbers. The Domain Name Service (DNS) translates Internet addresses into IP addresses. Security is very important on the Internet. Each user is assigned a username and password, which should be protected and changed often.

KEY WORDS AND CONCEPTS

Advanced Research Projects Agency (ARPAnet)
Application Layer
Archie
Browser
Channel
Chat
Client
Cyberspace
Domain
Domain Name System (DNS)
Domain root server
Download
E-mail
File server
File Transfer Protocol (FTP)
FTP site
Fully Qualified Domain Name (FQDN)
Gopher
Gopherspace
Graphical user interface (GUI)
Header
Hypertext
Hypertext Markup Language (HTML)
Information Superhighway
Internaut
Internet address
Internet host
Internet layer
IP address
Link
Local area network (LAN)
Lynx
Mosaic
Netscape
Network access layer
News
Newsgroups
Newsreader
Node
Offline
Packet
Post
Protocol
Router
Search engine
Stack
Surfing
Tag
Telnetting
Telnet session
Terminal
Terminal session
The Internet
Transmission Control Protocol/Internet Protocol (TCP/IP protocol)
Transport Layer
Usenet
Veronica
Virtual
Web site
Workstation
World Wide Web

MULTIPLE CHOICE

1. Which of the following statements about the Internet is true?
    (a) The Internet was started in the 1940s
    (b) The Internet is international in scope
    (c) The Internet is available only to the Department of Defense and large research universities
    (d) The number of Internet users is in the thousands

2. Which of the following is required to access the Internet?
    (a) A user ID
    (b) A password

(c) Both (a) and (b)
(d) Neither (a) nor (b)

3. Which of the following typically provides a graphical user interface to access the Internet?
   (a) Client software
   (b) A Unix shell account
   (c) A command-line prompt
   (d) All of the above

4. Users from which of the following organizations may access the Internet?
   (a) Government agencies
   (b) Nonprofit organizations
   (c) Commercial organizations
   (d) All of the above

5. Which of the following Internet services provides real-time interaction with other users?
   (a) Chat
   (b) E-mail
   (c) Usenet
   (d) All of the above

6. Which of the following products let(s) you browse the World Wide Web?
   (a) Mosaic
   (b) Netscape
   (c) Both (a) and (b)
   (d) Neither (a) nor (b)

7. E-mail allows you to send messages to:
   (a) Another user on your campus network
   (b) Another user on the Internet
   (c) Both (a) and (b)
   (d) Neither (a) nor (b)

8. Which of the following is the central authority of the Internet?
   (a) The Department of Defense
   (b) The Advanced Research Projects Agency
   (c) Both (a) and (b)
   (d) Neither (a) nor (b)

9. Which of the following is (are) the standard protocol(s) required for a computer to be connected to the Internet?
   (a) Pine
   (b) TCP/IP
   (c) POP
   (d) Windows

10. Which of the following statements about messages on the Internet is true?
    (a) The sending computer must run TCP/IP
    (b) The receiving computer must run TCP/IP

(c) Both (a) and (b)

(d) Neither (a) nor (b)

11. In the Internet address *postmaster@mercy.sjc.edu*, which is the highest level domain?

    (a) Postmaster

    (b) Mercy

    (c) Sjc

    (d) Edu

12. Which of the following will a search engine be able to locate?

    (a) Web documents

    (b) Gopher menus

    (c) FTP files

    (d) All of the above

13. Internet packages are broken into packets to:

    (a) Improve the load balance in the network

    (b) Help ensure the data gets through without error

    (c) Both (a) and (b)

    (d) Neither (a) nor (b)

14. Which of the following allows you to subscribe to a discussion group?

    (a) Usenet

    (b) Mailing lists

    (c) Both (a) and (b)

    (d) Neither (a) nor (b)

15. Which of the following is used to create Web documents?

    (a) Gopher

    (b) HTML

    (c) TCP/IP

    (d) Usenet

ANSWERS

1. b	6. c	11. d
2. c	7. c	12. d
3. a	8. d	13. c
4. d	9. b	14. c
5. a	10. c	15. b

Exploring the Internet

1. Use Figure 1.19 to match each Internet service with its description; a given resource may be used more than once or not at all. Some descriptions may have more than one matching resource.

Resource

a. Netscape
b. Pine
c. Eudora
d. Lynx

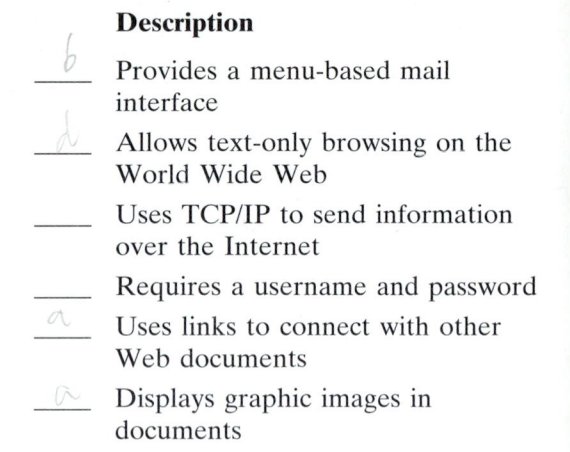

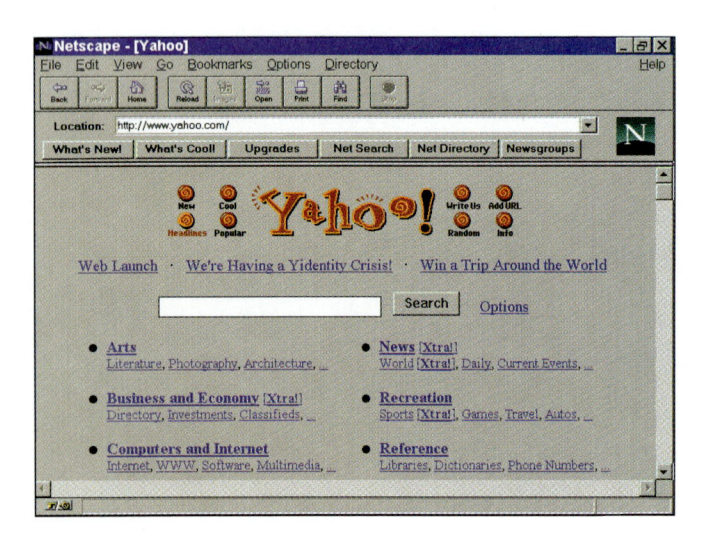

Description

_b_ Provides a menu-based mail interface

_d_ Allows text-only browsing on the World Wide Web

____ Uses TCP/IP to send information over the Internet

____ Requires a username and password

_a_ Uses links to connect with other Web documents

_a_ Displays graphic images in documents

(a) Netscape

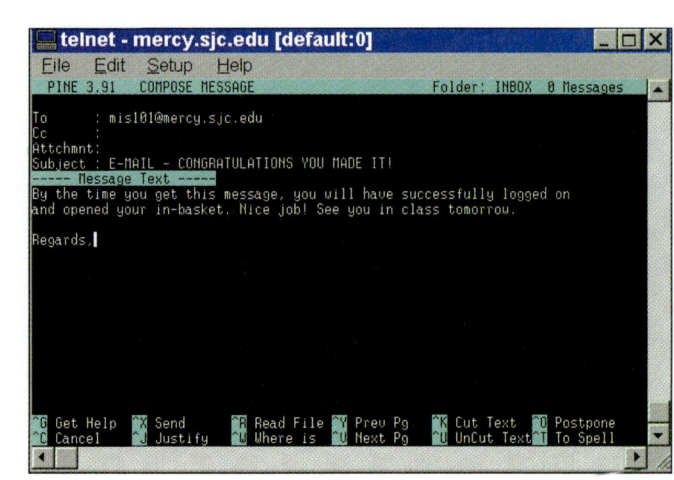

(b) Pine

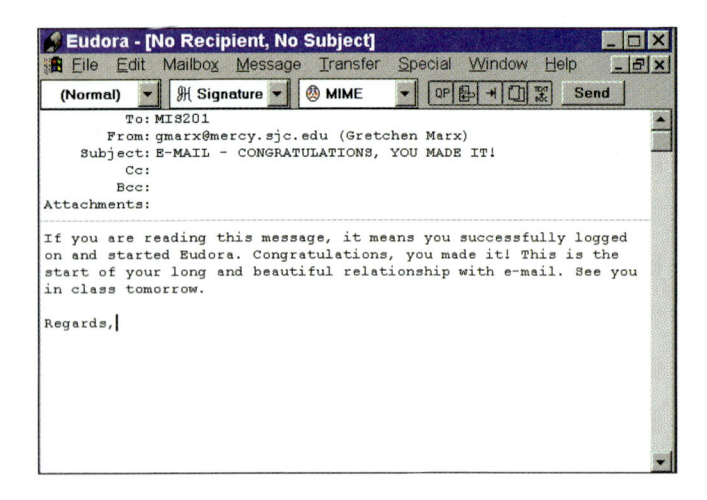

(c) A Message in Eudora

(d) Lynx

FIGURE 1.19 Figure for Exploring the Internet Exercise 1

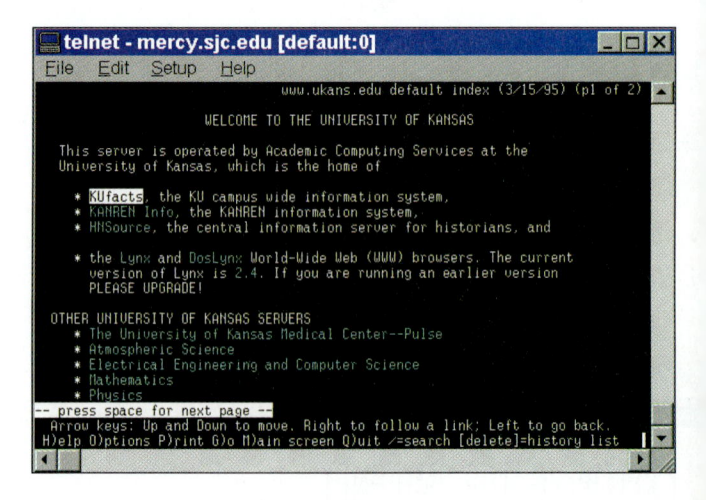

2. Examine the e-mail message shown in Figure 1.20 and answer the following questions.
   a. What is the sender's host name?
   b. What is the highest-level domain in the sender's Internet address?
   c. What is the sender's username?
   d. What is the recipient's host name?
   e. Can there be another person with the same username as the recipient at the same Internet address?
   f. Can there be another person with the same username as the recipient in the same domain?
   g. To what type of organization does the recipient probably belong? How can you tell?

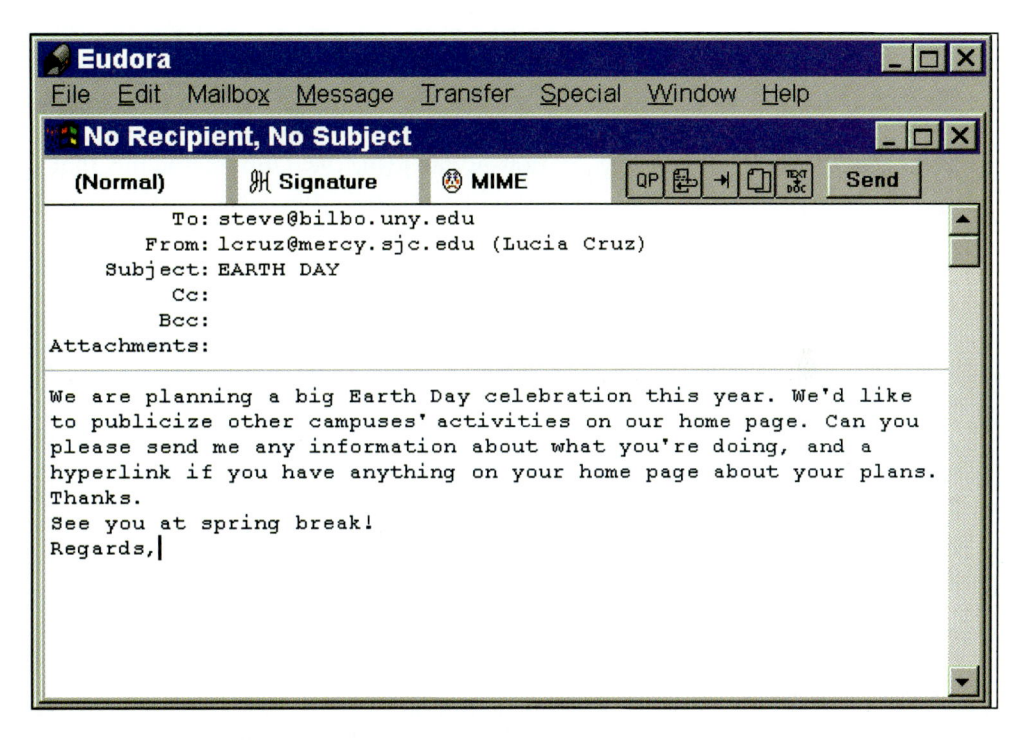

FIGURE 1.20 Figure for Exploring the Internet Exercise 2

3. Answer the following with respect to the Internet system at your college or university.
   a. Who is allowed access to Internet accounts?
   b. Do you have dial-in access?
   c. What e-mail program do you use?
   d. What is your username?
   e. What is your college or university's domain name?
   f. How often do you have to change passwords?
   g. Where do you go to get help?

4. Answer the following questions with respect to passwords:
   a. What advantage, if any, is there in choosing an eight-character password instead of one with four characters?
   b. What advantage (disadvantage) is there in choosing as a password a word found in the dictionary? Would it be better to use a nonsensical word, such as acissej (Jessica spelled backwards)?
   c. How often should you change your password? Why?

Practice with the Internet

1. **Practice Logging On:** Log on to your campus network, entering the wrong login name or ID. What error message do you get? What happens? Log on again, entering the correct login name or ID, but the wrong password. What happens this time? It is helpful to know what to expect in these situations, so that when you are under time pressure and make these common mistakes, you don't panic and assume something is wrong with your account. (Most computer problems are caused by human error.)

2. **Learn about Unix Help:** It helps to know more about Unix to do some of the things you will want to do on the Internet. Log on to your Unix server. At the Unix prompt type **man,** the Unix command to display the online Help manual. A list of available Unix commands is displayed. To learn more about a particular command, type **man commandname,** substituting the name of the command you want to review. For example, **man pwd,** displays information about **pwd,** the Unix command that displays the name of the current directory. Explore the Unix help manual by pressing the spacebar to move down a page. When you reach the end of the section you are reading you will automatically exit Help. When finished, log out using the Unix command appropriate for your computing environment.

3. **Learn about Unix Talk:** Most Unix systems provide an online dialog feature similar to Chat. With a classmate, go to the computer lab and each log on to your Unix accounts. Find out about the talk command by typing **man talk** at the Unix prompt. In particular, note how to end a talk session. After reading the help topic, type **talk username** at the Unix prompt, substituting the name of your classmate. Type a few messages to each other. Obviously this is not particularly useful if you are both in the same room, but it can be a lifesaver if you are communicating with someone on the other side of the campus. Quit the talk program and log out when finished.

4. **Find Out Who Is Logged On:** In the previous exercise you made arrangements to try the talk program with a classmate. At other times it is convenient to find out who is logged in at the same time you are. Log on and at the Unix prompt type **who.** A list of other users will be displayed. You may set up a talk session with any of them. However, just as you wouldn't randomly dial a phone number and start talking to whomever answered, you shouldn't disturb other users without good reason, and unless you know them.

Case Studies

Your Campus Computing Environment

Working with a friend or two from your class, interview your instructor, lab assistant, help desk specialist, LAN administrator, and anyone else who can provide information about your campus network. Draw a diagram of the network similar to Figure 1.12. Indicate which server or computer provides your Internet connection.

The Net Is Everywhere

Take a trip to a local pharmacy or bookstore that carries many types of magazines. Determine how many have the word *Internet* on the cover, and notice which types of magazines they are. (Are they all computer magazines, or are general-interest publications including articles about the Net?) Read the local paper for a week or two and watch for headlines about the Internet. You may find them on the front page, in the *Living* or *Business* sections, or just about anywhere else. Do a visual search in the periodical room at your campus or town library for references to the Internet. What did you find? Compare notes with classmates and write a brief report on the Internet and the media.

Is a Picture Worth a Thousand Words?

Much has been made of the World Wide Web and its ability to retrieve and display documents with embedded graphics. Review Figure 1.2 and compare the Netscape and Mosaic screens with the Lynx screen. Go back through this chapter and cover the illustrations and screens with a piece of paper, reading just the text. What value do graphics add to these documents?

The Commercialization of the Internet

The original design of the Internet precluded access to it by commercial organizations. That changed in the early 90s, and now it seems as though every company, from the multinational with its headquarters in Bahrain to the mom-and-pop grocery store on the corner, has a Web site. What reasons might the Department of Defense have had for limiting access initially? Why were commercial organizations eventually allowed access? Identify the pros and cons of commercial access to the Internet, and prepare a brief summary of your findings.

GLOBAL COMMUNICATION ON THE INTERNET: USING E-MAIL

OBJECTIVES

After reading this chapter you will be able to:

1. Discuss the general commands that are present in every e-mail system; send and receive an e-mail message.
2. Explain the differences between client- and server-based e-mail programs.
3. Create a distribution list to send the same e-mail message to many people.
4. Create a custom signature and mailbox.
5. Subscribe to an Internet mailing list.

OVERVIEW

Electronic mail (e-mail) is simply a means of sending messages by computer. One of the most widely used Internet services, it has changed the way we communicate. In many ways it is superior to the telephone. You send a message when it is convenient for you. The recipient reads the message when it is convenient for him or her. Neither of you has to be online for the other to access his or her e-mail system. Either of you can obtain a printed copy of the message. You can also use a mailing list capability to send the same message to many people. With very little training or effort, most people can understand the concepts involved with e-mail and learn to use it. And best of all, e-mail is a lot less costly than a long distance phone call.

In this chapter we describe two types of mail programs, Windows-based programs that run on a PC, and menu-based Unix programs. We begin by describing how e-mail is sent, received, and stored on your system. We show you how to send, receive, and reply to messages. We also discuss how to set up a custom mailbox, a distribution list, and a customized signature. Our examples use PC Eudora for Windows and the Unix mail program Pine, but the concepts apply equally well to any e-mail system.

A mailing list allows multiple people interested in exchanging mail about a subject to subscribe to the list and receive all the messages the members of the list generate. We show you how to request a list of all the mailing lists on the Internet, and how to get a list of all the mailing lists devoted to a specific topic. You will then subscribe to one or more lists, and within a few days (possibly hours) start receiving messages from other subscribers.

E-MAIL

Now that you know something from our discussion in Chapter 1 about how messages are transmitted on the Internet, let's find out how to send one. In essence, you use a text editor similar to a word processor to create a message, then you send it through the Internet, just as you would mail an ordinary letter. The message is delivered electronically to the recipient's *mailbox.* When the recipient checks his or her mailbox and finds the message, he or she can respond (or not) as he or she sees fit.

You do not have to be at home when the postman delivers a letter to your mailbox. In similar fashion your PC does not have to be on when an *e-mail* (electronic mail) system delivers a message to your electronic mailbox on your school's Internet host. All e-mail messages are stored in a central post office (an area on disk) that exists on the mail server at your college or university. Each user has a private mailbox on the mail server, which is analogous to a post office box in a regular post office. You have a key or combination lock to your post office box. In the same way you have a password for your e-mail mailbox. The electronic post office is controlled by a system administrator who monitors the e-mail system, provides access for individual users, and maintains the disk storage required to hold the electronic mail.

You can send e-mail in a variety of ways—across a local area network, by logging onto a remote computer at your school or university, or via an information service such as the Microsoft Network. There are many different types of e-mail programs, each with its own unique commands. It is impossible in any one text to cover the details of every system. All systems, however, provide the capability to send and receive mail. Our discussion will focus on the basic commands you can expect to find in any system. We demonstrate these commands using PC Eudora, a widely used Windows mail program, and Pine, a Unix mail program, but the discussion is sufficiently general so that you can apply the concepts to any other system.

The Structure of an E-mail Message

All e-mail messages contain certain basic elements as can be seen in Figure 2.1. Figure 2.1a shows the New Message window in PC Eudora, in which you compose an e-mail message. Figure 2.1b shows the Compose screen in Pine, a Unix-based e-mail program. You can see that while using two different types of computers and programs, the elements in the two screens are very similar.

The *header* area contains information pertaining to sending the message. The From and To lines contain the address of the sender and recipient, respectively. The Subject line is a one-line summary of the message. The Cc (*carbon copy*) line indicates the names of other people who are to receive copies of the message. Bcc, which stands for *blind carbon copy*, allows you to send a copy of the message to someone without the main addressee knowing you are doing so. The Attachments line lets you attach a file such as a Word document or Excel spreadsheet to your e-mail message. The e-mail message you are sending or receiving appears below the header.

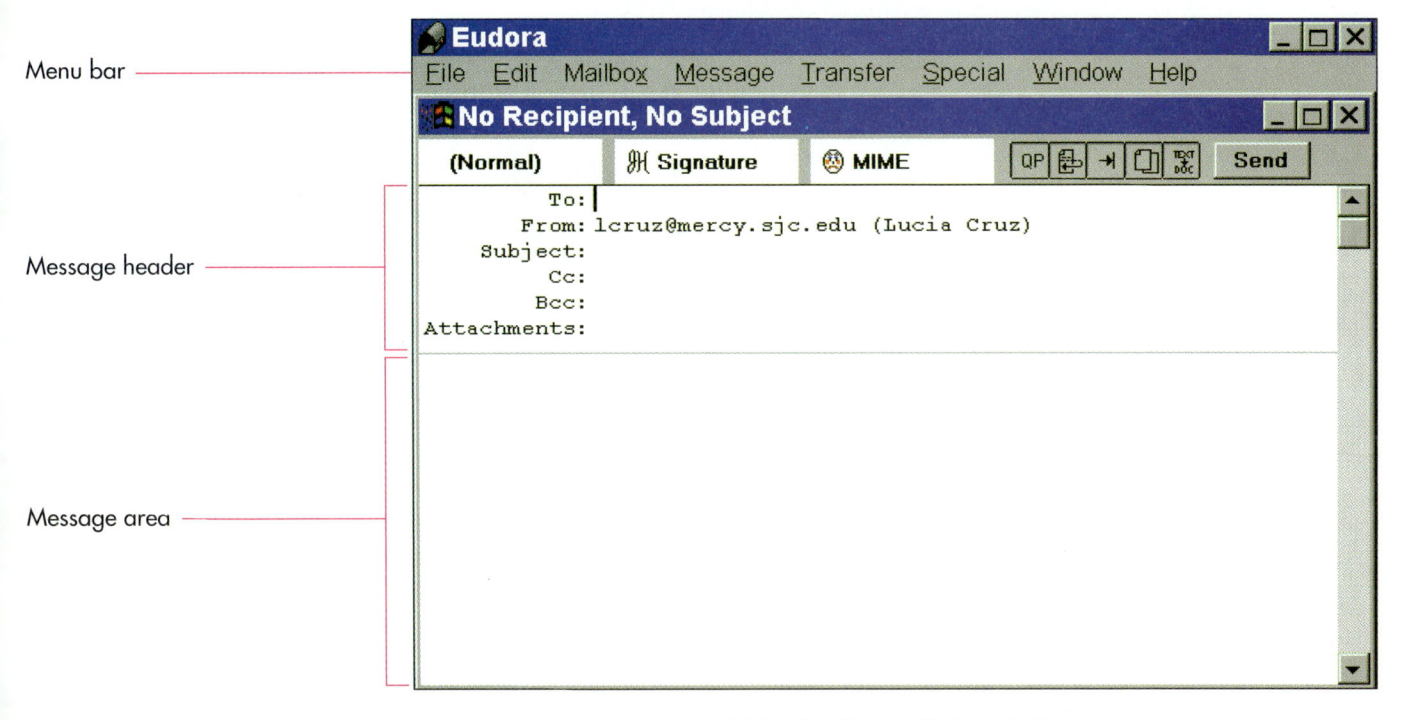

(a) The New Message Window in Eudora

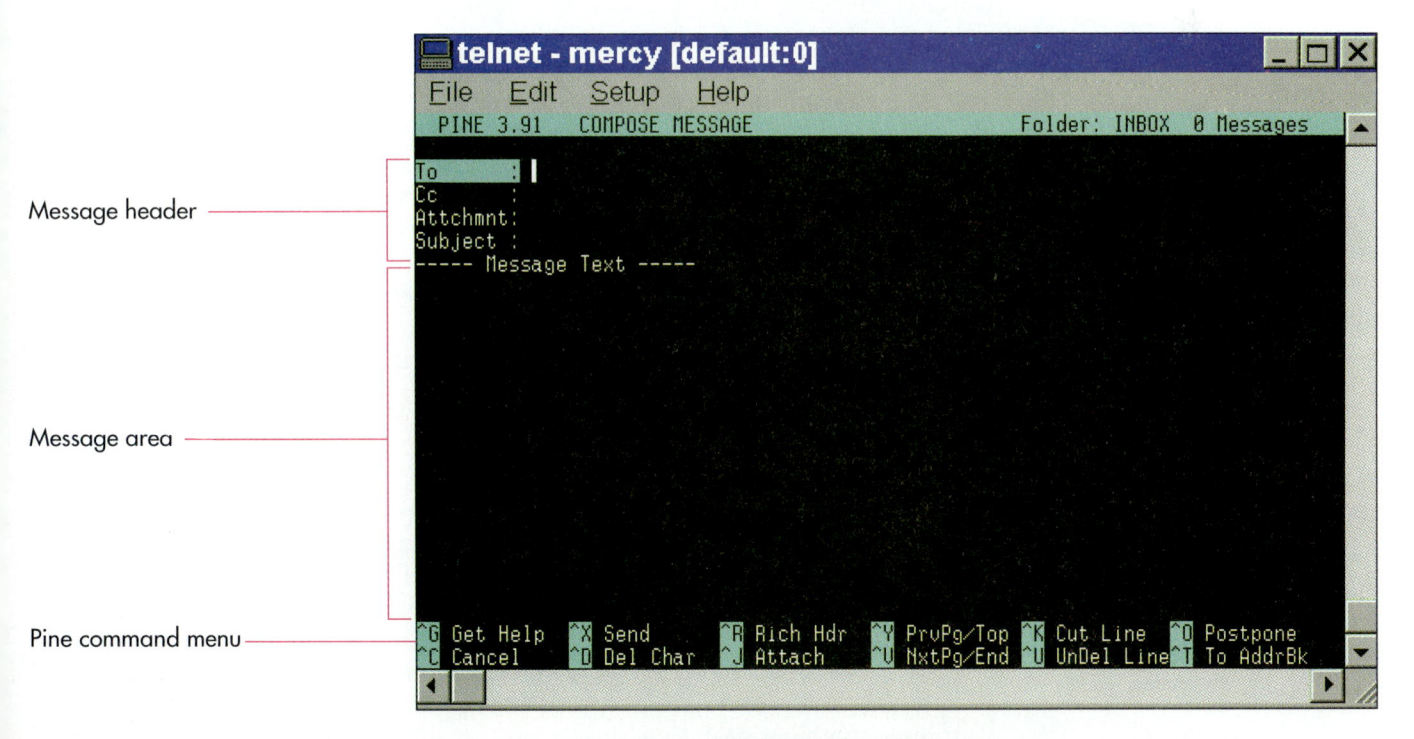

(b) The Compose Message Screen in Pine

FIGURE 2.1 Composing an E-mail Message

GLOBAL COMMUNICATION ON THE INTERNET

E-mail commands are executed by pulling down a menu, by clicking the corresponding icon on the toolbar, or by entering the appropriate command at the prompt in a command-driven system. The following commands (or their equivalent) are found in every system:

Compose:	To create a new message
Send:	To send a message that you created
Reply:	To respond to a message you received
Forward:	To send to another person a message you received

These commands are straightforward and will be illustrated in the hands-on exercises that follow.

Logins and Security

All e-mail systems let you send/receive messages to/from anyone on your network or information service. You can also send e-mail to individuals outside the network or information service, provided that they each have an Internet address and that your system has access to the Internet. You will need a userID and password to log on to your system. A **userID** is assigned to you and identifies you to the system. The **password** protects your account from unauthorized use by others. (As discussed in Chapter 1, you may actually have two or more userIDs and passwords, depending on how many systems you access on campus.) Your userID for the e-mail system will be the username you use in your Internet address. If Melissa Boyer is attending AnyU and uses an Internet host in the psychology department called Freud, her e-mail address would be *mboyer@freud.anyu.edu*. She would log on to the Unix system using the userID *mboyer*.

Many people choose passwords that are easy to remember, but what is easy for you is also easy for someone trying to break into your account. Thus, you should choose a password consisting of at least six characters, preferably letters *and* numbers or special characters. Keep the password to yourself and change it periodically. Do your LAN administrator a favor, and remember your password. If every user frequently forgets his or her password, the academic computing staff will have time to do little else but change user passwords!

PROTECT YOUR PASSWORD

Many computer break-ins occur because of a poorly chosen password consisting of only four characters. A hacker's computer is fast and it doesn't get discouraged if its first several attempts at guessing a password are rejected. A four-letter password has fewer than 500,000 combinations, which can be solved in only 30 seconds of computer time. Opting for eight letters increases the number of combinations to more than 200 billion, which makes the hacker's job much more difficult. And if you include numbers in addition to letters, an eight-character password (letters and numbers) has more than 2 trillion combinations! You should also avoid proper names and common words, as a hacker will use a program that goes through the dictionary trying common words until it finds one that allows the hacker in.

Mailboxes

Mail programs keep track of your mail by having default mailboxes, one for incoming messages (generally called the In-box or something similar), and one for outgoing messages (called the Out-box or sent-mail). In Figure 2.2a, the Eudora In-box folder is selected. It contains previously received messages (which the mailbox owner has decided to keep), as well as new messages waiting to be read. A bullet in the first column on the left indicates that the message in that row is

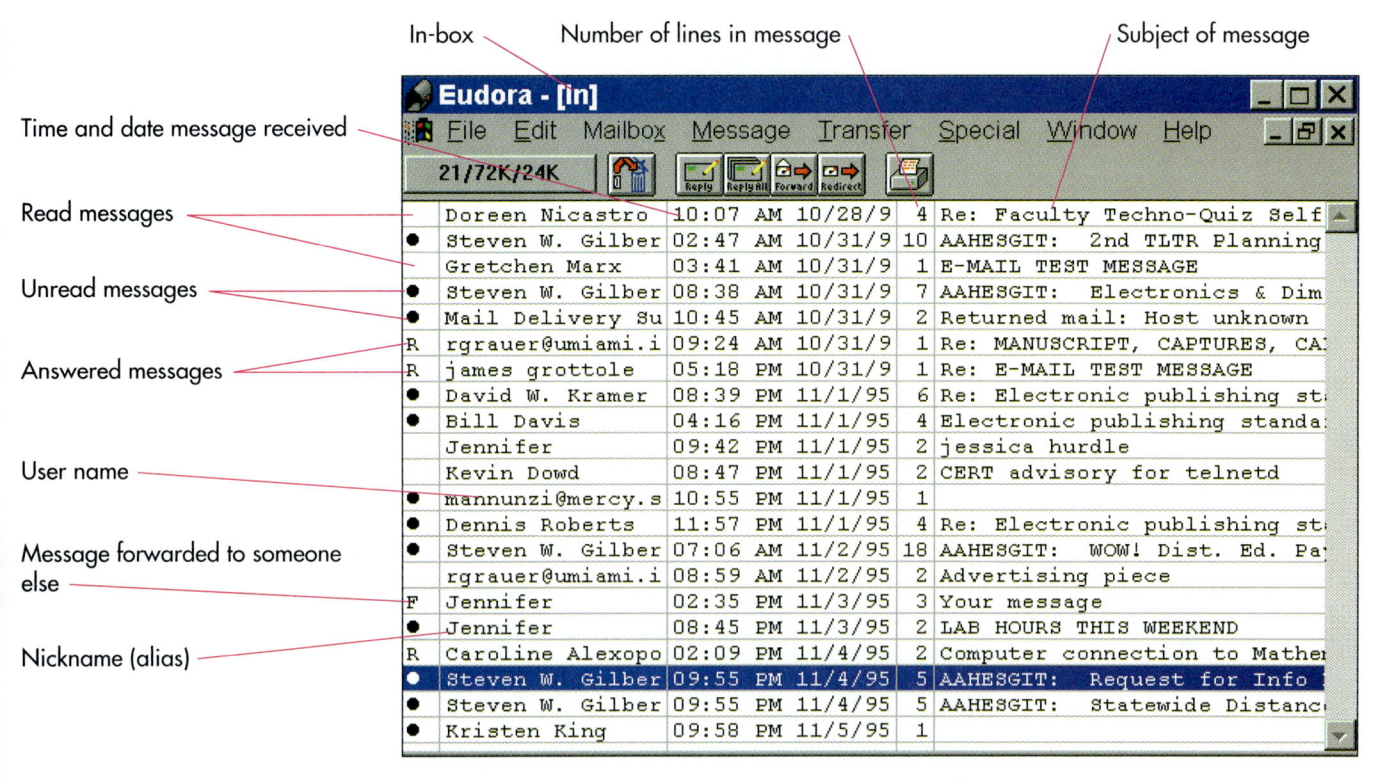

(a) The Eudora In-box

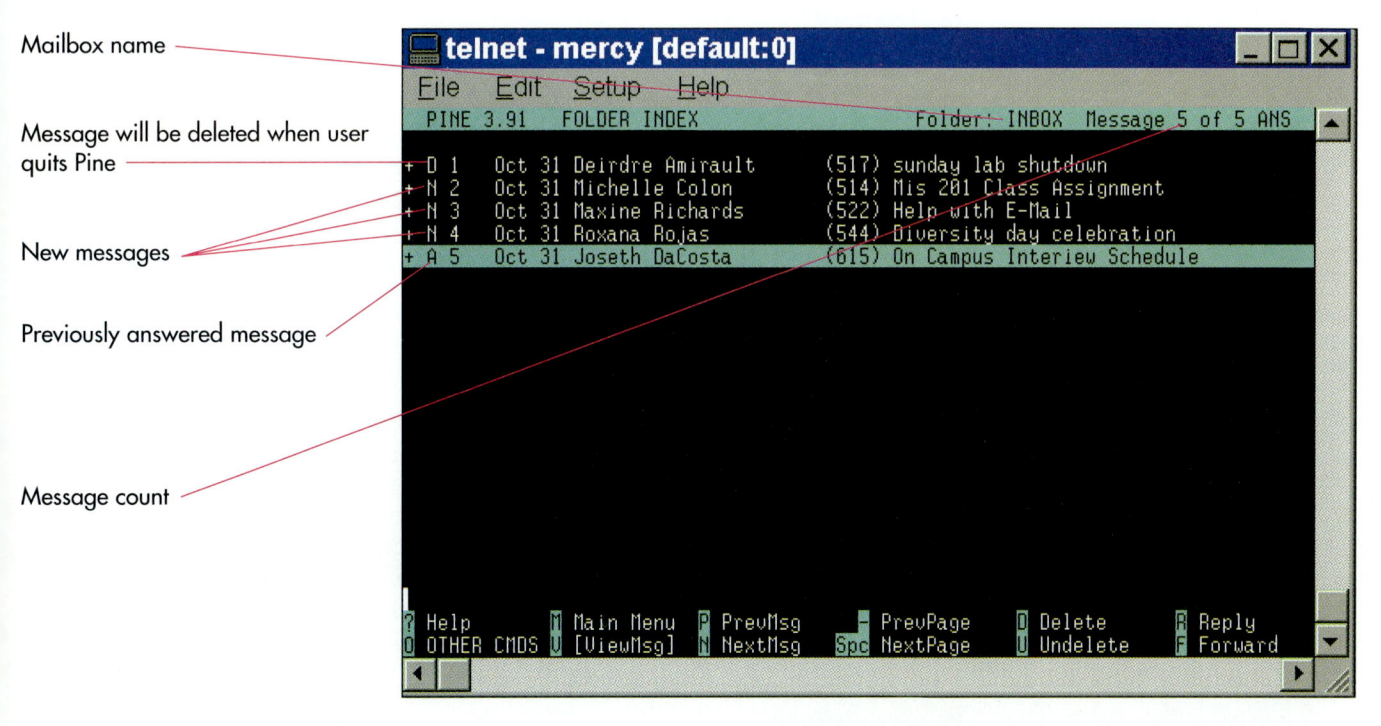

(b) The Pine In-box

FIGURE 2.2   The E-mail In-box

unread mail. An "R" indicates the message has been read and replied to. A blank field means the recipient has read the message without responding to it. The second column shows the sender's username or *alias.* (An alias is a nickname that is converted to a username by the e-mail system the sender is using.)

Figure 2.2b shows the INBOX folder in Pine. Messages are numbered and marked according to their status. Messages marked with a "D" will be expunged, or permanently deleted when you exit Pine. Messages marked with an "N" are new, unread messages, with an "A" are those you have read and replied to, with a "+" are those for which you are the sole recipient. Depending on how your system administrator has configured Pine, you may be able to flag a message as important, in which case you will see an asterisk "*" next to it. The *folder index,* which is what is shown in Figure 2.2b, also shows the date the message was sent, the name of the sender, the size of the message, and the subject, if any.

After reading a message you may decide to "throw it away" by moving it to a trash basket or marking it for deletion. When you exit Eudora, messages in the trash basket will be emptied, and the messages in it will be discarded. When you exit Pine, messages marked for deletion will be expunged.

SENDING AND RECEIVING E-MAIL

There is more than one way to send and receive e-mail on the Internet; which you use depends on your campus network environment. By far the easiest way is through the use of a Windows-based **mail client,** or e-mail program, running on your PC. The **client software** presents a graphical user interface (GUI) on the screen, which lets you point and click to select mail options and commands. If you don't have access to client software on your PC, you will access e-mail using a Unix-based mail program such as Pine. (Unix is a multipurpose operating system used in most campus Internet systems.) We will discuss both methods, and present two hands-on e-mail exercises that allow you to use whichever type of interface you have in your campus computing environment.

E-mail with a POP Mail Client

The process of sending and receiving mail using a PC-based mail client is illustrated in Figures 2.3a and 2.3b, respectively. The client software uses a protocol known as the **Post Office Protocol (POP)** to send and receive mail. When you use a POP mail client, your incoming mail is kept on the **mail server,** or Unix-based host, until you connect and request it. The mail client on your PC communicates with the mail server and **downloads** (retrieves) the inbound messages. It places them in a mailbox on your local PC disk drive (or in your personal mail directory on a network drive on a different file server).

You can read the messages when they are downloaded, or, because they are stored locally, you can read them at a later time without being logged on to the mail server. Outbound messages are composed on the PC using the POP mail client, **uploaded** (forwarded) to the Unix mail server, and also stored in your personal mailbox on your PC or network mail directory. The mail server sends the outbound messages through the router to the Internet by using a protocol known as **Simple Mail Transfer Protocol (SMTP).** (Hence the mail server is known as an SMTP server.)

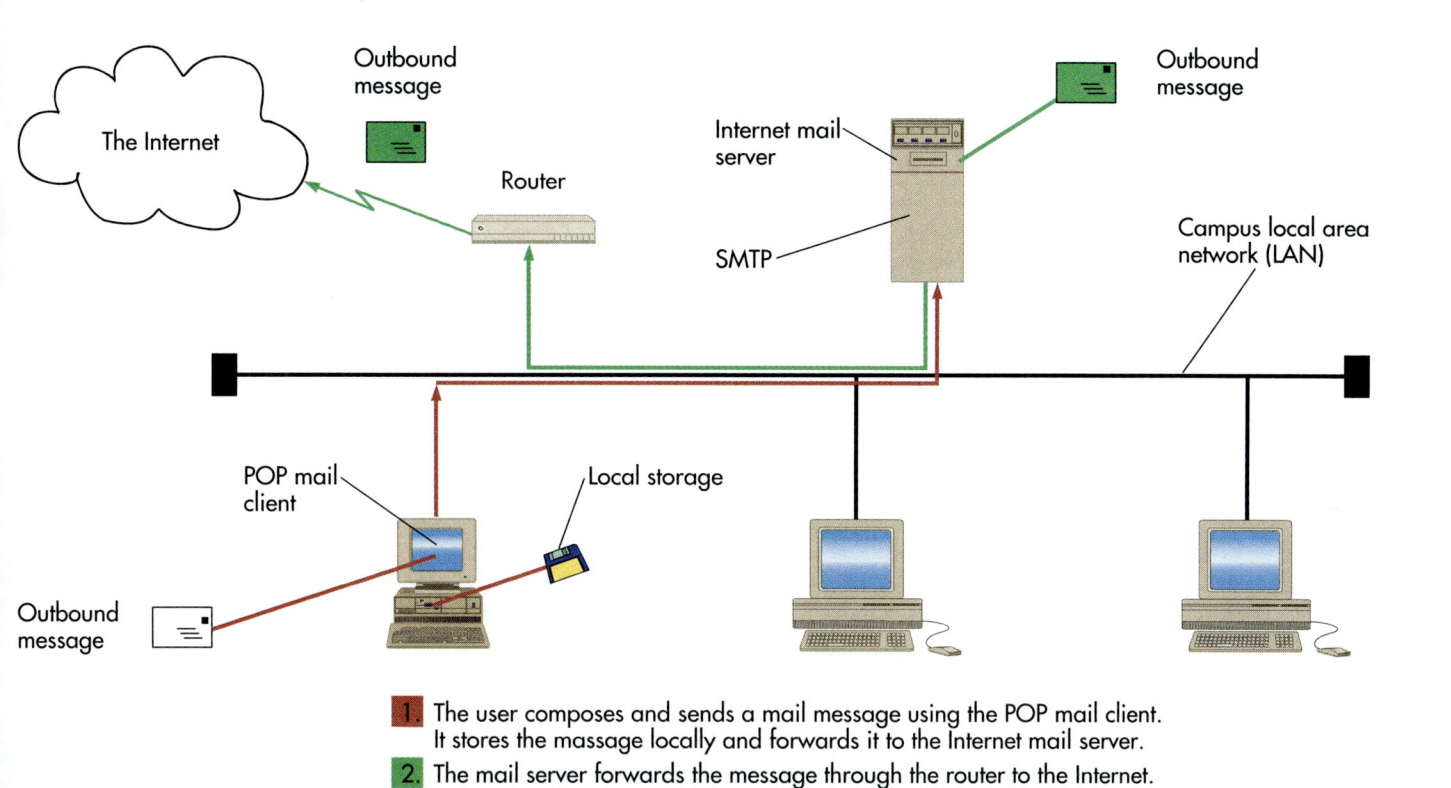

(a) Sending a Message with a POP Mail Client

1. The user composes and sends a mail message using the POP mail client. It stores the massage locally and forwards it to the Internet mail server.
2. The mail server forwards the message through the router to the Internet.

(b) Receiving a Message with a POP Mail Client

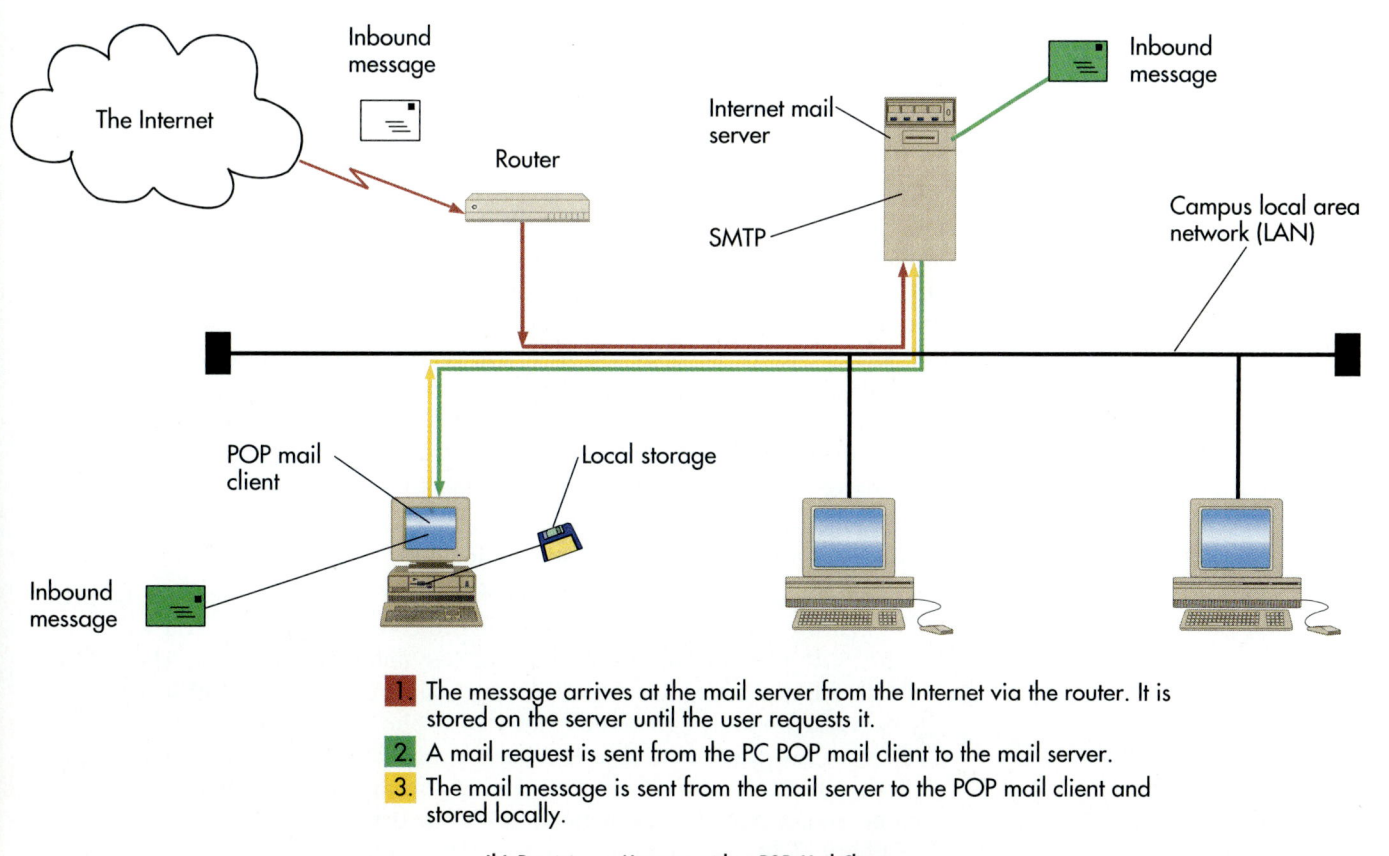

1. The message arrives at the mail server from the Internet via the router. It is stored on the server until the user requests it.
2. A mail request is sent from the PC POP mail client to the mail server.
3. The mail message is sent from the mail server to the POP mail client and stored locally.

FIGURE 2.3 Sending and Receiving E-Mail

GLOBAL COMMUNICATION ON THE INTERNET **45**

LEARNING BY DOING

The following exercise demonstrates the basics of e-mail in the context of PC Eudora. Although the commands in the exercise are specific to Eudora, they are sufficiently general that you should be able to adapt the exercise to any PC-based POP mail client. See your instructor, lab assistant, or help desk for assistance. And remember, the programs used to access the Internet are constantly changing. What you see on your screen may differ (possibly substantially) from the figures that follow.

FIND A PEN PAL

Everyone likes to get mail, especially when using e-mail for the first time. Find a classmate and exchange e-mail addresses so that you can practice sending and receiving mail. Do the following exercise with your partner. Find a pen pal at another school so you can practice sending mail across the Internet.

HANDS-ON EXERCISE 1

Welcome to E-mail with PC Eudora

Objective: Send and receive an e-mail message. The exercise is written for PC Eudora, but it can be done with any e-mail system. Use Figure 2.4 as a guide in the exercise.

STEP 1: Log On

> Log on to the local area network that you will use for e-mail.

STEP 2: Configure Your Mail Program

> Open the icon on your desktop that contains your Internet tools and start Eudora (or other POP mail client). Before you can use it, you will have to customize Eudora on your PC so it will recognize your username and password. *The instructions provided here give you a general overview of what you need to do to configure Eudora. See your instructor or LAN administrator for specific instructions for your computing environment. You will have to complete the configuration only once. It will be saved for future use.*

- Press the **Esc** key to ignore the password message shown in Figure 2.4a, which is displayed when you start Eudora.
- Select **Configuration** from the **Special** menu shown in Figure 2.4b. The Configuration dialog box shown in Figure 2.4c is displayed. You will enter your POP account (Internet address), real name (First Name, Middle Initial, and Last Name), your SMTP server name (your Unix mail server), and your return address (Internet address) in the dialog box. PC Eudora will use your full name to create an alias, or nickname, for your mail messages. (See your instructor or lab assistant if you are not sure what your username and/or SMTP server name is.) Your dialog box should look similar to Figure 2.4d when complete. Click **OK** when you have finished entering the required fields.

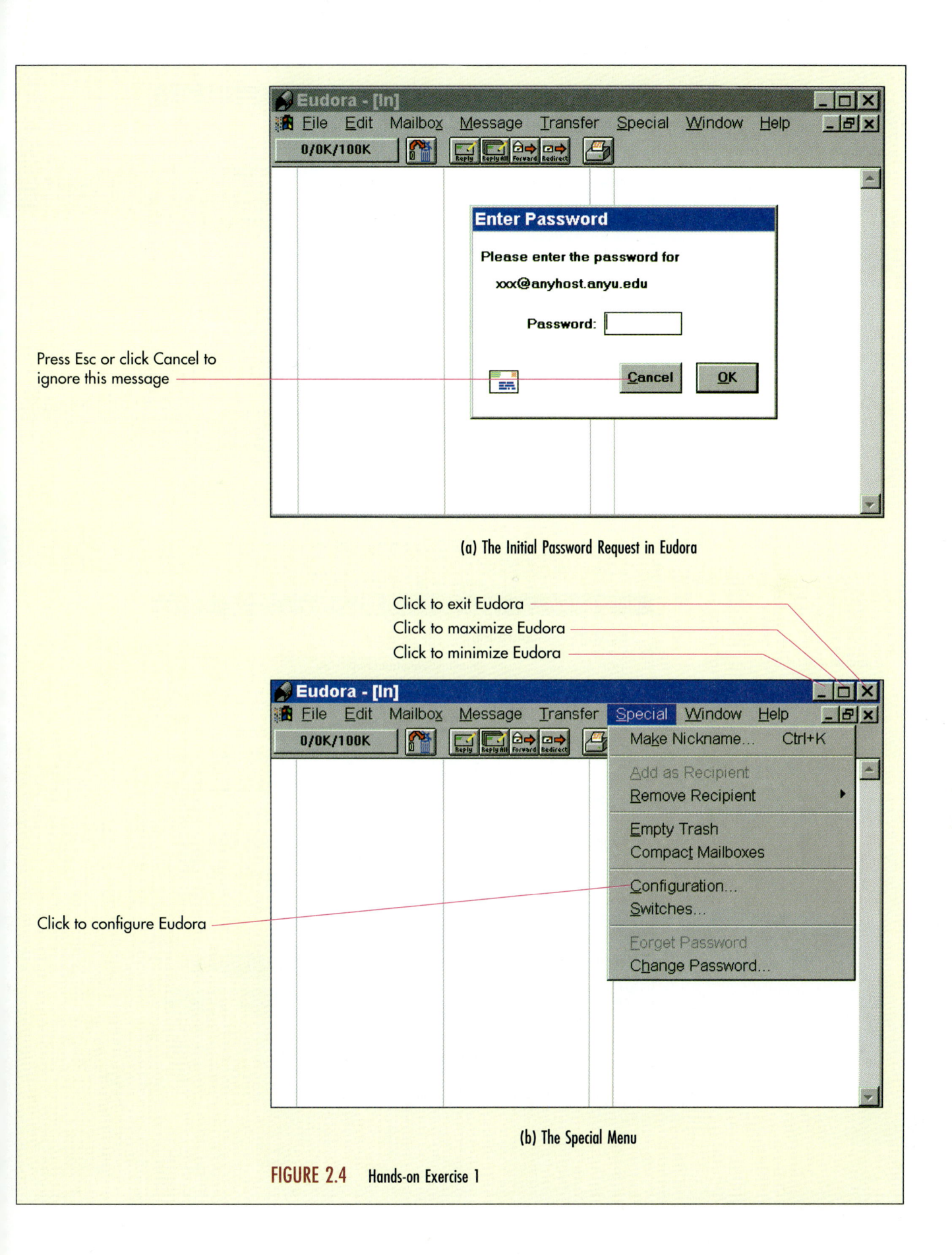

Press Esc or click Cancel to ignore this message

(a) The Initial Password Request in Eudora

Click to exit Eudora
Click to maximize Eudora
Click to minimize Eudora

Click to configure Eudora

(b) The Special Menu

FIGURE 2.4　Hands-on Exercise 1

GLOBAL COMMUNICATION ON THE INTERNET

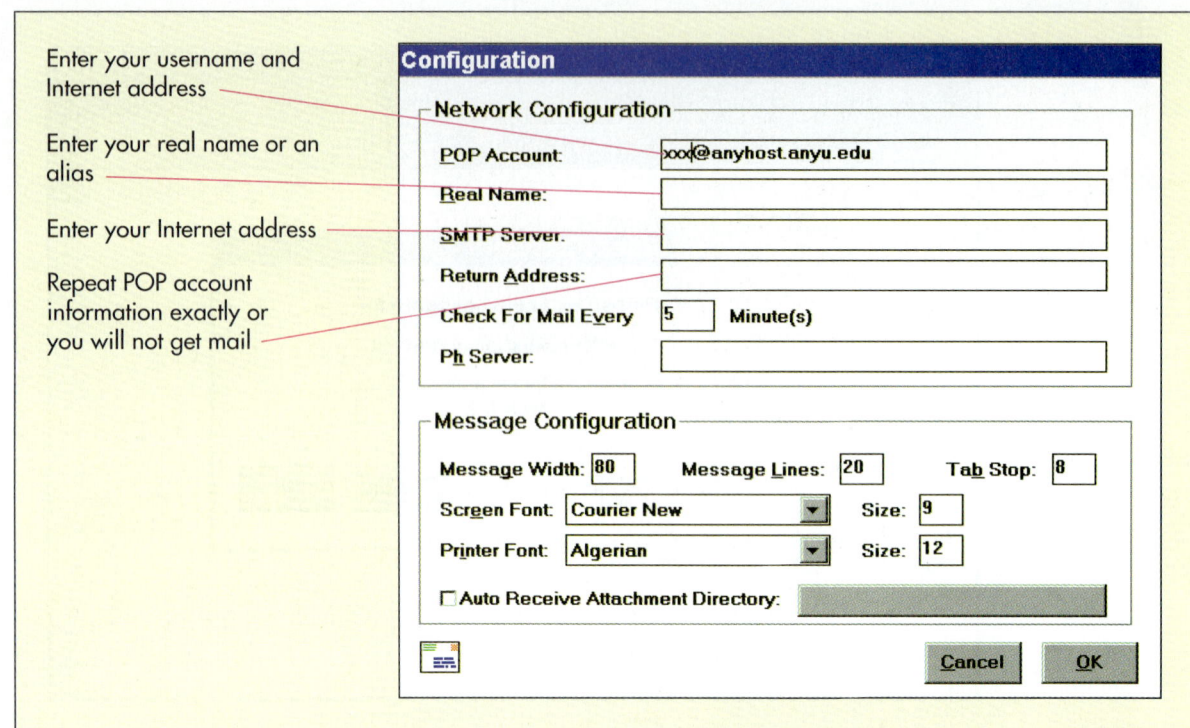

Enter your username and Internet address

Enter your real name or an alias

Enter your Internet address

Repeat POP account information exactly or you will not get mail

(c) The Configuration Dialog Box

A nickname or alias can be used instead

Change to increase/decrease frequency with which Eudora checks mail server for messages

Click when finished

(d) The Completed Configuration Dialog Box

FIGURE 2.4 Hands-on Exercise 1 (continued)

48 EXPLORING THE INTERNET

- Select **File** then **Exit,** and leave Eudora; then start it again. (This step is required to update the system with the information you just entered.) This time at the password screen enter your e-mail password, which you should have obtained from your instructor or LAN administrator. *For security reasons, the password is not displayed on the screen as you enter it.*
- Select **Special** then **Change Password,** and enter a new password. You will be asked to enter the new password a second time to verify it. Again, the password is not displayed on the screen as you type it. (Check with your instructor to be certain this is the correct method to change a password in your environment.)

STEP 3: Send a Message

➤ Sending messages in Eudora is simple. Pull down the **Message** menu, click **New Message,** and the New Message window in Figure 2.4e is displayed. You will fill in the username and Internet address of the recipient, send a copy of the message to a second person, and type the message in the message portion of the screen. Your completed message will look similar to Figure 2.4e after you have completed this step.

- The insertion point should be blinking next to To:. Type the Internet address(es) of the person(s) to whom you are sending the message. For instance, if you were sending e-mail to the authors, you would enter **gmarx@mercy.sjc.edu,** or **rgrauer@umiami.miami.edu.** (If you have not

Click to change passwords   *Click to send message*

Recipient's name and Internet address

Sender's name is automatically entered by Eudora

Send confirmation copy to yourself

(e) The Completed Message

FIGURE 2.4   Hands-on Exercise 1 (continued)

GLOBAL COMMUNICATION ON THE INTERNET   **49**

made arrangements to send a message to a classmate, you can type your own username and Internet address in the To field.) To send the message to more than one person, separate the usernames with a comma. The From address is automatically entered by the system, and should show your Internet address. Usernames and Internet addresses may be case sensitive; use lowercase for both unless instructed otherwise.

INTERNET ADDRESSES SIMPLIFIED

If you are sending e-mail to someone on the same mail server you're on, the message doesn't have to go out to the Internet through the router, the device that provides your school's Internet connection, but can be processed locally. You can simply type the recipient's username, without the host and domain information. For example, if the author and series editor were on the same host, one could simply address the other as gmarx or rgrauer, respectively.

- Press the **Tab** key to move the insertion point (or click in) to the **Subject** line. It is advisable to enter a subject for every message you send (unless instructed to leave the Subject line blank); many e-mail users assume that messages without a subject are "junk mail," and automatically delete them. Type the subject of your message and press the **Tab** key again to move to the **Cc** field.

- If you are going to copy the message to additional people, enter their usernames in the Cc field (for "carbon copy"—now that's old technology!), separated by commas. Enter your **username** in the **Cc** field now so you will get a confirming copy, and so you will have mail in your in-box for a later step.

- Skip the Bcc and Attachments fields for now. The Bcc field, which stands for blind carbon copy, allows you to send a copy of the message to someone without the recipient knowing you are doing so. The Attachments field lets you attach a file such as a Word document or Excel spreadsheet to your e-mail message. You will use this field in an end-of-chapter exercise.

- Press the **Tab** key until the insertion point is blinking in (or click in) the message area. Type your message as you would using any word processor, correcting any mistakes as you go. Many word processing cursor movement keys will work in e-mail messages. For instance, you can use the Backspace and Delete keys to delete left and right, respectively. Move the insertion point one word at a time by using **Ctrl+Right Arrow** or **Ctrl+Left Arrow.**

- When you are satisfied that the message is complete, click the **Send** button at the top of the document window. Your message will arrive at its destination within seconds! (It is possible that the recipient will not receive it immediately, however. The recipient may not be logged on, his or her mail server may be down, there may be network problems, or the mail server may be configured to check for mail at periodic intervals.)

MOVING ABOUT THE EUDORA SCREEN AND EDITING TEXT

You can correct mistakes in Eudora just as you can in other Windows programs. Use the Backspace and Delete keys to remove small amounts of unwanted text. Select larger amounts by using the mouse. Move forward and backward through the fields by pressing Tab and Shift+Tab, respectively. Click in any field you want to change, then delete the appropriate text and reenter.

STEP 4: Read and Print a Mail Message

➤ When you start Eudora and enter your password, the program will check the mail server for new mail, notify you if you have any, and automatically download it and open your in-basket if you do. While you are using Eudora, it will check the mail server for new mail every five minutes (or whatever interval is specified in the configuration information), and notify you if any has arrived. You can also manually check for new mail by selecting Check Mail in the File menu.

- Select **Check Mail** on the **File** menu. Any messages you have received should be displayed in the In-box document window as shown in Figure 2.4f.
- There are three ways to display a message that you want to read.
  1. Press the **Down Arrow** until you select the message you want to read, then press **Enter** to open it;
  2. Click on the message, then press **Enter;** or
  3. Double click the message.
- Use the **PageUp** and **PageDown** keys and scroll bars to scroll through and read the message.
- Print the message by selecting **Print** on the **File** menu.
- When you have finished reading the message, double click the Windows icon at the left of the message window (*not the blue title bar at the top of the screen that says Eudora*), or select **Close** on the **File** menu, as shown in Figure 2.4g.
- You will return to the In-box window. If you have no need to do anything further with the selected message, you can discard it by clicking on the **Trash button** (the blue trash can with the red arrow). The message is stored in the trash can and may be recalled at any time before you end this Eudora session. **Trash** the message now.
- Retrieve the message from the trash by pulling down the **Mailbox** menu, then selecting **Trash,** then clicking on the message you want to retrieve from the trash. Select **In** on the **Transfer** menu, and the message is moved to your in-box. Do this now so the message is available for later use.

Click to check for new mail

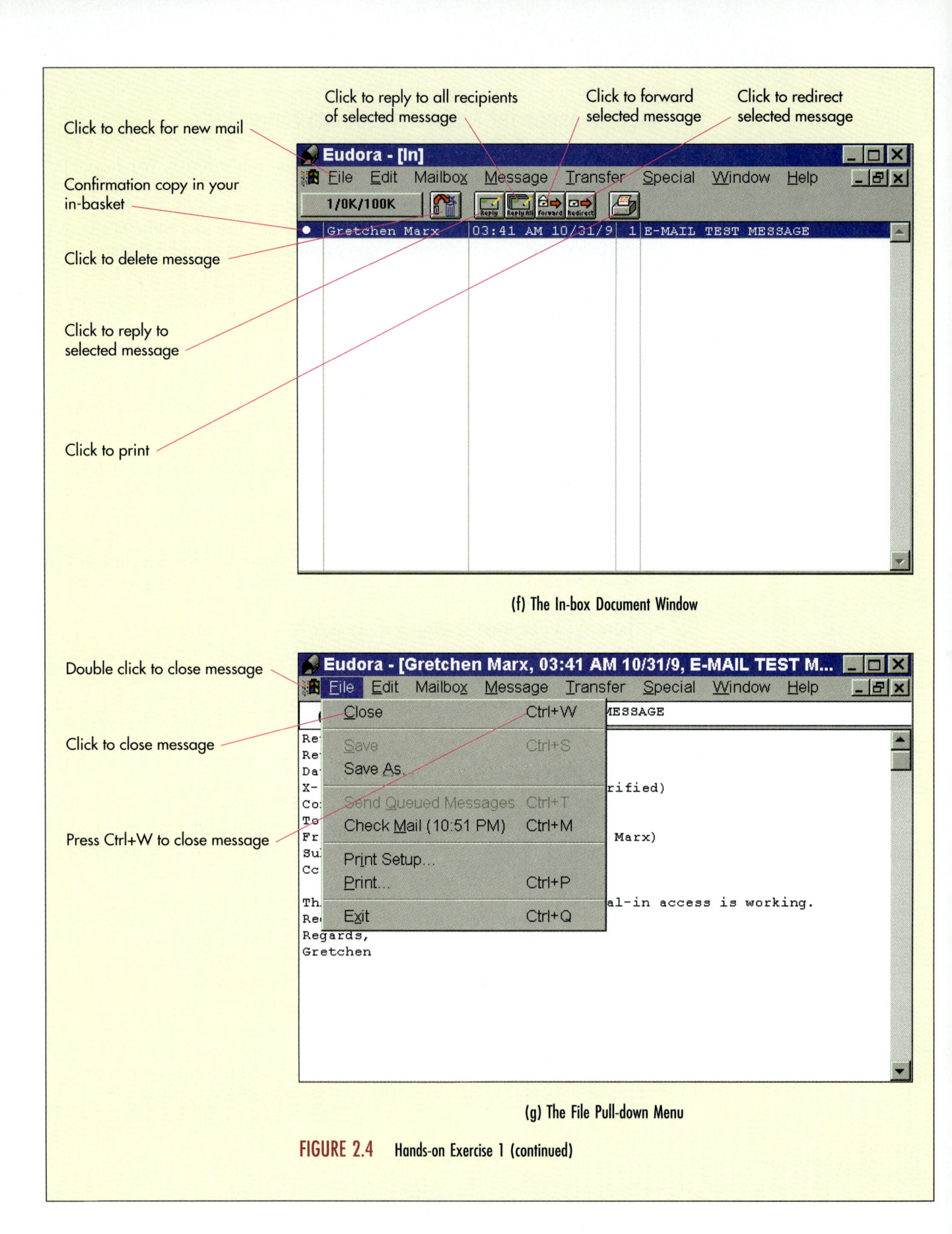

Confirmation copy in your in-basket

Click to delete message

Click to reply to selected message

Click to print

Click to reply to all recipients of selected message

Click to forward selected message

Click to redirect selected message

(f) The In-box Document Window

Double click to close message

Click to close message

Press Ctrl+W to close message

(g) The File Pull-down Menu

FIGURE 2.4   Hands-on Exercise 1 (continued)

52   EXPLORING THE INTERNET

REJECTED MAIL

You will occasionally get returned mail with a message indicating it could not be delivered. There are two common causes of returned mail—the receiving site was down, or you used the wrong username or Internet address.

STEP 5: Reply to a Message

➤ After you have read your e-mail message, you may reply to the sender as shown in Figure 2.4h.

- If your in-box is not visible, select **In** on the **Mailbox** pull-down menu.
- With your in-box on the screen, single click on the e-mail message you want to reply to, then click the **Reply** button. Eudora will display the standard message screen with the To address already filled in with the sender's username, and the From address filled in with your username. The message area of the screen contains the original e-mail message sent to you. Each line of the original message is preceded by a greater than sign (>). This indicates the text was part of the original message.
- Press the **Tab** key several times until the insertion point is blinking at the left edge of the first line of text. You may press the **Enter** key two or three times to give yourself a few blank lines above the original message in which to enter your reply. Press the **Up Arrow** key to move the insertion point back to the first line of the message area, then type your response. (The original text will be included with your message. You may

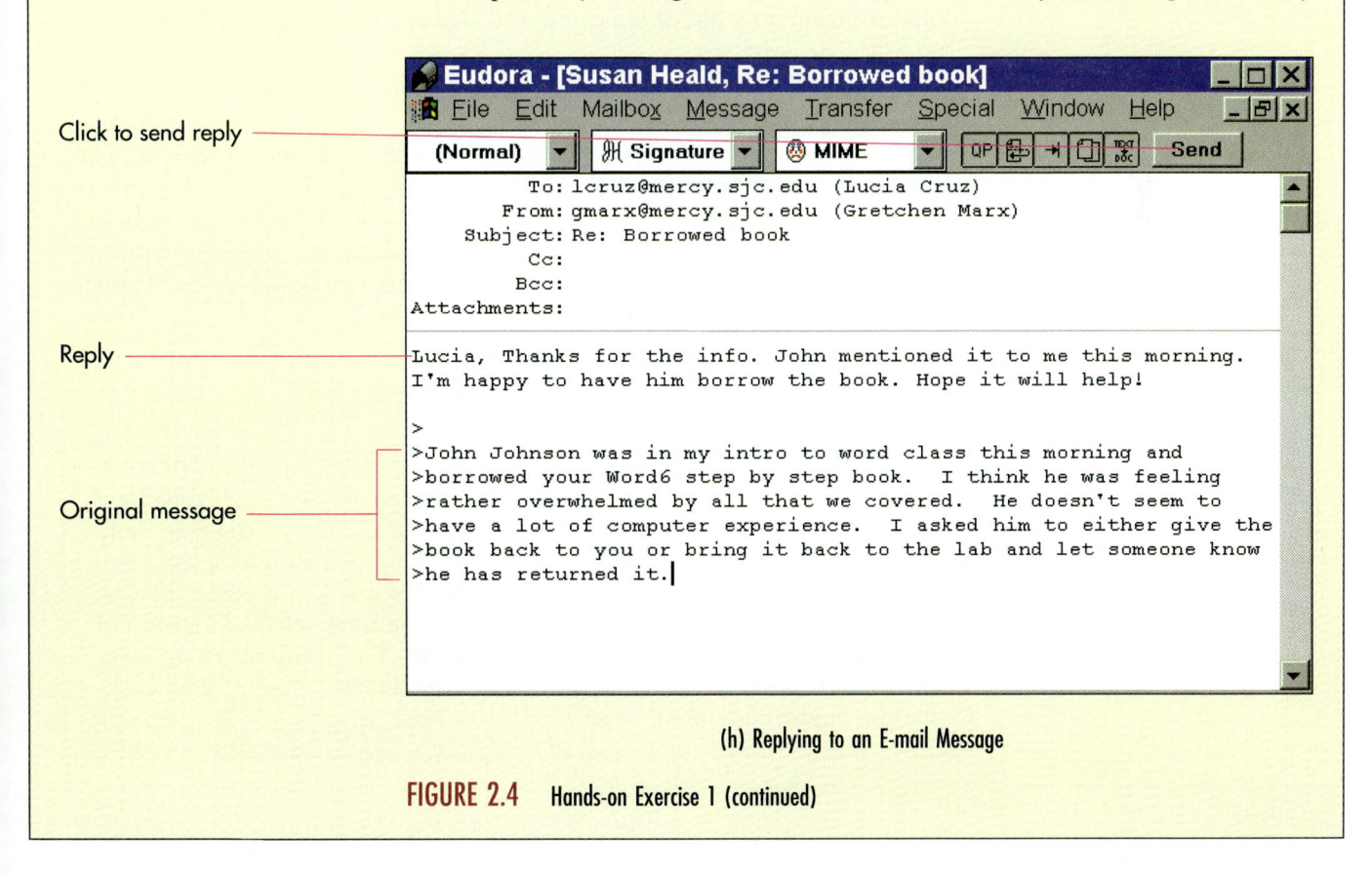

(h) Replying to an E-mail Message

FIGURE 2.4   Hands-on Exercise 1 (continued)

GLOBAL COMMUNICATION ON THE INTERNET   53

choose to delete all or part of the original text instead. To do so, select the text (click and drag) and press the **Delete** key as you would in any word processor.)

- Click the **Send** button, and off goes your reply. The original message will remain in your in-box until you transfer or trash it. The reply will be in your out-box.

> **FORWARDING AND REDIRECTING MAIL**
>
> You can forward a message to someone else by choosing the Forward button instead of the Reply button. The recipient will see your username in the From field, but will also see the orginal sender information. You can add comments to a forwarded message just as you do to a reply. You can redirect the message to someone else by choosing the Redirect button. The recipient will see the original sender's username in the From field, and you will not add comments to the redirected message. (This is analogous to redirecting U.S. mail that arrives at your house or apartment addressed to a previous occupant—you write a new address on the front and send it on unopened.)

STEP 6: Check Your Mailboxes and Delete Messages

➤ You can review your messages at any time by selecting **Mailbox** from the pull-down menu, then clicking **In** or **Out** as appropriate (In for messages you receive, Out for message you send). Keep your mailbox from overflowing (and from running out of allocated disk space) by deleting messages that are no longer necessary.

- To see both the In and Out mailboxes on the screen at the same time first pull down the **Mailbox** menu and select **In,** then pull down the **Mailbox** menu and select **Out.** Both mailboxes are open, but one is on top of the other so you do not see both.
- Click on the **Window** pull-down menu, then click on **Tile** to see both windows together as shown in Figure 2.4i. Transfer any message from one mailbox to the other by selecting the mailbox name from the **Transfer** menu.

> **SELECTING MULTIPLE FILES**
>
> You can select multiple files from your mailboxes the same way you select multiple lines of text in a Windows application. Click the first file, hold the Shift key, then click the last file in the group you wish to select. You can select multiple nonadjacent files by clicking one file, holding the Ctrl key, then clicking the additional files. Once you have selected a group of files, you can delete them all by clicking the Trash button, or transfer them all to another mailbox by selecting the Transfer menu, then clicking the appropriate mailbox name.

Click to move message from one mailbox to another

Click to delete selected message

Double click to open selected message

(i) The Tiled In- and Out-boxes

FIGURE 2.4   Hands-on Exercise 1 (continued)

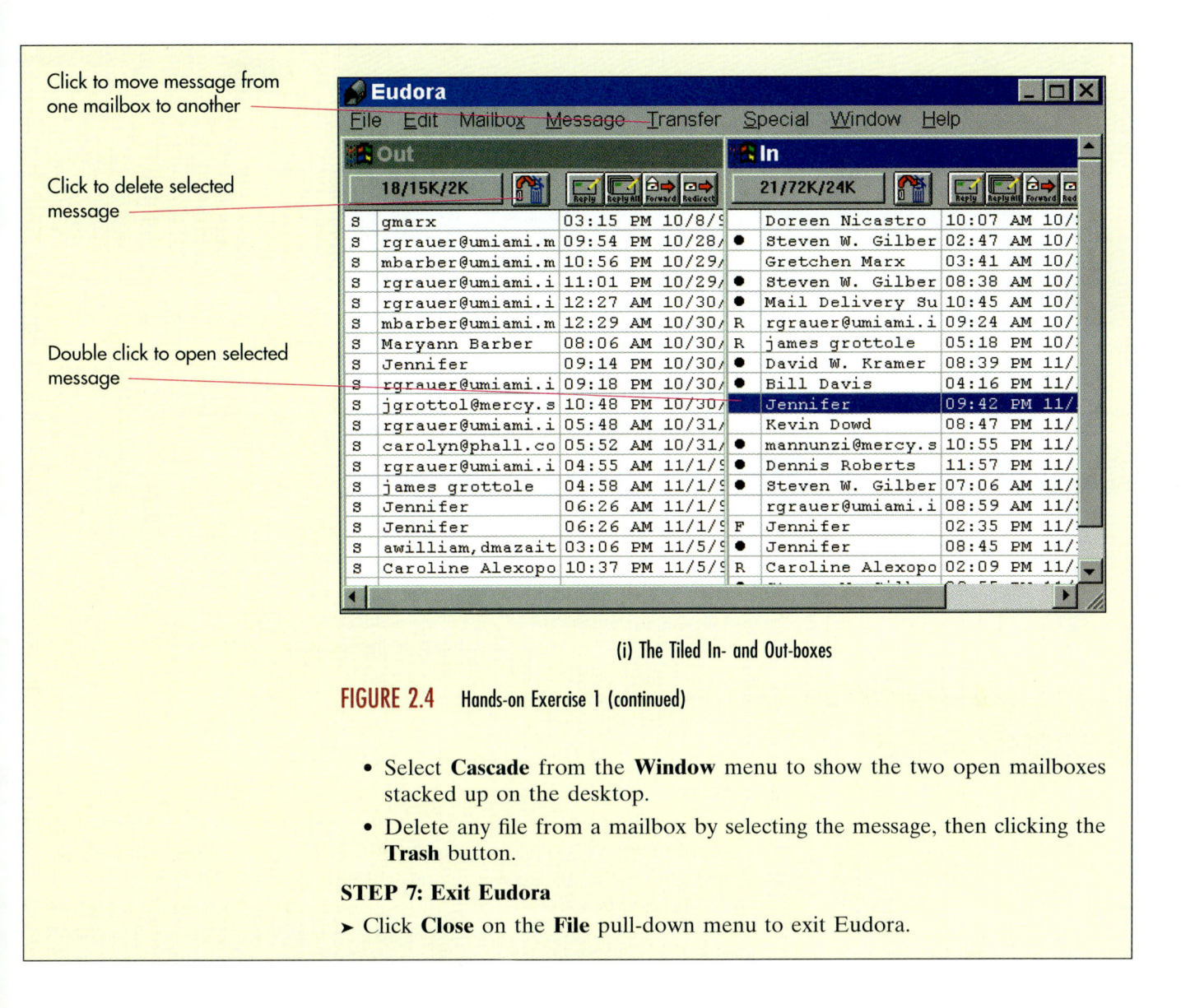

- Select **Cascade** from the **Window** menu to show the two open mailboxes stacked up on the desktop.
- Delete any file from a mailbox by selecting the message, then clicking the **Trash** button.

STEP 7: Exit Eudora

➤ Click **Close** on the **File** pull-down menu to exit Eudora.

E-mail Using a Unix Mail Program

While it is easier to compose and send mail using a Windows-based POP mail client, it involves a fairly complex setup for both you and your college computing staff. Therefore, your college may choose to have you access your e-mail by using a Unix-based *shell account* instead. Unix accounts work with a *command-line interface,* not a graphical user interface, which means you will have to enter commands at the Unix system prompt to retrieve your mail. Typically you will enter a command to start a menu-driven mail program such as Pine, which was illustrated in Chapter 1.

Your incoming messages are not downloaded from the mail server and stored on your PC. Instead, they reside on the mail server, and can be viewed only when you are logged in to your account on the mail server. In the post office analogy this is similar to having a post office box and being required to read your mail at the post office. Using your Unix shell account to access e-mail is illustrated in Figure 2.5. In the following hands-on exercise you will send an e-mail message with Pine, a Unix-based mail program that lets you compose, send, and retrieve mail messages using your mail server.

1. The incoming message is stored on the Internet mail server.

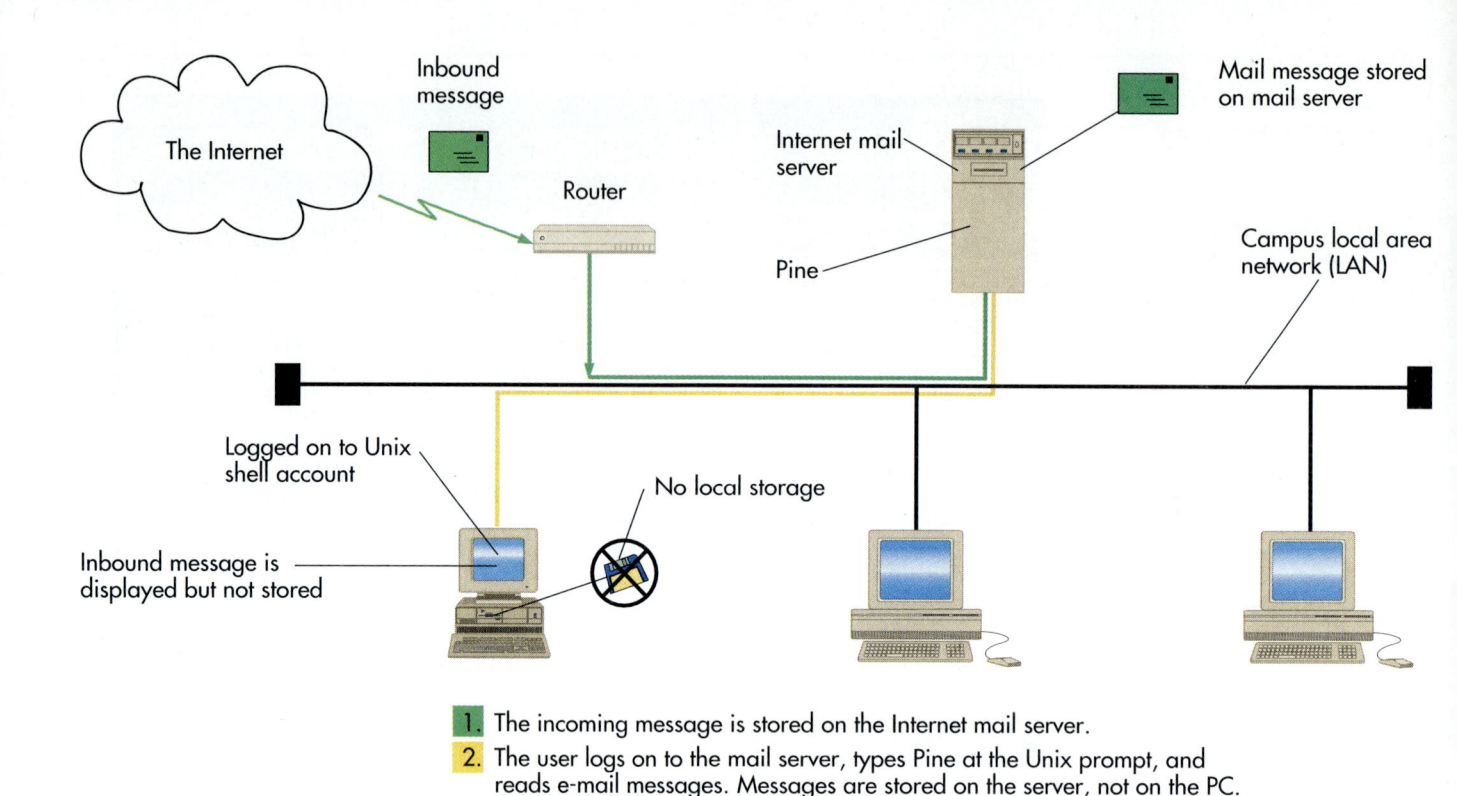

2. The user logs on to the mail server, types Pine at the Unix prompt, and reads e-mail messages. Messages are stored on the server, not on the PC.

FIGURE 2.5 Using Your Unix Shell Account and a Menu-Driven Program to Retrieve E-mail

LOST MAIL

If you have a post office box at your local U.S. mail substation, you can go there and get new mail. However, you will not see mail that was delivered to you yesterday, because it is already in a stack on your kitchen counter at home. In a similar way you may be able to dial into your Unix shell account from home and read your new mail by using Pine or other Unix-based mail software. You will not be able to see any old mail that you already retrieved while you were on campus. Don't despair—it is not lost. When you retrieved it, the POP mail client downloaded it from the Internet mail server to your personal mail directory on your campus PC or file server hard drive. You can read it by using your POP mail client when you log on next time you are on campus.

HANDS-ON EXERCISE 2

E-mail Using Pine

Objective: Send and receive an e-mail message using your Unix shell account. The exercise is written for Pine, but is general enough that you can apply the instructions to other menu-driven e-mail software. Use Figure 2.6 as a guide in completing the exercise.

STEP 1: Log On

➤ Log on to the system you will use for e-mail.

- If you are using a local area network at school, you will need an account (userID) and a password, which your instructor or LAN administrator should provide for you. You may need a second account (userID) and password to access your mail server.

STEP 2: Send a Message

➤ At the Unix prompt (see your instructor or LAN administrator for information on how to get to the Unix prompt if you have not already done so), type **Pine** and press **Enter.** You will see the menu interface shown in Figure 2.6a. Notice the menu options across the bottom of the screen. They identify what actions you can take at this point.

- Type the letter **C** to select the Compose Message command. You will see the Compose Message screen shown in Figure 2.6b. Note that there is a new menu at the bottom of the screen. Each option is preceded by the ^ character, which stands for the Ctrl key.

- Fill in the **To** field with the Internet address of the person to whom you are sending mail. (If you have not made arrangements to do this exercise with a classmate, enter your own username and address.)

- Press **Tab** once to go to the Cc field. Enter the Internet address of anyone to whom you want to send a copy. In this case enter your username so you will have a confirmation of the message, and so you will have new mail.

- Press **Tab** twice to move to the Subject field. Type the subject of your message.

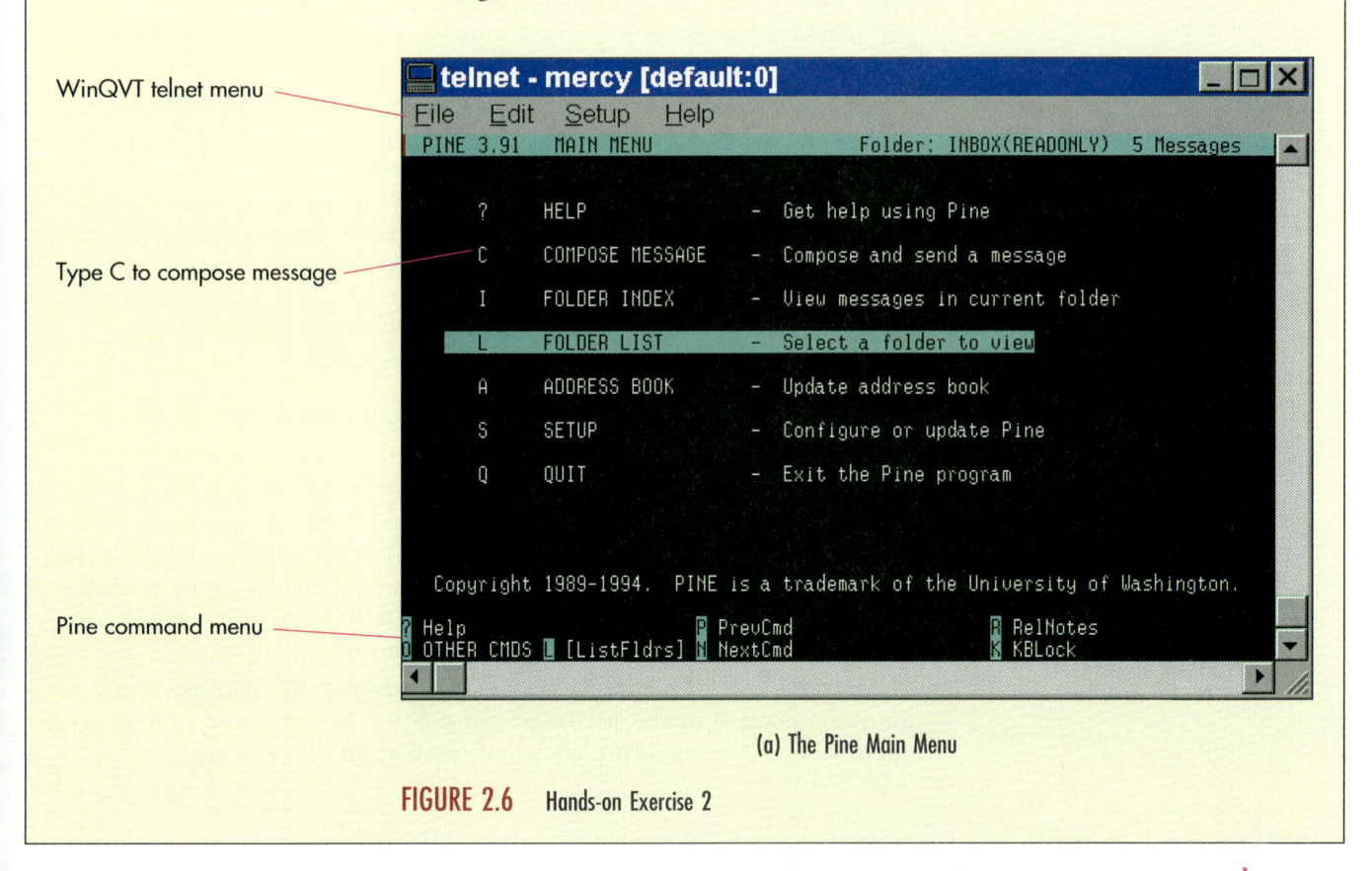

(a) The Pine Main Menu

FIGURE 2.6 Hands-on Exercise 2

Enter recipient's Internet address

Enter message

Command menu has changed

Press Ctrl+X to send message

(b) The Compose Message Screen

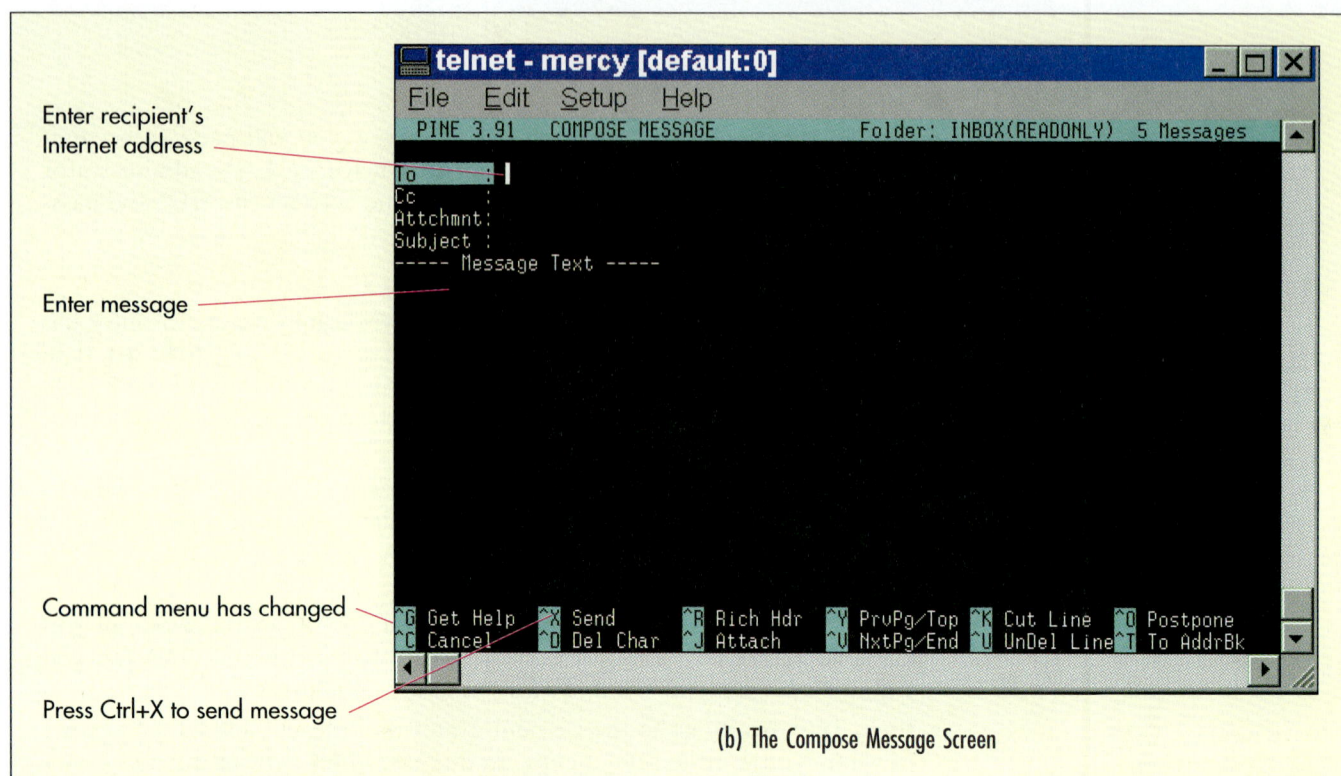

FIGURE 2.6 Hands-on Exercise 2 (continued)

- Press **Tab** again to move to the message area. Type the e-mail message as you would any word processing document, correcting mistakes as you go by using the **Backspace** and/or **Delete** keys.
- When your message is complete, press **Ctrl+X** to send the message, as indicated in the menu at the bottom of the screen. You will get a confirmation request, to which you reply by typing **Y** if you want to send the message, or **N** if you don't. The message will reach its destination within seconds! (While the Internet has the capability to deliver messages almost instantaneously, the recipient may not get it instantly. His or her system may be down, or may be configured to deliver mail once a day.) Once your message has been sent, you will be returned to the main menu.

STEP 3: Read Your Mail

➤ Now that you have sent yourself a message, you should have mail in your mail folder. You will read it now.

- From the main menu, type **I** to view messages in the current folder, which by default is the INBOX folder.
- Your e-mail messages will be displayed as a numbered list similar to the one shown in Figure 2.6c (although you may not have as many messages yet!). Use the arrow keys to scroll down to the message you want to read. When it is selected, press **Enter**. The message will be displayed.
- Move to the second page of a message by pressing the spacebar. Move to the next message in the list by pressing **N** for Next message. Other frequently used commands are shown at the bottom of the screen.

Mailbox name   Message count

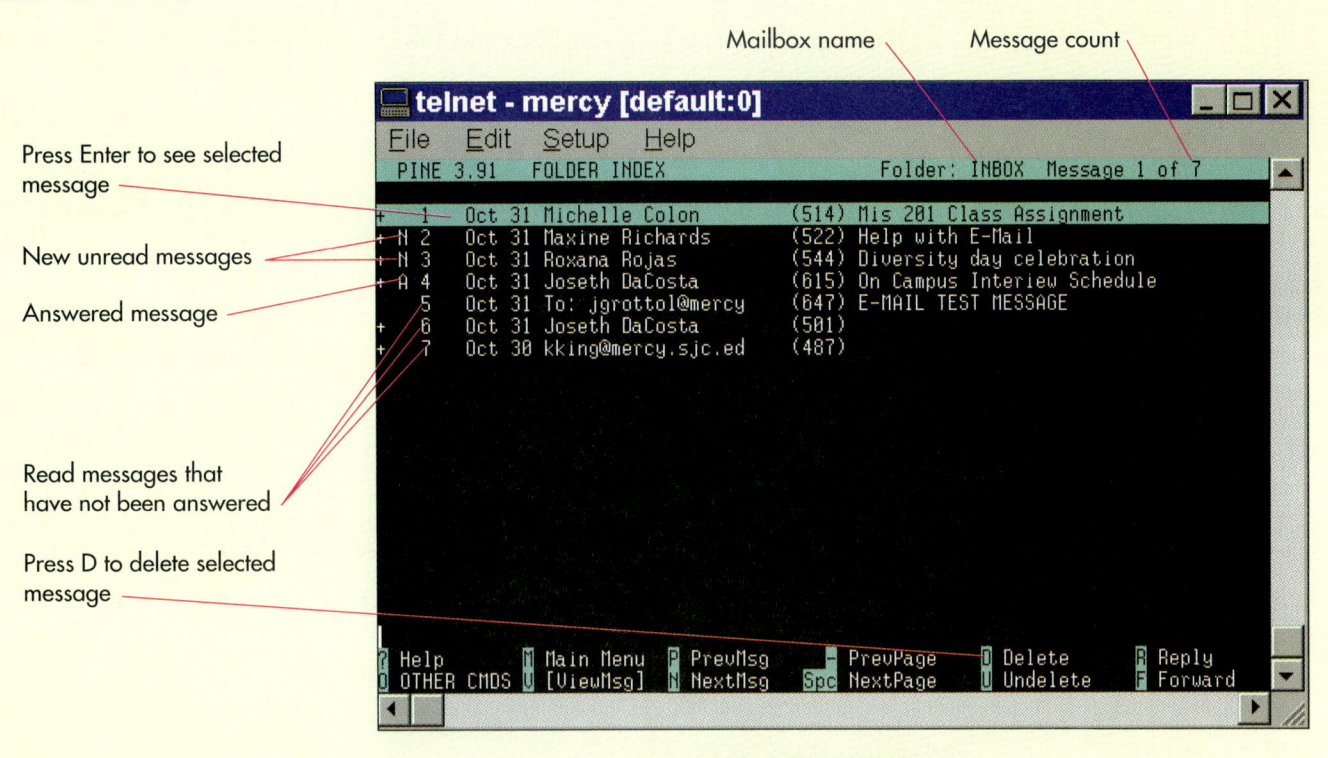

```
telnet - mercy [default:0]
File  Edit  Setup  Help
PINE 3.91   FOLDER INDEX              Folder: INBOX  Message 1 of 7
+   1   Oct 31  Michelle Colon      (514) Mis 201 Class Assignment
+ N 2   Oct 31  Maxine Richards     (522) Help with E-Mail
+ N 3   Oct 31  Roxana Rojas        (544) Diversity day celebration
+ A 4   Oct 31  Joseth DaCosta      (615) On Campus Interiew Schedule
    5   Oct 31  To: jgrottol@mercy  (647) E-MAIL TEST MESSAGE
+   6   Oct 31  Joseth DaCosta      (501)
+   7   Oct 30  kking@mercy.sjc.ed  (487)

? Help        M Main Menu   P PrevMsg   - PrevPage   D Delete    R Reply
O OTHER CMDS  V [ViewMsg]   N NextMsg  Spc NextPage  U Undelete  F Forward
```

- Press Enter to see selected message
- New unread messages
- Answered message
- Read messages that have not been answered
- Press D to delete selected message

(c) The List of Mail Messages

FIGURE 2.6   Hands-on Exercise 2 (continued)

STEP 4: Reply to a Message

▶ You can send a response to the person who sent you a message.
- If necessary, press **M** to return to the main menu.
- From the main menu, type **I** to select a message in your in-box.
- While reading the message, press the letter **R** to reply. Pine will display a message asking whether you want the text of the original message included in your reply.
- Enter **Y** to include the text, **N** to leave the message area blank. The Reply message screen will be shown (which is the same as the New Message screen), with the To and From fields filled in with the original senders' name and your name, respectively.
- Enter the text of your reply in the message area, and press **Ctrl+X** to send the reply.

STEP 5: Delete a Message

▶ You can delete messages while viewing the folder index.
- Press **M** to return to the main menu if necessary.
- Type **I** to return to the in-box.
- Use the **Up/Down Arrow** keys to select the message you want to delete, then press **D**. The message is marked for deletion, but remains in the folder until you quit Pine. (When you quit, Pine will warn you that it is going to "expunge" deleted messages, that is, permanently delete them, and let you change your mind. If you want the message deleted, respond with a **Y** to

expunge the message. Enter **N** to quit Pine without expunging the marked messages.)

STEP 7: Exit Pine

➤ Getting out of Pine is easy.

- Return to the main menu, if necessary, by pressing the letter **M**.
- Type **Q** to quit. You will see a message asking if you really want to quit.
- Answer by typing **Y.** If you have deleted any messages, you will be warned that they will be expunged.
- Answer **Y** if that is OK, **N** if you don't want deleted messages removed from your In-box. You will be returned to the Unix prompt.

ADDITIONAL E-MAIL CAPABILITIES

Most e-mail programs have additional capabilities beyond sending and receiving mail. You can customize the program to create a distribution list, a personal signature, and multiple folders in which to store your mail.

Distribution Lists

In the exercise you just completed, you composed a message for a specific person. What if you often compose and send the same message to a group of people with whom you frequently correspond? It would be an unfortunate waste of time to type and send the message several times. Instead you can create a **distribution list,** or **nickname list,** which contains the Internet addresses of all the recipients in the group. You can then send the message once, addressed to the distribution list. The mail program reads the list or nickname and automatically retrieves the e-mail addresses of the recipients from a nickname file, which is set up when you create the list.

Customizing Your Signature

You can create a custom *signature* (minus the actual handwriting sample!) that will be placed at the end of each message you send. Some people type their name,

---

SIGNATURE NETIQUETTE

No one wants to read an endless soliloquy attached to your messages, so keep your signature short, preferably to four or fewer lines. Also, it is not considered good form to use four-letter words, racial slurs, or other unacceptable text in your signature. Such inappropriate use may cause you to lose your computer privileges. Remember, your e-mail is not really private, and has the potential to be read by many people. Use common sense and good manners in all you write.

title, address, telephone, and fax number. Others use a closing, their name, and a short, pithy saying. For example:

> Regards and good surfing,
> Sarah Goodall
> If you think education is expensive, consider the alternative.

Others give themselves colorful nicknames surrounded by simple graphics created from standard keyboard characters. Your signature can be as unique as you are and convey something personal about you.

Personal Mail Folders

Think, for a moment, about how you process your regular mail. You bring it into your house from the mailbox and you read it at your leisure. Some mail will be junk mail, which you will immediately throw away. Other mail will be important and you will want to file it with your important papers. And there may be letters that you will want to share with others in your household, and so you may leave those on the kitchen table to reread at a later time.

After you have been sending and receiving e-mail for some time, and have subscribed to several mailing lists (covered in the next topic), you will discover that you are receiving too much mail to save it all in your in-box. Like the kitchen table, the in-box simply gets too crowded with messages. You can alleviate the mess by setting up different mailboxes, or *folders,* for each type of mail you receive, then transferring messages you want to save to the appropriate mailboxes. Figure 2.7a illustrates these mailboxes as they are implemented in PC Eudora. Figure 2.7b shows Pine folders.

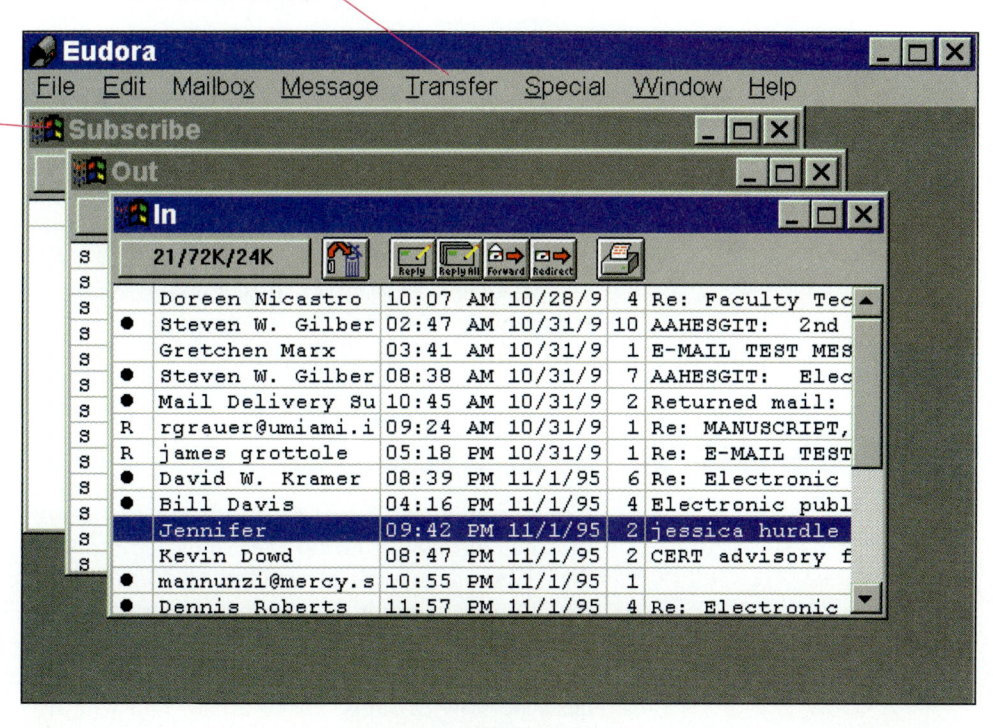

(a) Multiple Mailboxes in Eudora

FIGURE 2.7   E-mail Mailboxes

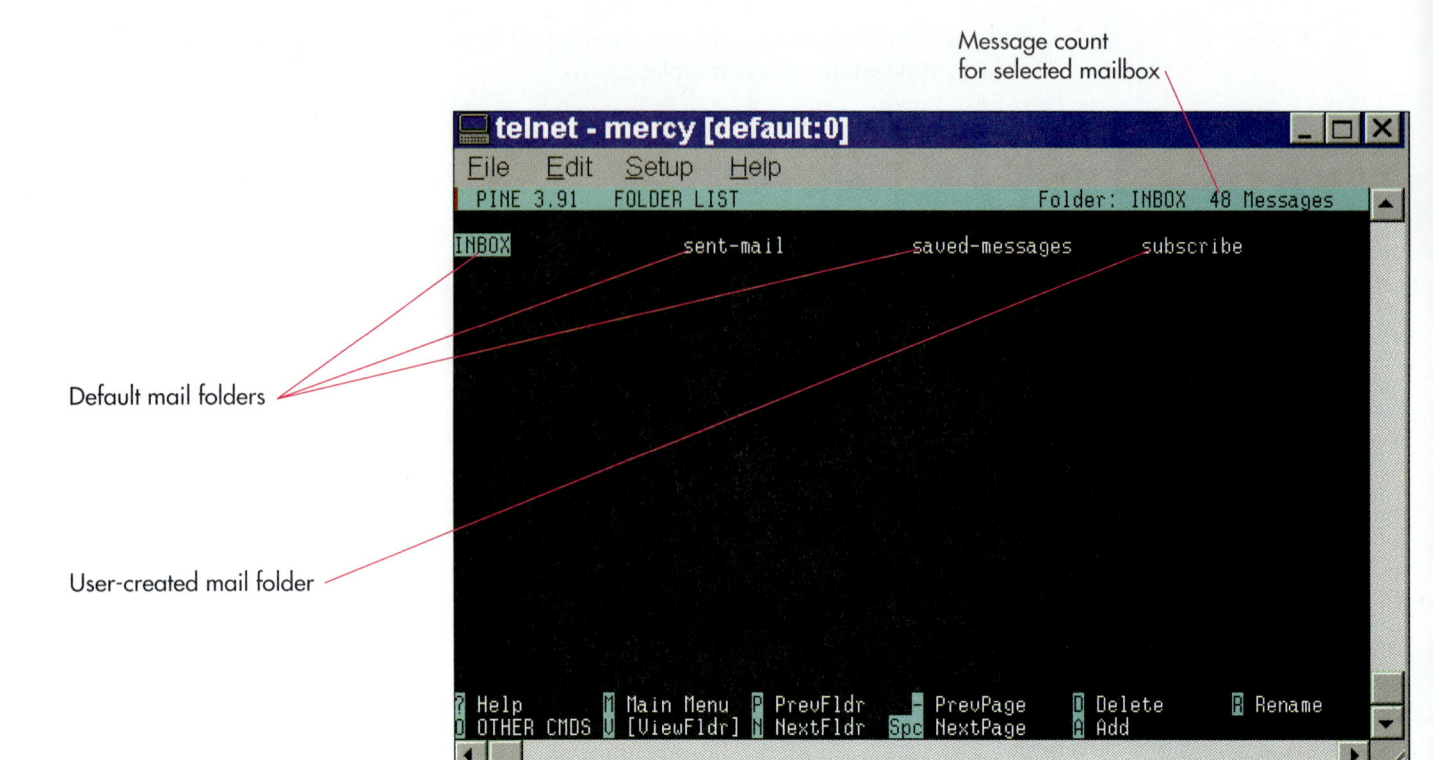

Default mail folders

User-created mail folder

Message count for selected mailbox

(b) The Folders List in Pine

FIGURE 2.7 E-mail Mailboxes (continued)

ATTACHING FILES

Many e-mail systems provide the capability to attach a file to the message you're sending. Suppose you are assigned a group project, and are working on a section of the final report. You could attach your section to a mail message, and mail it to the rest of your group for their review and comment. Check with your instructor or system administrator to find out if your system has this capability. Also, be advised that, just because you can attach and send a document, this doesn't mean the recipient will receive it correctly!

MAILING LISTS

Access to mailing lists is an important feature of the Internet. A *mailing list* is an Internet discussion group that operates much like a magazine subscription—you find a list on a topic of interest to you and subscribe. You then get all the mail sent to and from people on the subscription list. The big difference between this and a magazine subscription is that you get to help write the news! There are thousands of mailing lists that cover every conceivable topic. In this section we'll describe how to subscribe to a list. You will also want to know how to *suspend* a subscription—while you are on spring break, for instance—and how to unsubscribe. All this is done via e-mail messages.

Participating in mailing lists generally requires that you know two addresses, and send different types of messages to each. The first address is that of the computer that manages the list, usually called a *listserv, listproc,* or *majordomo.* This address is where you will send subscription information, such as your initial request, a suspend request, or an unsubscribe request. This is analogous to the subscription department at a magazine.

The second address is the mail address where you will send your contributions to the discussion on the list. All mail you send to this address will be broadcast to the entire list, so be sure you really want to send the message! Sending a message to the list is analogous to sending a letter to the editor, which will in turn be published for all subscribers to see. Many lists have a *list owner* or *moderator* who reads and rejects messages that do not relate to the general topic discussed by the list.

Be sure you understand the difference between the list and the listserv. Just as you would not send a subscription hold or cancellation notice to every reader of *Time* or *Newsweek*, you should not send an unsubscribe message to the list, but rather to the listserv. You will find that many new users do not understand the difference, and you will receive annoying unsubscribe letters in your e-mail once you are on a list.

ADDING YOUR TWO CENTS

It is a good idea to read the messages being sent to a mailing list for a while before sending one yourself. Known as *lurking,* this allows you to discover the tone and subject matter of the discussions so what you add will be appropriate to the conversation. Some lists are quite friendly and patient with newcomers' "dumb questions." Others have a very low tolerance for new members and the introduction of topics that do not meet the group's approval. Should you send an inappropriate comment or question to one of these lists, your mailbox may be flooded with very derisive replies. Called *flaming,* this can be a very unpleasant experience for the recipient. Be forewarned!

Finding Mailing Lists

There are thousands of mailing lists on the Internet. You can retrieve a (very long) list of mailing lists by sending mail to **listserv@bitnic.educom.edu.** In the message area type **list global** and nothing else. You will receive a message listing thousands of mailing lists. You will have an opportunity to try this in the following hands-on exercise. You can get a list about a specific subject—skiing, for instance—by sending the message **list global/skiing** to the same address.

Subscribing to a List

Once you have found the list to which you want to subscribe, you do so by simply sending an e-mail message to the *list server* requesting that your name be added to the subscription list. The message will generally follow the form *subscribe listname,* where you substitute the name of the list in the message. The listserv software automatically adds your name to the list (and generally sends you a confirmation). You will start receiving e-mail messages from other subscribers within a day or two.

DON'T OVERSUBSCRIBE!

Be careful about subscribing to too many lists—you will find yourself reading hundreds of messages a day if the lists are active. If you don't routinely read your messages and dispose of them, your disk space on your mail server will quickly overflow, and you will have to contact your system administrator to resolve the problem.

Subscription Options

As indicated earlier, you may suspend a subscription so you will remain on the list but not receive mail until you release the suspension. You should do this before going on any school breaks. Many, if not most, lists keep an archive of all messages sent, so you can find out later what happened while your subscription was suspended. Where the archive is and how you can access it is generally described in a message you receive from the list manager when you subscribe. You can turn your mail off temporarily by sending a message in the form *set listname nomail.* To resume receiving mail, you can use the command *set listname mail.* You should, of course, send these messages to the list server, not to the list itself.

You can set your subscription to send you all messages in **digest** form. This is particularly useful on a very active list, from which you receive more than 10 to 15 messages per day. The digest option will notify the list server to send all the messages as one file, which reduces the time it takes you to open, read, and dispose of the messages.

When you sign on to a mailing list, the list server keeps a record of your e-mail address (how else would it be able to send you mail?). Anyone subscribing to the list can get a list of all subscribers by sending the list server the command *review listname* (where the actual listname is substituted for *listname*). You can send the message *set listname mail conceal* to the list server to hide your name, and maybe keep Internet "junk mail" out of your mail box.

SAVING SUBSCRIPTION INFORMATION

You should set up a mailbox called SUBSCRIBE or something similar in which to retain the subscription confirmations you will receive after subscribing to mailing lists. The confirmation messages will tell you how to suspend and digest mail, and how to unsubscribe or sign off the lists. If you save all these messages in one SUBSCRIBE or CONFIRM mailbox, you will be able to find them easily at a later time when you want to change a subscription.

HANDS-ON EXERCISE 3

Customizing E-mail and Subscribing to Mailing Lists Using a PC Mail Client

Objective: Create a distribution list (nickname), signature, and mailbox, and subscribe to a mailing list. Use Figure 2.8 as a guide in the exercise.

STEP 1: Create a Distribution/Nickname List

➤ Log on to your system and open Eudora (or other PC mail client).

➤ Select **Window,** then **Nicknames,** then click the **New** button at the bottom of the screen as shown in Figure 2.8a. The New Nickname dialog box shown in Figure 2.8b is displayed. Enter your course number (such as MIS201) in the New Nickname dialog box, then click **OK.**

- The nickname is shown in the Nickname list at the left of the screen. Click in the Address(es) area. Type each recipient's Internet username on a new line in the Address text box. Enter three or four classmates' usernames, as shown in Figure 2.8c.

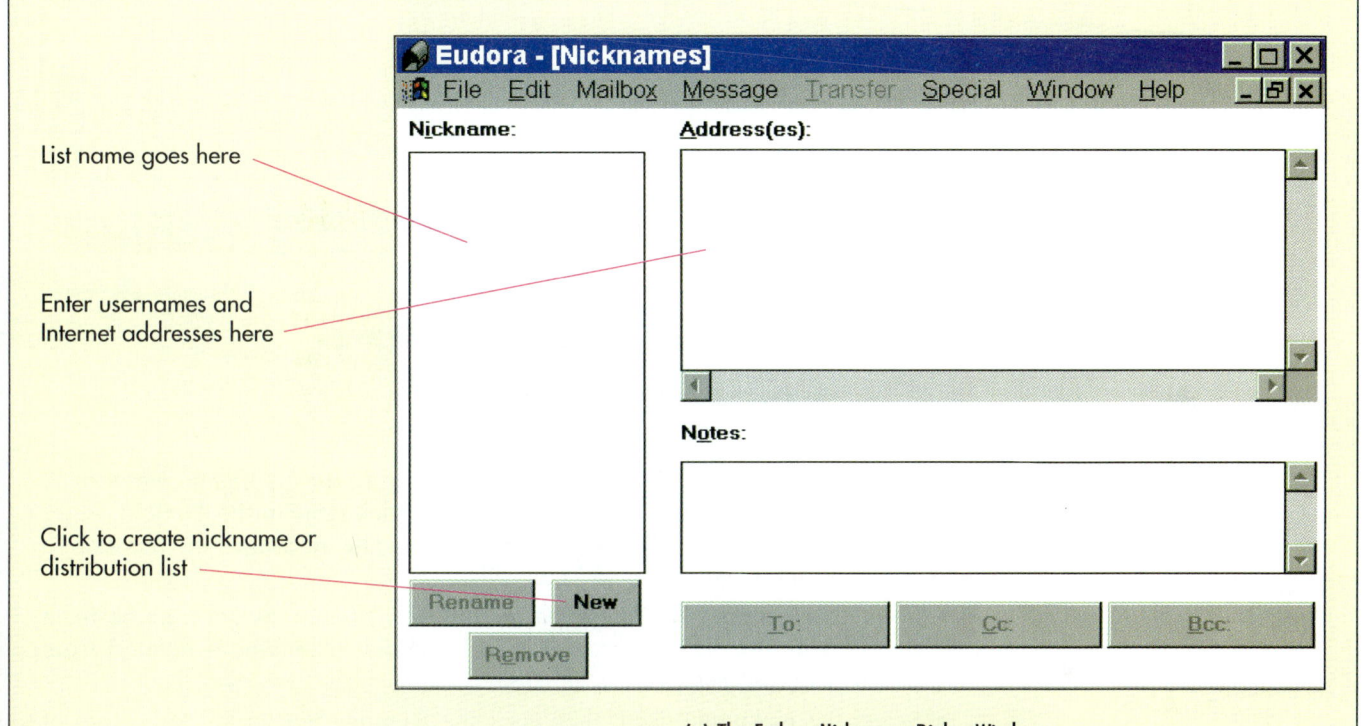

(a) The Eudora Nicknames Dialog Window

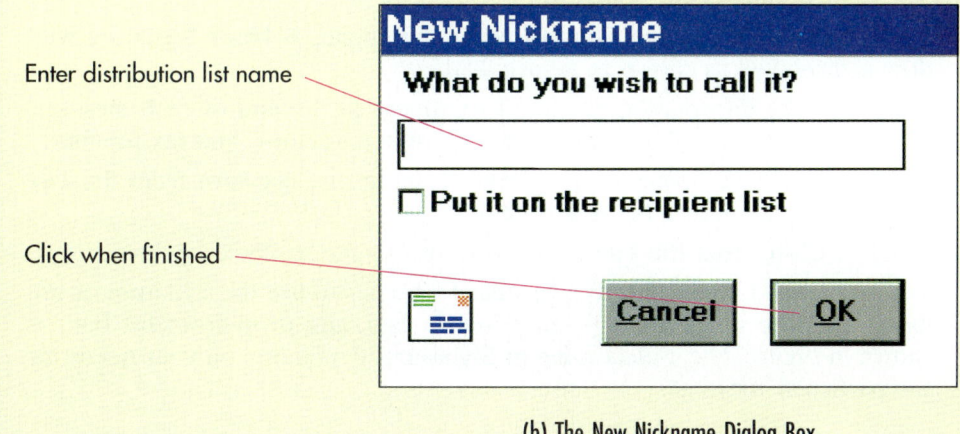

(b) The New Nickname Dialog Box

FIGURE 2.8 Hands-on Exercise 3

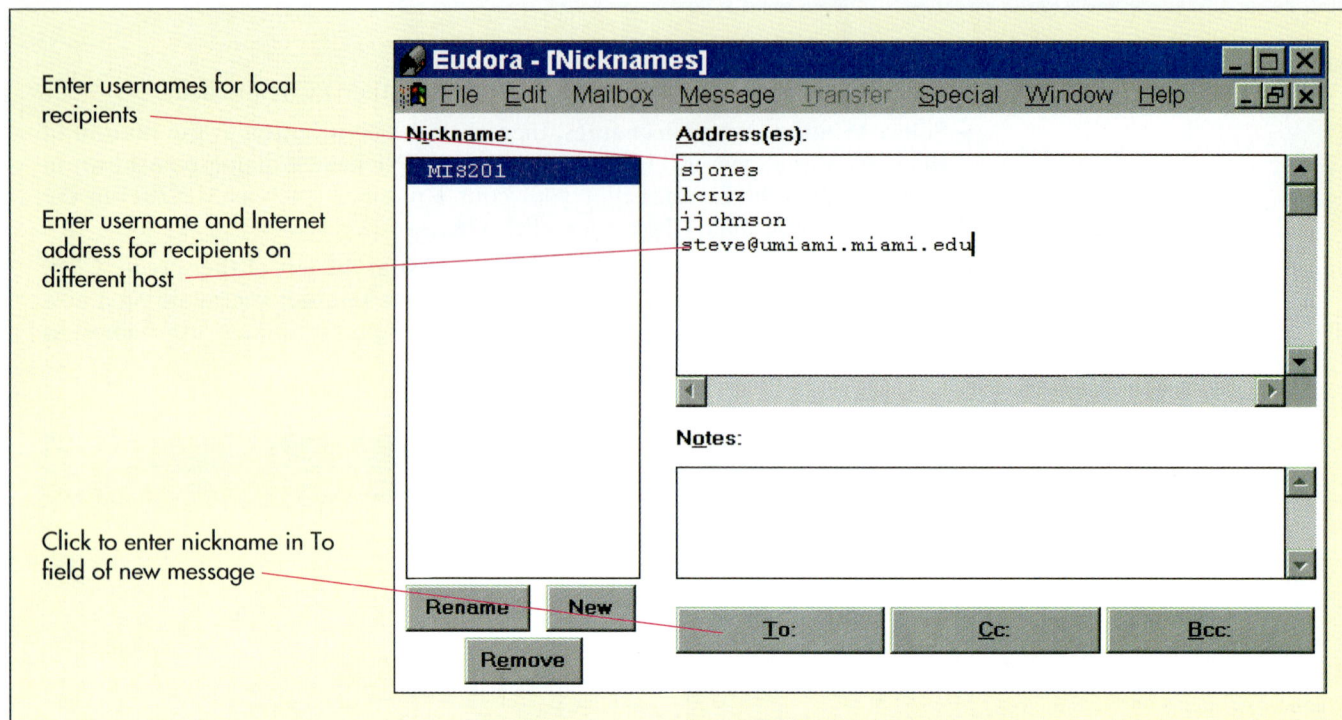

Enter usernames for local recipients

Enter username and Internet address for recipients on different host

Click to enter nickname in To field of new message

(c) The Completed Nicknames Dialog Window

FIGURE 2.8   Hands-on Exercise 3 (continued)

- Select the nickname, then click the **To** button in the Nickname window. A New Message window is displayed, with the nickname in the To field. After typing the message, click the **Send** button. The message will be sent to everyone included in the nickname list.
- Select **Nickname** from the **Window** pull-down menu. Select a name from the list you just entered and press **Delete.** That username is deleted from the distribution list.
- Select the nickname itself, then click the **Remove** button at the bottom of the screen. The nickname is deleted.

STEP 2: Customize Your Signature

➤ Select **Signature** from the **Window** pull-down menu. A blank Signature window is displayed as shown in Figure 2.8d.

- Type in the information you want to appear at the end of each message. Some people type their name, title, address, telephone, and fax number.
- When you have finished typing your signature, select **Save** from the **File** menu. The signature file is updated.
- Select **Close** from the **File** menu to return to the mailbox window.

➤ When you send a message you can select whether to use the signature or not by clicking the down arrow in the Eudora signature drop-down list box, as shown in Figure 2.8e. Select **none** or **Signature,** depending on your needs for the particular message.

Click to save new signature

Enter your signature here

(d) The Signature Window

Select None if you are subscribing to a mailing list

(e) The Signature Drop-down List Box

FIGURE 2.8 Hands-on Exercise 3 (continued)

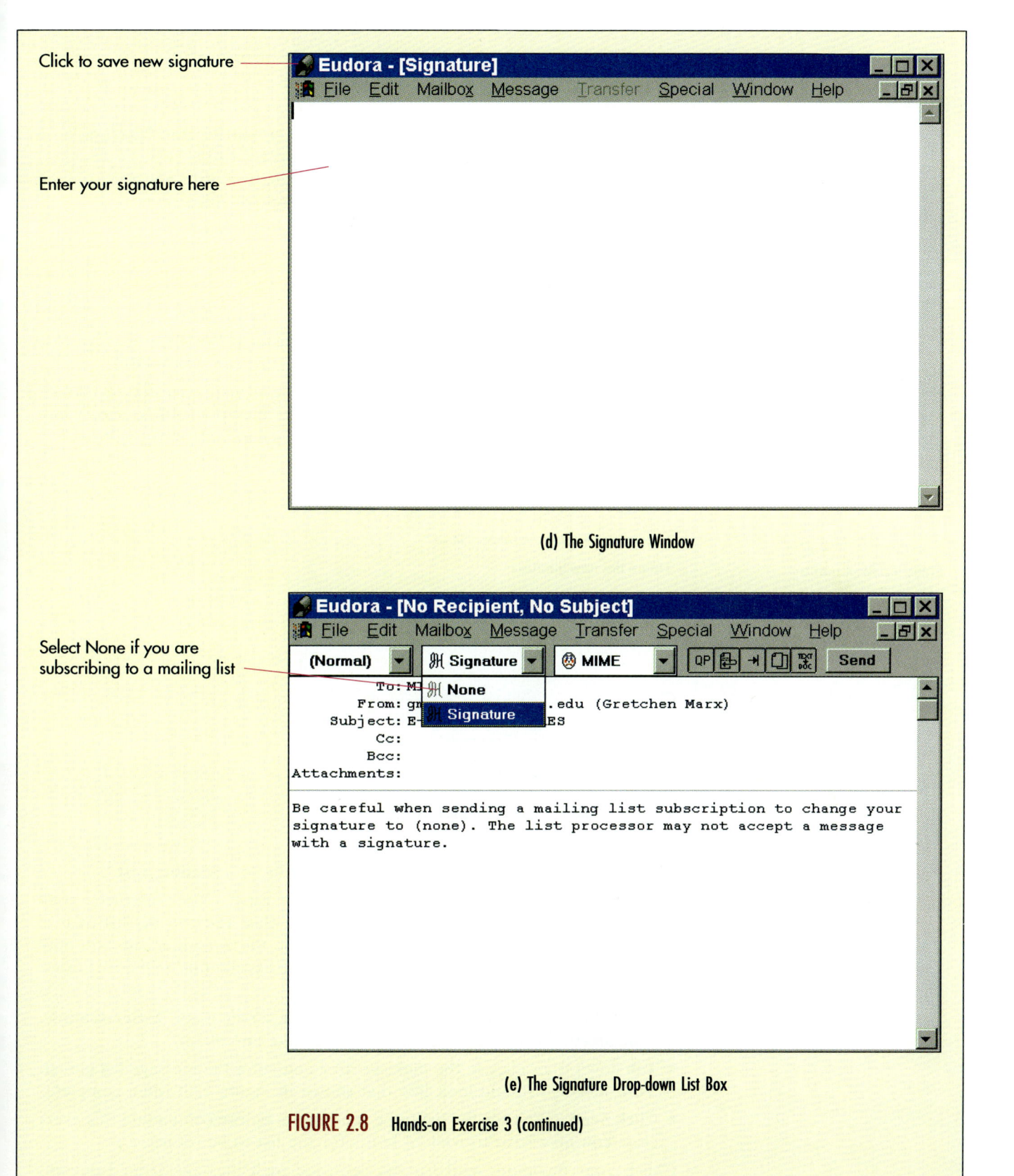

WATCH THAT SIGNATURE

Commands sent to a list server must follow a certain format. Inserting a signature in your message may cause the list server to reject it. To avoid this problem, be sure to select **None** in the Signature drop-down list box before sending any message to a listserv, listproc, or majordomo.

STEP 3: Create a Mailbox

➤ Select **Mailbox** from the pull-down menus, then select **New.**
- Enter the name of the new mailbox, **subscribe,** in the text box displayed in the New Mailbox dialog box, as shown in Figure 2.8f. Click **OK.**
- Select **Mailbox** again. You should see your new mailbox listed, as shown in Figure 2.8g. You can now use the Transfer command to move any selected mail from any of your other mailboxes to your new mailbox.

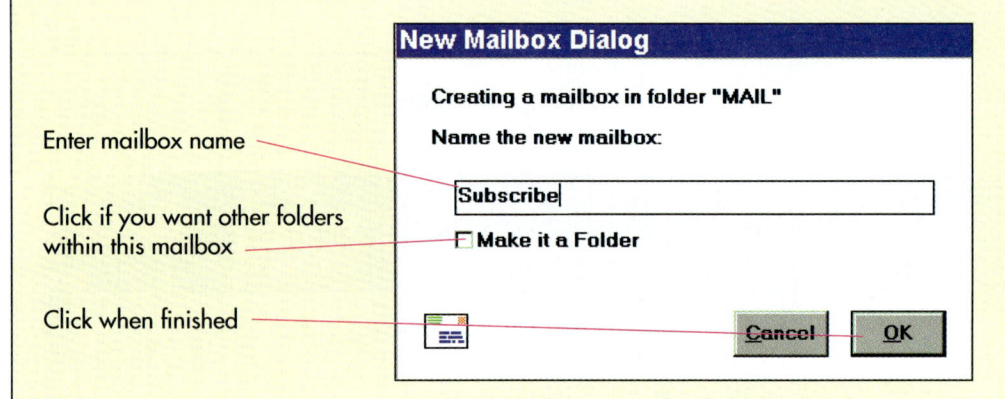

Enter mailbox name

Click if you want other folders within this mailbox

Click when finished

(f) The Completed New Mailbox Dialog Box

FIGURE 2.8 Hands-on Exercise 3 (continued)

STEP 4: Retrieve the "List of Lists" and Subscribe to a Mailing List

➤ Send an e-mail message to retrieve the "list of lists." (Your instructor may choose to have only one or two people in the class retrieve the list as it is quite long. If a copy of it is already available in the computer lab, you may not need to retrieve it at all. Check with your lab assistant or help desk before proceeding.)
- Select **Message,** then **New** and enter the list server name **listserv@bitnic.educom.edu** in the To field. Leave the Subject line blank.
- **Tab** down to or click in the message area and enter the message **list global.** Your message should look like that shown in Figure 2.8h when complete.
- Click **Send.** (Wait for the list to be sent to you before completing this exercise. You may have to wait 24 hours for the list to be returned.)

➤ Check your incoming mail for the returned mail message from Educom, which is an organization formed to promote technology in education. Select the message, then select **File** and **Print** to print the list.

➤ Choose a list to which you want to subscribe.

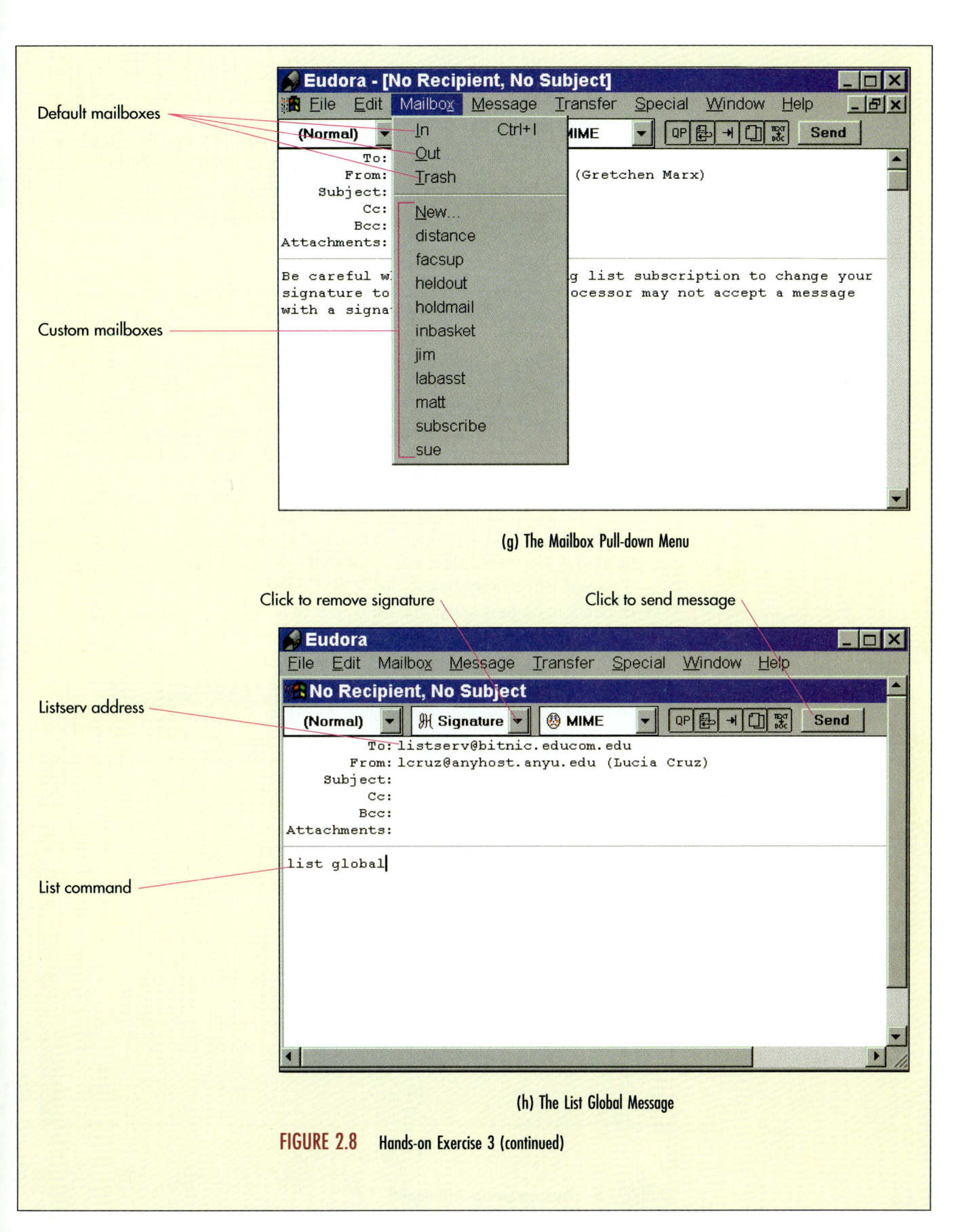

Default mailboxes — In, Out, Trash

Custom mailboxes — distance, facsup, heldout, holdmail, inbasket, jim, labasst, matt, subscribe, sue

(g) The Mailbox Pull-down Menu

Click to remove signature

Click to send message

Listserv address — To: listserv@bitnic.educom.edu
From: lcruz@anyhost.anyu.edu (Lucia Cruz)

List command — list global

(h) The List Global Message

FIGURE 2.8   Hands-on Exercise 3 (continued)

GLOBAL COMMUNICATION ON THE INTERNET

- Subscribe to the list. The following instructions assume you want to know more about biking, and want to find other people interested in the sport. You want to try the bicycling list, *bicycle,* owned by Chris Tanski. You should use the following instructions, substituting the name of the list and the list server address to which you wish to subscribe where appropriate in the message.
  - Select **New Message** from the **Message** menu.
  - In the To field, enter **listproc@list.cren.net.** That is the address of the list server.
  - Leave the Subject field blank.
  - Tab to the message area, and type the message **subscribe bicycle your real name,** substituting the listname and your real name (not your username) where appropriate, as shown in Figure 2.8i.
  - Click **Send.** Your subscription to the list called *bicycle* (or whichever list you subscribed to) will be entered. You should get a confirmation back from the list server within 24 hours.
  - Save the confirmation message. It will explain how you can unsubscribe and/or suspend your mail, and should have the name and e-mail address of the list manager or moderator to write to should you have problems. (Do not send e-mail about problems with the list to the entire list, or to listserv. Instead, send a message to the manager's or moderator's Internet address.) Select the confirmation message in your in-box. Select the **Transfer** pull-down menu, then select **Subscribe.** Your subscription information is moved from the in-box to the SUBSCRIBE mail folder.
  - Depending on how active the list is, you may start getting mail right away. Check within 24 hours to see your messages from the list.

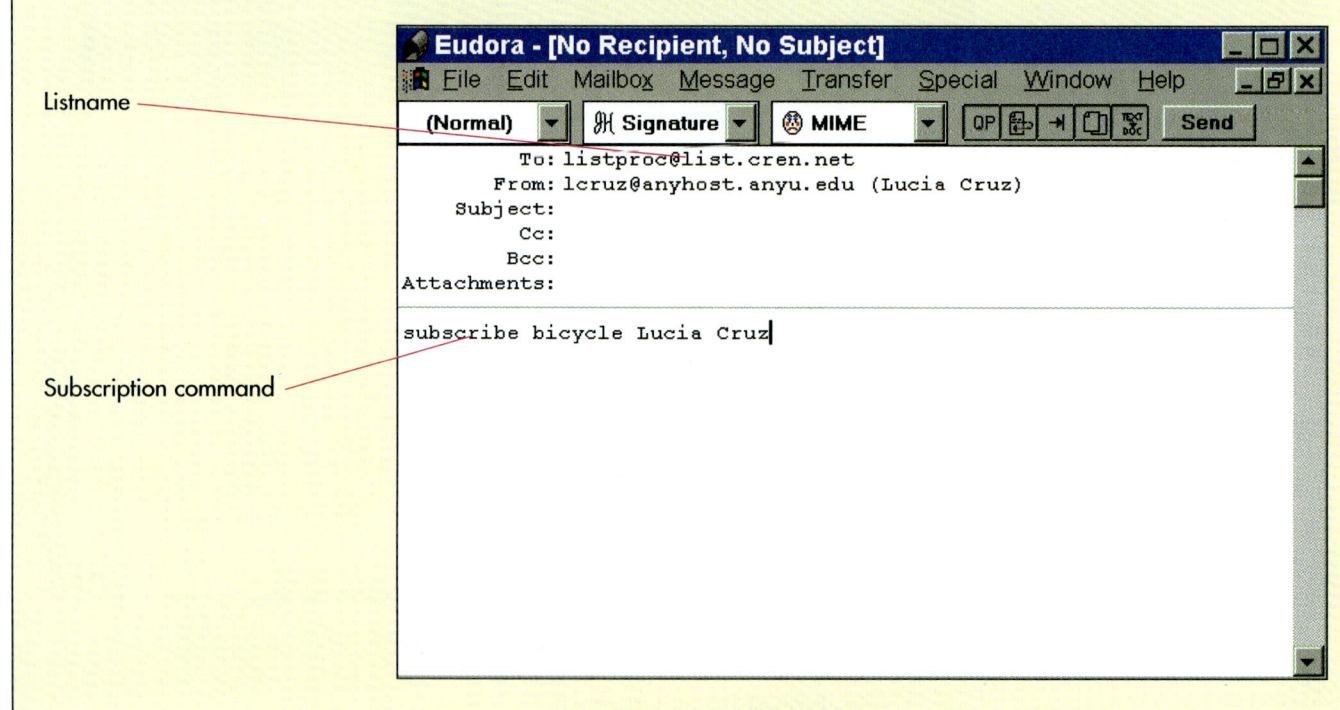

(i) Subscribing to a List

FIGURE 2.8   Hands-on Exercise 3 (continued)

HANDS-ON EXERCISE 4

Customizing E-mail and Subscribing to Mailing Lists Using Pine

Objective: Create a distribution list and folder, and subscribe to a mailing list. Use Figure 2.9 as a guide in the exercise.

STEP 1: Create a Distribution/Nickname List

➤ Log on to your system and type **Pine** at the Unix prompt.

- At the main menu type **A** to update your *address book*. The blank Address Book screen shown in Figure 2.9a is displayed.

- Type **S** to create a distribution list (this and other available commands are shown at the bottom of the screen). A message is displayed at the bottom of the screen requesting the long name/description of the list as shown in Figure 2.9b. Enter a descriptive name for the list, such as **MIS201 Class List** (substitute the course number for your class), and press **Enter.**

- Next enter the list nickname (a one-word abbreviation for the distribution list). This is the name you will later enter in the To field when you send a message to the list. Enter **MIS201** or something similar and press **Enter.**

- You will be prompted to enter the first address in the distribution list as shown in Figure 2.9c. Enter the username of someone in your class, then press **Enter.** (If you are creating a distribution list of people using the same Internet host as you, you can simply enter their usernames. If they are at another site, enter their usernames and Internet addresses.)

- Continue entering usernames and pressing **Enter** until you have entered all the names you want on the distribution list.

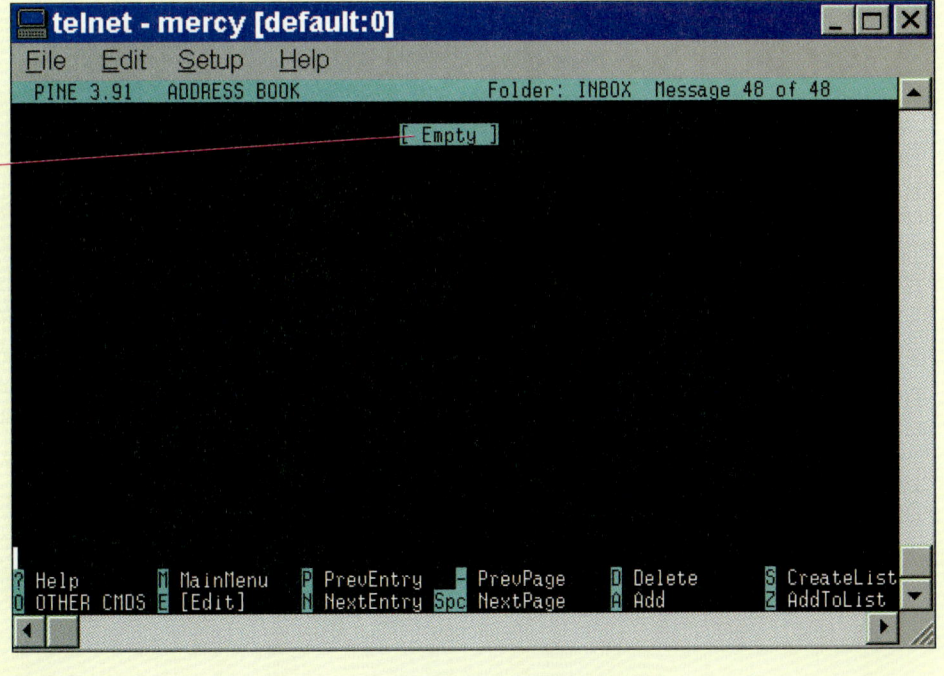

There are no distribution lists

(a) The Blank Address Book

FIGURE 2.9 Hands-on Exercise 4

Enter full name (description) of distribution list

(b) The Long Name/Description Message

Leave blank after last name is entered

Enter username and Internet address of first person on distribution list

(c) Entering the First Address in the List

FIGURE 2.9 Hands-on Exercise 4 (continued)

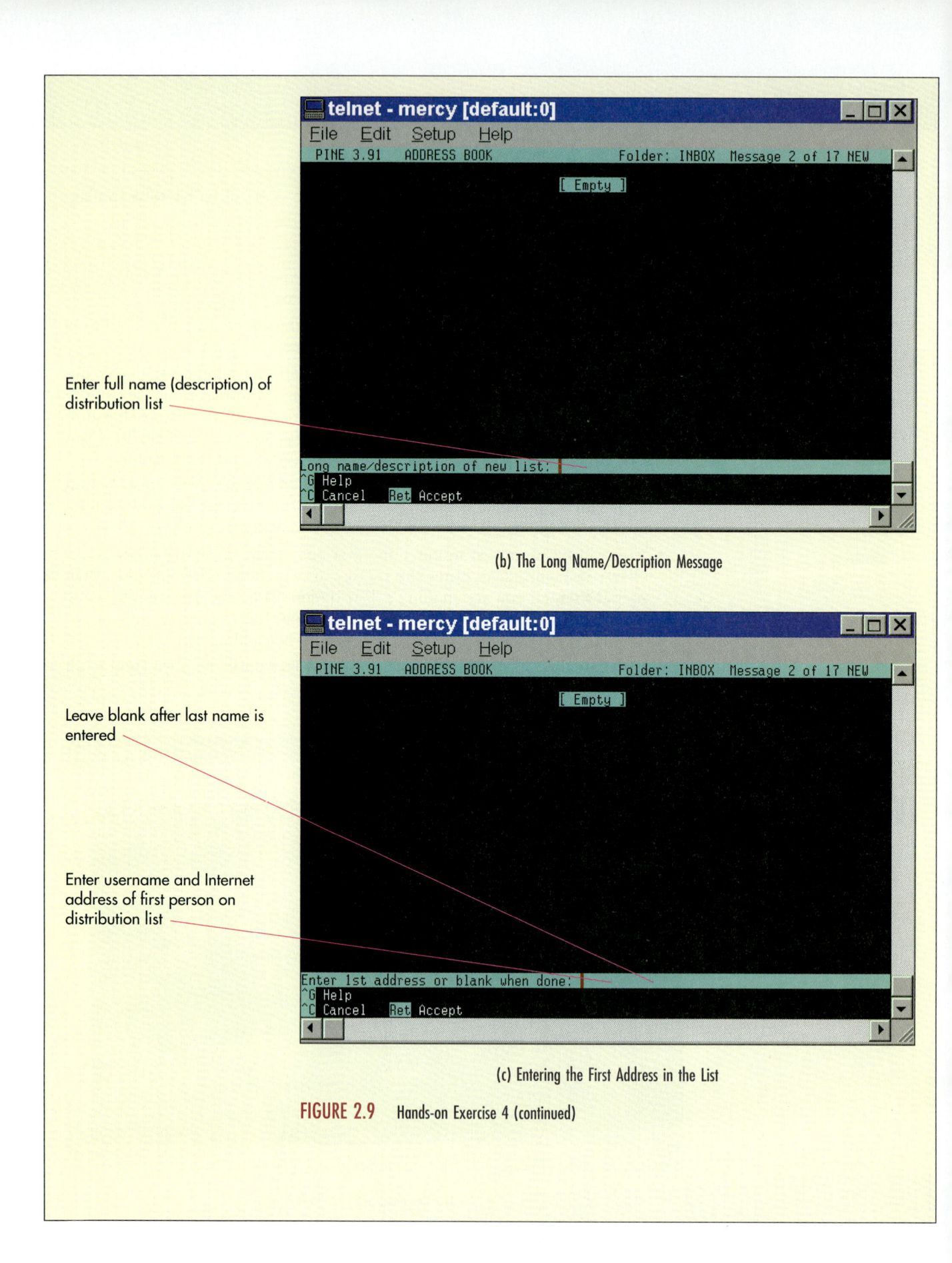

- When you have no more names, leave the address line blank and press **Enter** one more time. (The blank address field tells Pine you have reached the end of the list.) A message is displayed briefly, indicating that Pine is updating the address book. You should now see a screen similar to that shown in Figure 2.9d, displaying the distribution list you just created.
- Press **M** to return to the main menu.

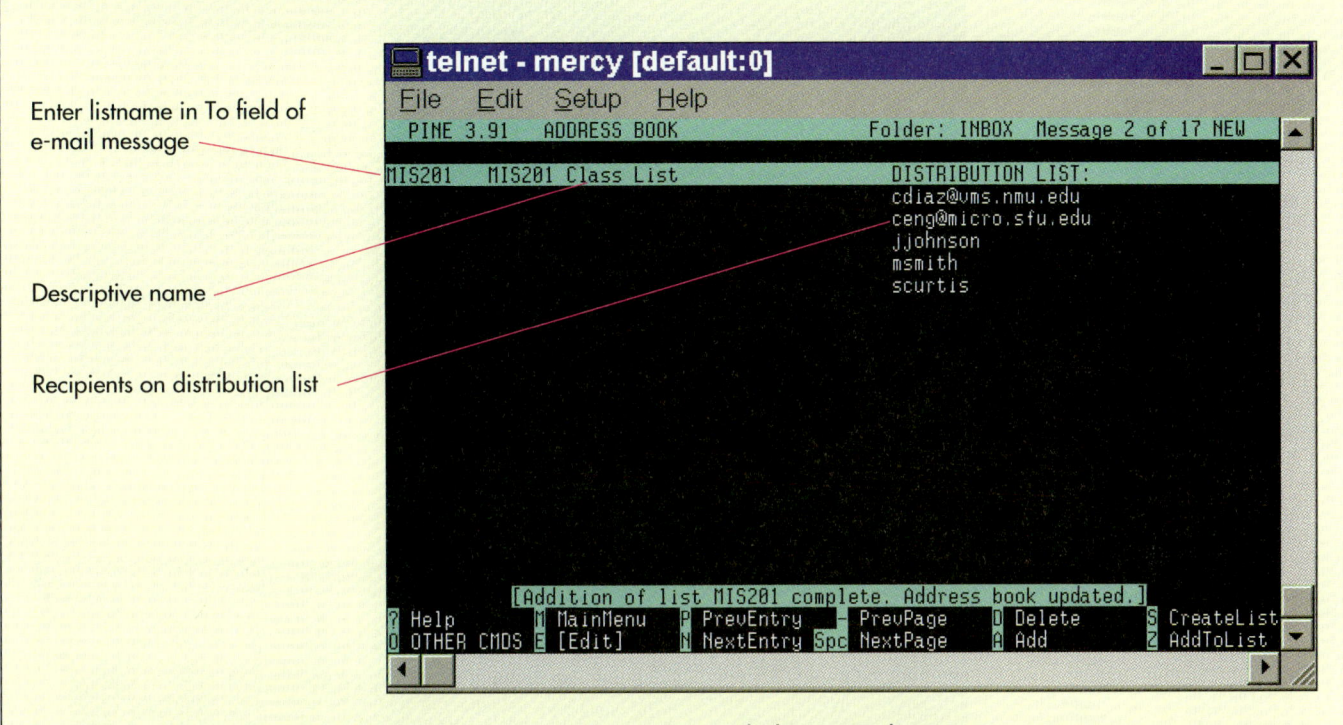

Enter listname in To field of e-mail message

Descriptive name

Recipients on distribution list

(d) The New Distribution List

FIGURE 2.9 Hands-on Exercise 4 (continued)

STEP 2: Create a New Mail Folder and Move a Message to It

➤ You will want to customize Pine to organize mail messages you want to save indefinitely, as opposed to having them cluttering your in-box.
- At the main menu type **L** to display a list of existing mail folders as shown in Figure 2.9e.
- When you see the list, which by default includes INBOX, sent-mail, and saved-messages, type **A** to add a folder. You will be prompted for the name of the folder you want to add, as shown in Figure 2.9f.
- Type the name of the folder you want to add, **subscribe,** and press **Enter.** You will see the new folder displayed in your folder list.

➤ Press **M** to return to the main menu, then type **I** to see an index of messages in the current folder, which by default is INBOX.

➤ Select a message to transfer to the **SUBSCRIBE** folder. Type **S** to save the message, then enter the name of the folder to save to, **subscribe,** as shown in Figure 2.9g. The message will be marked for deletion in the INBOX, and saved to the new folder.
- Type **M** to return to the main menu.

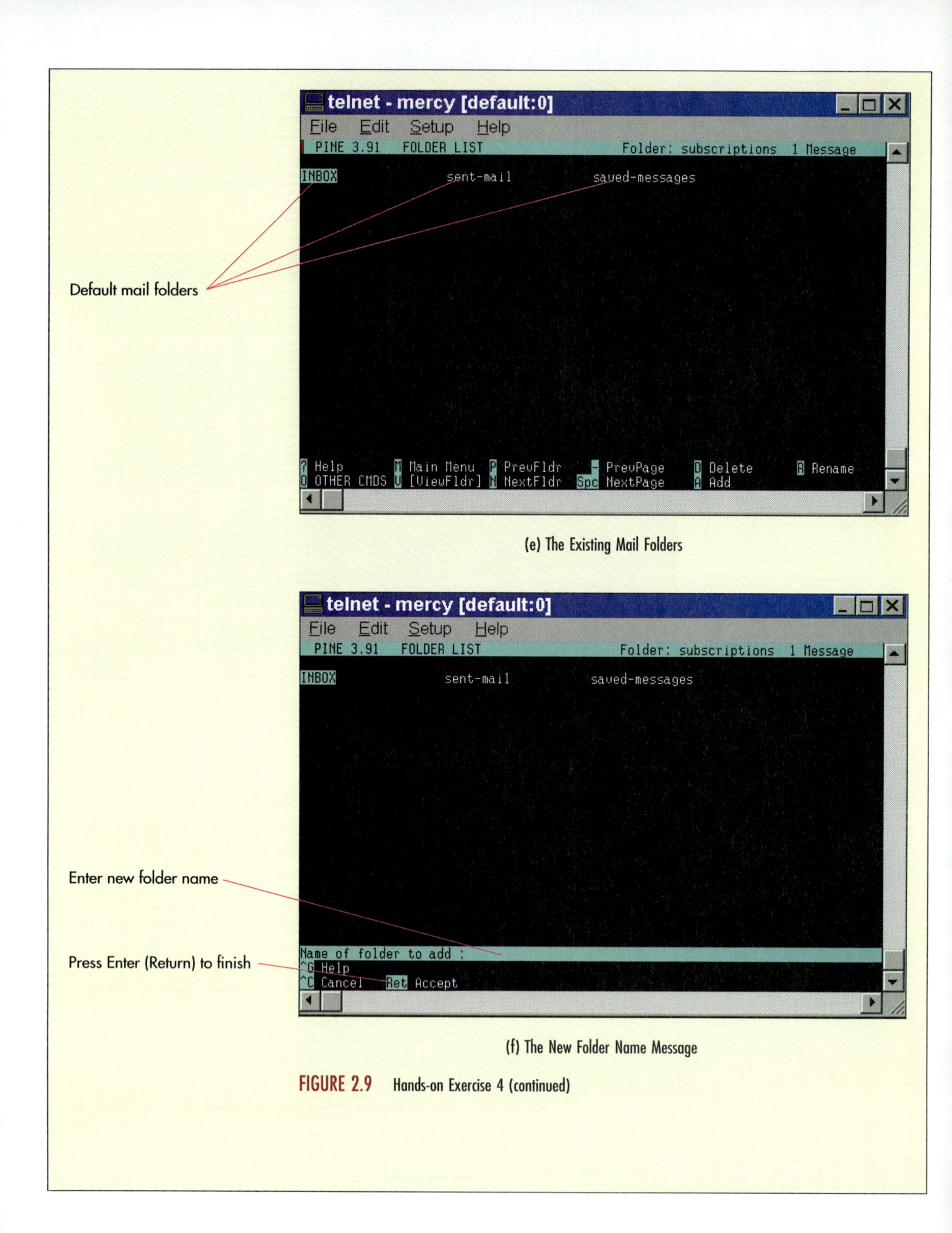

(e) The Existing Mail Folders

(f) The New Folder Name Message

FIGURE 2.9   Hands-on Exercise 4 (continued)

Selected message

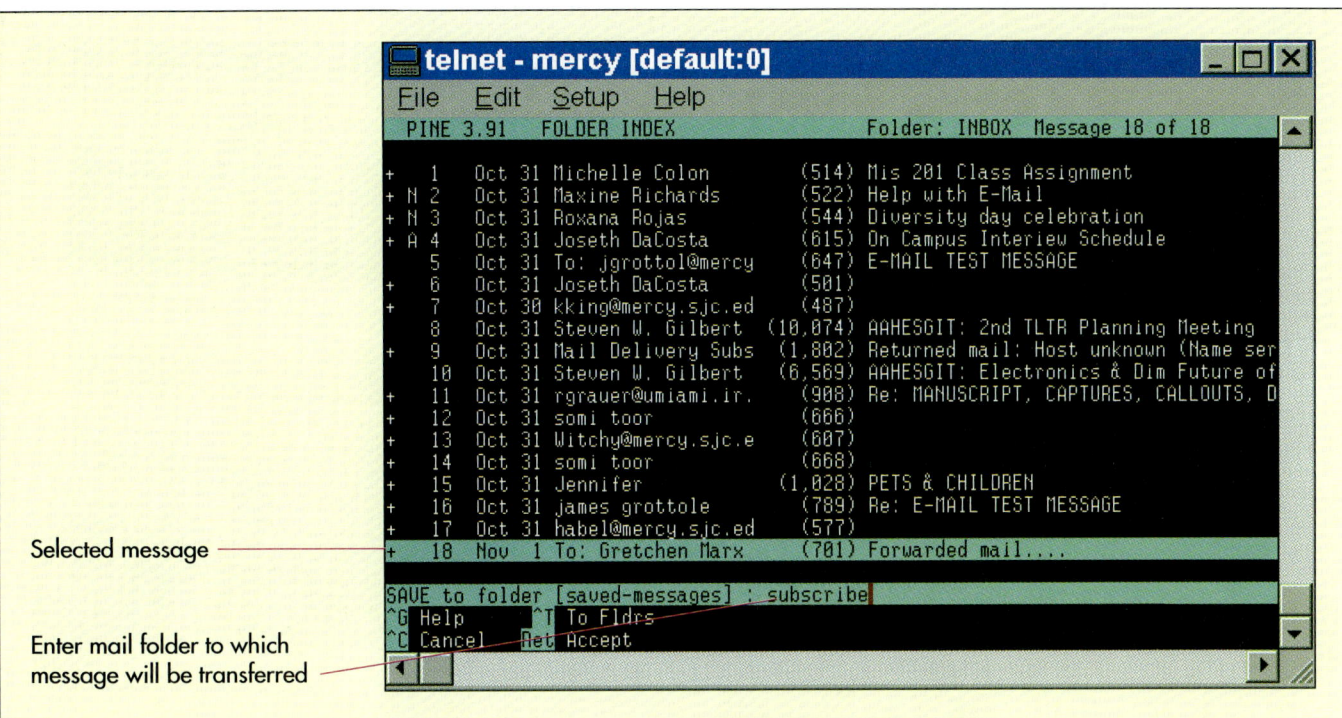

Enter mail folder to which message will be transferred

(g) Saving a Message to a Folder

FIGURE 2.9 Hands-on Exercise 4 (continued)

STEP 3: Retrieve the "List of Lists" and Subscribe to a Mailing List

➤ Send an e-mail message to retrieve the "list of lists." (Your instructor may choose to have only one or two people in the class retrieve the list as it is quite long. If a copy of it is already available in the computer lab, you may not need to retrieve it at all. Check with your lab assistant or help desk before proceeding.)

- Type **C** at the Pine main menu and enter the list server name **listserv @bitnic.educom.edu** in the To field in the message screen. Leave the Subject line blank.
- **Tab** down to the message area and enter the message **list global.** Your message should look like that shown in Figure 2.9h when complete.
- Press **Ctrl+X.** (Wait for the list to be sent to you before completing this exercise. You may have to wait 24 hours for the list to be returned.)

➤ Check your incoming mail for the returned mail message from Educom, which is an organization formed to promote technology in education. Select the message, then select **File** and **Print** to print the list.

➤ Choose a list to which you want to subscribe.

➤ Subscribe to the list. The following instructions assume you want to know more about biking, and want to find other people interested in the sport. You want to try the bicycling list, *bicycle,* owned by Chris Tanski. You should use the following instructions, substituting the name of the list and the list server address to which you wish to subscribe where appropriate in the message.

- Type **C** at the main menu to compose your subscription message.
- In the To field, enter **listproc@list.cren.net.** That is the address of the list server.

GLOBAL COMMUNICATION ON THE INTERNET   **75**

Listserv address

Leave subject blank when requesting list

List global command

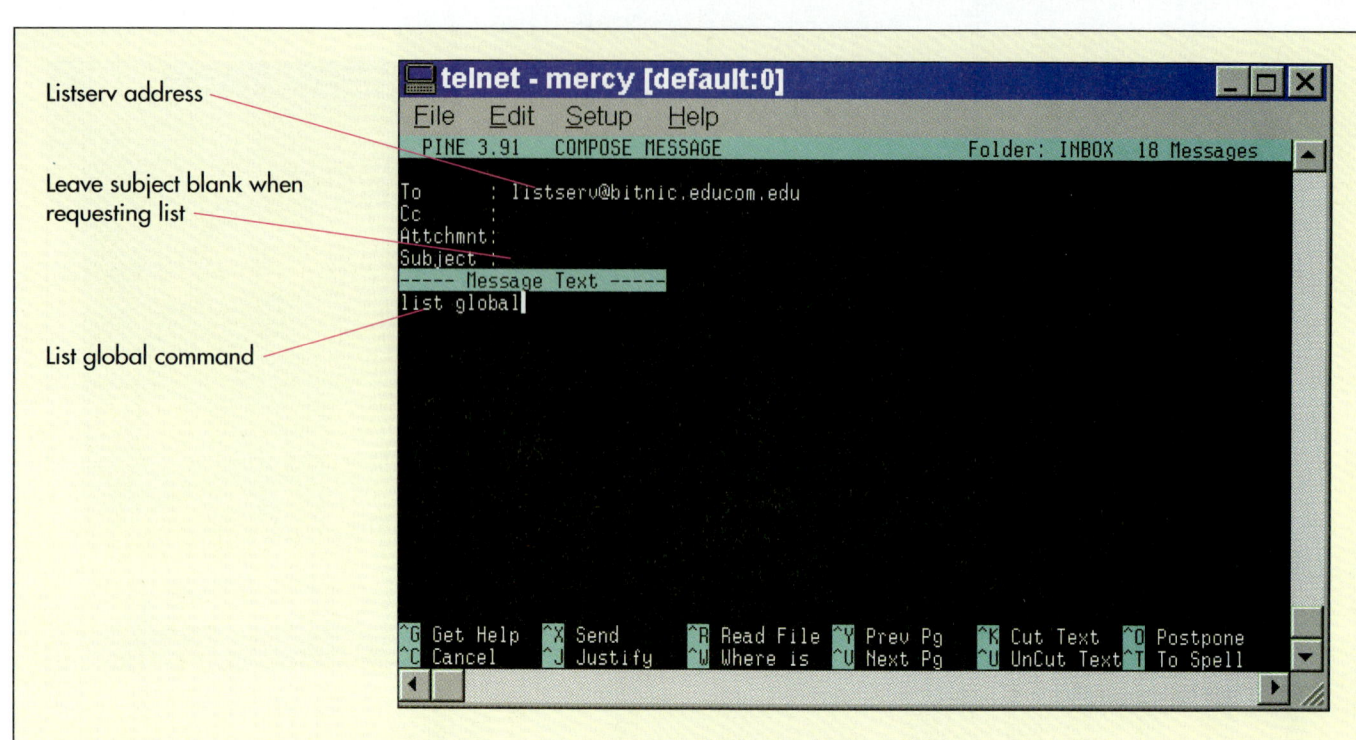

```
telnet - mercy [default:0]
File  Edit  Setup  Help
PINE 3.91    COMPOSE MESSAGE          Folder: INBOX  18 Messages

To      : listserv@bitnic.educom.edu
Cc      :
Attchmnt:
Subject :
----- Message Text -----
list global

^G Get Help  ^X Send     ^R Read File  ^Y Prev Pg  ^K Cut Text    ^O Postpone
^C Cancel    ^J Justify  ^W Where is   ^V Next Pg  ^U UnCut Text  ^T To Spell
```

(h) The Completed List Global Message

FIGURE 2.9 Hands-on Exercise 4 (continued)

- Leave the subject field blank.
- Tab to the message area, and type the message **subscribe bicycle your real name,** substituting the listname and your real name (not your username) where appropriate, as shown in Figure 2.9i.
- Type **Ctrl+X.** Your subscription to the list called *bicycle* (or whichever list you subscribed to) will be entered. You should get a confirmation back from the list server within 24 hours.
- Save the confirmation message. It will explain how you can unsubscribe and/or suspend your mail, and should have the name and e-mail address of the list manager or moderator to write to should you have problems. (Do not send e-mail about problems with the list to the entire list, or to listserv. Instead, send a message to the manager's or moderator's Internet address.) Select the confirmation message in your INBOX folder. Type **S** to save the message. When you see a message asking what folder to save to, enter **subscribe,** or whatever name you gave your subscription information folder in the previous step. Your subscription information is copied to the SUBSCRIBE mail folder and marked for deletion in the in-box.
- Depending on how active the list is, you may start getting mail right away. Check within 24 hours to see your messages from the list.

List server

Leave subject field blank when subscribing to list

Press Ctrl+X to send

(i) Subscribing to the Bicyle Mailing List

FIGURE 2.9   Hands-on Exercise 4 (continued)

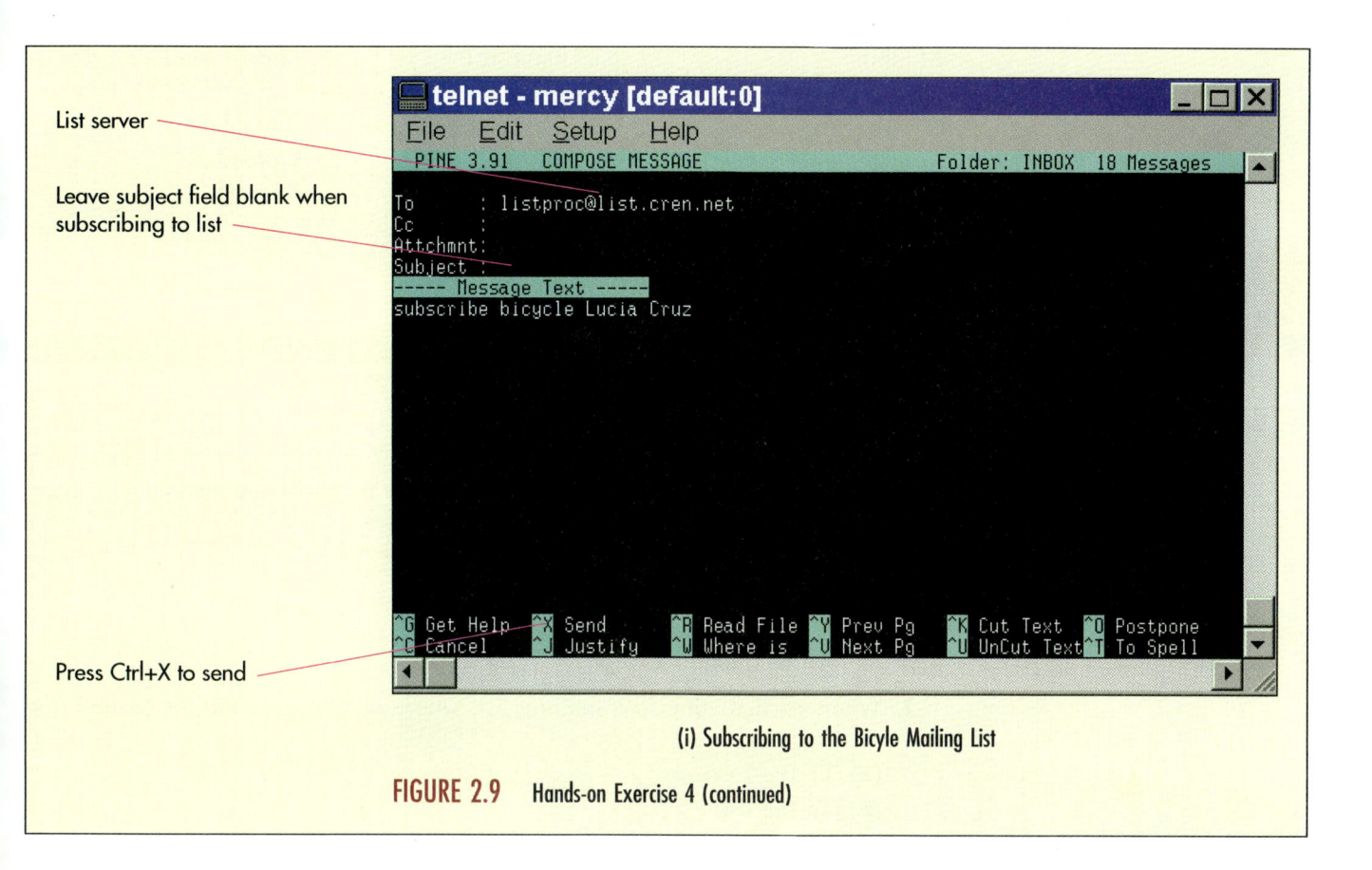

SUMMARY

Using e-mail you can send a message to anyone on the Internet in a matter of seconds (although they, for various reasons, may not immediately receive it). All e-mail systems give you the capability to compose and send messages; to receive, reply to, and forward mail; and to set up custom distribution lists. You can also subscribe to mailing lists, which will automatically send you messages sent by other subscribers to the list. Many people subscribe to mailing lists and correspond about their favorite subjects with other people from all over the world.

How you send and retrieve your mail depends on whether you are using a POP mail client or a Unix mail program. A POP mail client retrieves mail from the Internet server and stores it on your PC or the file server in the computer lab. A Unix mail program leaves the mail on the Internet server. However, both provide the capabilities described above.

KEY WORDS AND CONCEPTS

Alias	Distribution list	Header
Blind carbon copy	Download	List owner
Carbon copy	E-mail	Listproc
Client software	Flaming	Listserv
Command-line interface	Folder	List server
Digest	Folder index	Lurking

GLOBAL COMMUNICATION ON THE INTERNET **77**

Mailbox
Mail client
Mailing list
Mail server
Majordomo
Moderator

Nickname list
Password
Post Office Protocol (POP)
Shell account
Signature

Simple Mail Transfer Protocol (SMTP)
Suspend
Upload
UserID

Multiple Choice

1. Which of the following typically provides the user with a graphical user interface to access the Internet?
   (a) Client software
   (b) A Unix shell account
   (c) A command-line prompt
   (d) All of the above

2. When participating in a mailing list, where would you send an unsubscribe message?
   (a) To the Listserv
   (b) To the list
   (c) Both (a) and (b)
   (d) Neither (a) nor (b)

3. If you often send messages to the same group of recipients at your college, which of the following should you do?
   (a) Subscribe to a mailing list
   (b) Set up a distribution list
   (c) Both (a) and (b)
   (d) Neither (a) nor (b)

4. Which of the following capabilities is available in most e-mail systems?
   (a) Compose
   (b) Send
   (c) Forward
   (d) All of the above

5. E-mail allows you to send messages to:
   (a) Another user on your local area network
   (b) Another user on the Internet
   (c) Both (a) and (b)
   (d) Neither (a) nor (b)

6. Which of the following downloads your mail to be stored on your local PC when requested?
   (a) Post Office Protocol (POP) software
   (b) Pine
   (c) A Unix mail program
   (d) All of the above

7. Which e-mail program allows you to create a distribution list?
   (a) Pine
   (b) Eudora
   (c) Both (a) and (b)
   (d) Neither (a) nor (b)

8. Which symbol is used in an e-mail address to separate the username from the host computer name?
   (a) *
   (b) @
   (c) .
   (d) #

9. If you use a POP mail client, where is the mail stored while enroute to you?
   (a) On the Unix server
   (b) On local storage on the PC
   (c) Both (a) and (b)
   (d) Neither (a) nor (b)

10. Which of the following statements regarding Internet e-mail programs is true?
    (a) You may move a message from one folder to another
    (b) You may create an alias for your username
    (c) You can define your own distribution lists
    (d) All of the above

11. Which of the following allows you to send an e-mail message to a second person without the first recipient knowing it?
    (a) The To field
    (b) The Cc field
    (c) The Bcc field
    (d) All of the above

12. If you choose to redirect an e-mail message, what happens to it?
    (a) It is automatically sent back to the originator
    (b) It is sent to the new recipient with your username in the From field
    (c) It is sent to the new recipient with the originator's name in the From field
    (d) It goes into the trash folder for deletion at the end of the mail session

13. Which of the following statements regarding Eudora mailboxes is true?
    (a) The user cannot create mailboxes
    (b) Mail transferred to the Trash folder cannot be recalled
    (c) Mailboxes can be viewed only one at a time
    (d) None of the above

14. Which of the following guidelines should be used when creating an e-mail signature?
    (a) Keep the length to a minimum
    (b) Use appropriate verbiage
    (c) Both (a) and (b)
    (d) Neither (a) nor (b)

15. To which of the following mailing list programs would you recommend sending a signature with the Subscribe command?
    (a) Listserv
    (b) Listproc
    (c) Majordomo
    (d) None of the above

ANSWERS

1. a	**6.** a	**11.** c
2. a	**7.** c	**12.** c
3. b	**8.** b	**13.** d
4. d	**9.** c	**14.** c
5. c	**10.** d	**15.** d

EXPLORING THE INTERNET

1. Using Figure 2.10, match each action with its result; a given action may be used more than once or not at all.

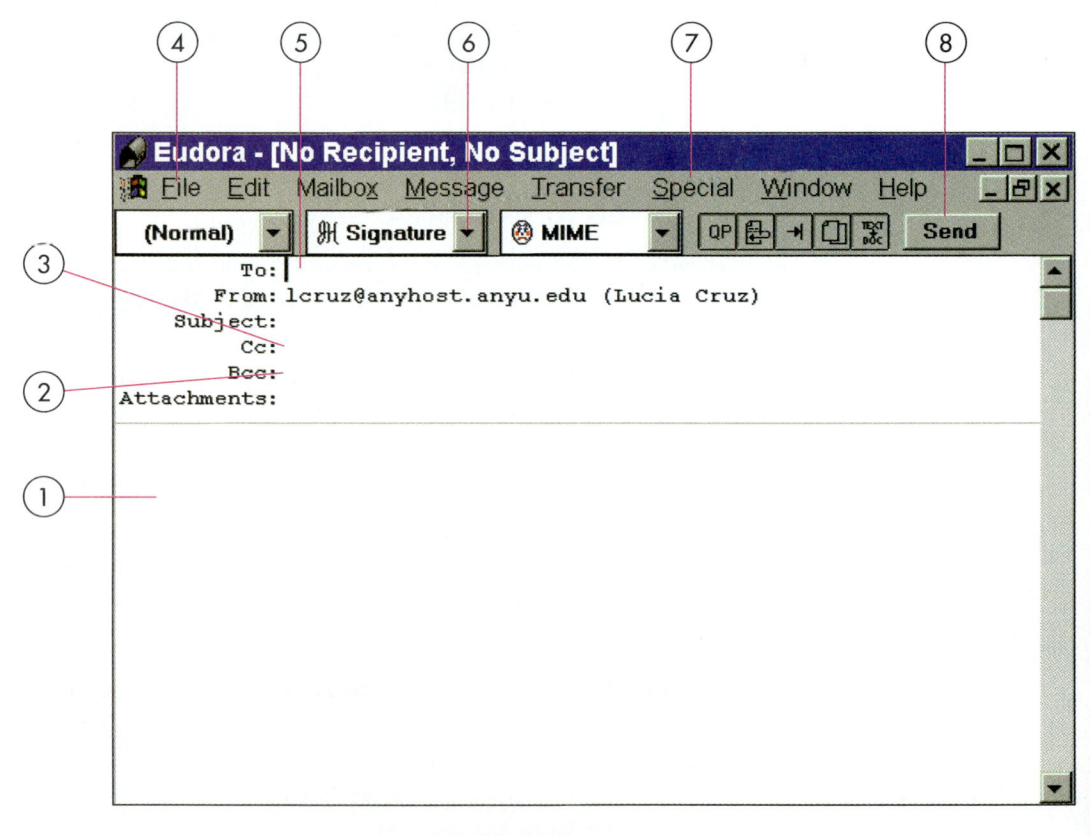

FIGURE 2.10   Figure for Exploring the Internet Exercise 1

Action	Result
a. Click at 1	____ Enter the text of the message
b. Click at 2	____ Change your password
c. Click at 3	____ Send a copy to someone without the addressee's knowledge
d. Click at 4	
e. Click at 5	____ Send a copy; the addressee will know the copy has been sent
f. Click at 6	
g. Click at 7	____ Send the message
h. Click at 8	____ Remove your signature from the message
	____ Check for incoming mail
	____ Enter the recipient's username

2. The messages shown in Figure 2.11 appeared (or could have appeared) in conjunction with one of the hands-on exercises in this chapter. Explain the nature of each message and indicate the necessary corrective action (if any).

(a) Message 1

(b) Message 2

FIGURE 2.11 Messages for Exploring the Internet Exercise 2

GLOBAL COMMUNICATION ON THE INTERNET

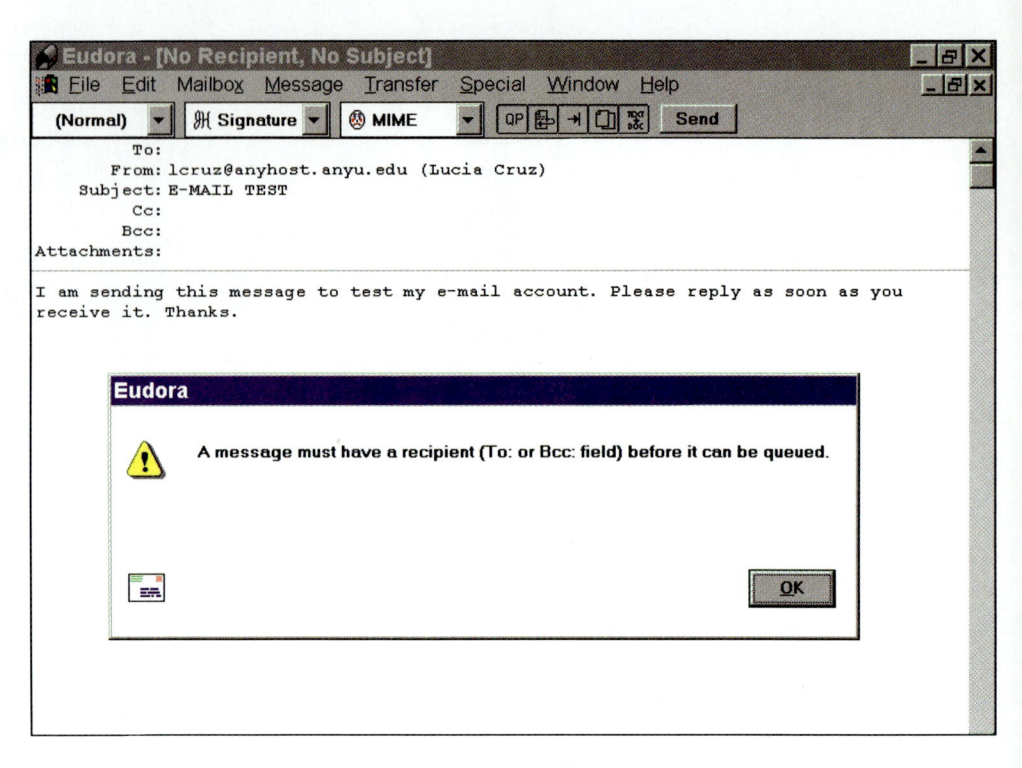

(c) Message 3

FIGURE 2.11 Messages for Exploring the Internet Exercise 2 (continued)

3. Answer the following questions regarding e-mail. Compare your answers to those of your classmates.
    a. What mailing lists, if any, are sponsored by your college or university?
    b. Do the faculty members at your school use e-mail to communicate with (a) each other, (b) colleagues at other institutions, (c) administrators, or (d) students?
    c. What are some of the advantages/disadvantages of communicating with faculty members via e-mail?
    d. Distance learning is a hot topic at many colleges. Could a course be successfully taught entirely through e-mail? Why or why not?

4. Learn More about Pine: Log on to your Unix server and type **Pine.** Once you are at the main menu, type a question mark (**?**). The main Pine Help screen will appear. Read through the overview about Pine, pressing the **spacebar** to move down a screen at a time. Pine Help is context sensitive. Press **I** to move to the INBOX folder index, and press **?** again. This time you will see information about various options in using the index. For instance, you will learn that you can jump to a specific message in the index by pressing the letter **J,** then entering the message number. You can press the **Tab** key to move to the next unread message. Press **E** at any time to exit Help.

PRACTICE WITH E-MAIL

1. Find a Pen Pal: Find a pen pal in the class or at another university and send that person an e-mail message describing how you plan to use the Internet

this semester. Send a copy of the message to your instructor as proof that you did the exercise.

2. Subscribe to a Mailing List about the Internet: Send the message **list global/internet** to the listserv at **listserv@bitnic.educom.edu.** Wait for the reply and then choose a list about the Internet to which to subscribe. For example, you could subscribe to the Scout Report, a weekly update on new and interesting sites and Net developments. To subscribe to the Scout Report, send e-mail to **majordomo@is.internet.nic.** In the message area enter **subscribe scout-report Your Real Name.** When you get your subscription confirmation, transfer it to the **SUBSCRIBE** mailbox you set up in Hands-on Exercise 2.3 or 2.4.

3. Attach a File: Eudora, other POP mail programs, and some versions of Pine provide the capability to attach a file to the message you're sending. Suppose you are assigned a group project, and are working on a section of the final report. You could attach your section to a mail message, and mail it to the rest of your group for their review and comment. The following instructions describe how to attach a file in Eudora. See your instructor for attaching files in Pine.

   a. Log on and start Eudora. Select **New Message** from the **Message** menu.

   b. While you are preparing the e-mail message, click on **Attach Document** in the **Message** menu. You will see a dialog box, shown in Figure 2.12a, that requests information about the document you wish to attach to the message. Eudora wants to know on which drive the document is found. First click the **down arrow** next to the drive name, to see a drop-down list box of all the disks attached to your system. Select the disk on which the document is stored.

   c. If your document is in a subdirectory, double click the desired subdirectory in the directories list, and a list of all files in the subdirectory will be displayed at the left of the window.

(a) The Attach Document Dialog Box

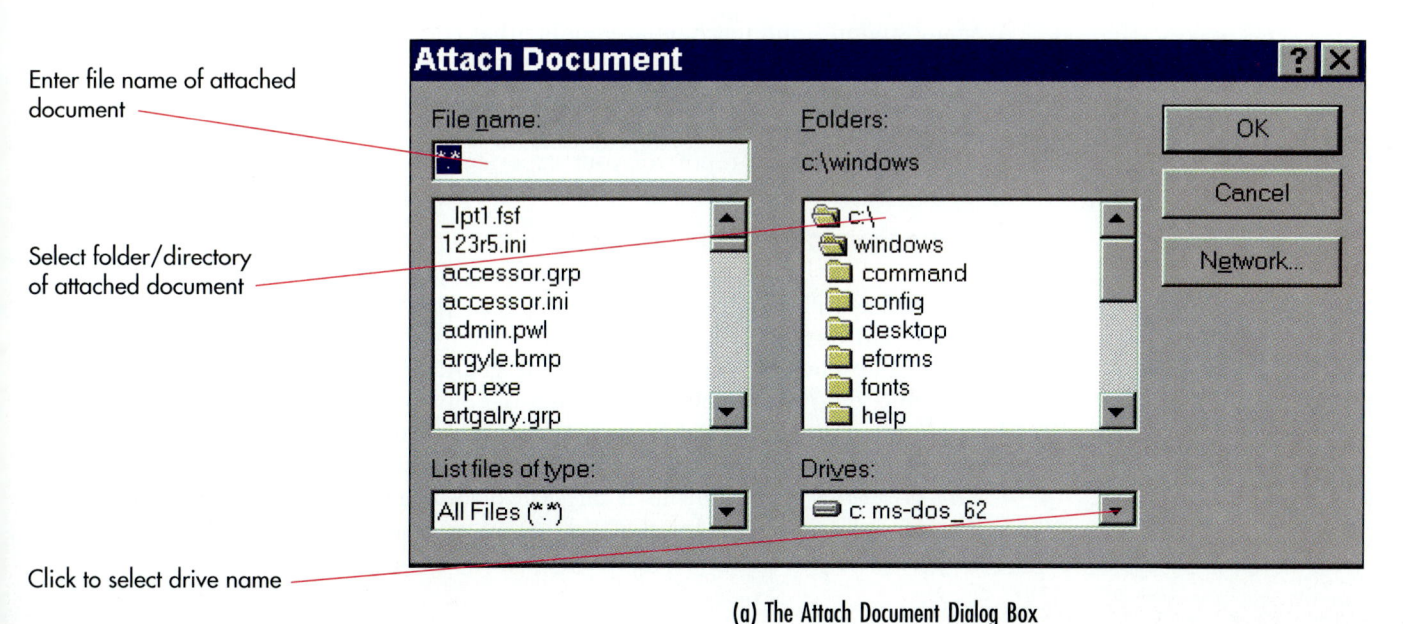

FIGURE 2.12 Figure for Practice Exercise 3

d. Click the file you want to attach, then click **OK.** You will be returned to the mail message window. The Attachments field will contain the name of the file you want to attach.

   e. Complete your message, click **Send,** and the document, in its original form, is sent as an attachment with the message.

4. Send a Message to a List: Subscribe to a mailing list that interests you, and read the messages posted to the list for a few weeks. After you have been on a mailing list for a while and feel comfortable with the types of messages being sent to the list, compose a message or a reply to someone else's question or statement. Remember to send the message to the list address, not the listserv.

CASE STUDIES

Finding a List

Assume you want to find a mailing list on a particular subject—Shakespeare, for example. Send a message to **listserv@bitnic.educom.edu** with the command **list global/shakespeare** in the message area. You will receive an e-mail message showing the mailing lists on the topic in which you are interested. Find mailing lists for two or three topics of interest to you and subscribe to them. ***Be sure to send the subscribe message without a signature.*** Save the subscription confirmations in your **SUBSCRIBE** mailbox (set one up if you have not already done so).

Collaborative Learning Using E-mail

Many students and teachers are finding that collaborative learning helps everyone learn better. Set up a distribution list for one or more of your classes, and invite people to join an online study group for the course. How many of your peers respond? Do they know about e-mail? Can you use e-mail for group work and studying? Prepare a report of your experience.

Participatory Democracy

As a citizen, participating in the democratic process is your right, and an obligation of citizenship. However, with the advent of the Internet, you don't have to wait for an election. Your voice can be heard with an immediacy not previously available. Find out the e-mail addresses of your Congressional representatives, and send them e-mail about an issue that concerns you—perhaps legislation regarding government funding of student financial aid. Remember, however, that e-mail is just as serious a medium as a physical document. You will not be anonymous. Therefore, it is important that you compose your thoughts and send a clearly worded, finely crafted message.

Analyzing E-mail Content

Subscribe to a list of interest to you, and read the e-mail daily for a week. Analyze the content of the e-mail for its information-to-noise ratio. How much of the traffic provides useful information, and how much is sent just so the sender can expound to thousands of people? Noise can be a problem everywhere on the Net.

3
FINDING THINGS ON THE WORLD WIDE WEB: NETSCAPE AND LYNX

OBJECTIVES

After reading this chapter you will be able to:

1. Explain the basic terminology of the World Wide Web, and explore the Web using a graphical browser such as Netscape.
2. Describe what a URL is and use one to find a specific Web document or home page.
3. Explain how to navigate through the Web using hypertext and hypermedia links.
4. Create a bookmark for a Web site; save and print a Web document.
5. Use a search engine to find Web resources that match a specific query.
6. Understand the differences between a graphical browser and a text-based browser such as Lynx.

OVERVIEW

The World Wide Web (WWW, W3, or simply the Web) is the newest, hottest tool on the Internet, and what's more, it couldn't be easier to use. The Web is a means of information storage and retrieval that has captivated millions of people and thousands of companies around the globe, and it is critically important that you understand how to make productive use of it. Any document on any Web server, anywhere in the world, is accessible using a Web browser on your PC or Unix server. Learning how to use a Web browser, software that lets you locate and retrieve these documents, is the key to a vast library of millions of references, including audio, video, and graphic files.

In this chapter we show you how to surf the Web using Netscape Navigator, a graphical Web browser that lets you locate text, graphics, video, sound, and other files. You will use hypertext links to jump from document to document and site to site. You will also learn to use Web search engines to conduct directed searches, or queries.

The millions of files and documents available on the Web can also be accessed with a text (rather than graphical) browser. We show you how to use Lynx, a text-based browser that allows those who do not have a GUI client such as Netscape to access the Web and use hypertext links from the Unix prompt.

THE WORLD WIDE WEB

In Chapter 2 we discussed e-mail, and you learned to send and receive messages over the Internet. However, the Internet is much more than a message switching network for e-mail. It connects computers around the globe and lets users access a vast array of text, graphic, audio, video, and programming files from wherever they are connected anywhere in the world.

The original language of the Internet was uninviting to say the least. You needed a variety of esoteric programs (e.g., Telnet, FTP, Archie, Gopher, and so on), which were derived from the Unix operating system. You had to know the precise syntax of those programs. And, even if you were able to get what you wanted, everything was communicated in plain text (graphics and sound were not available).

The **World Wide Web (WWW)** was developed in 1991 at the European Particle Physics Laboratory (CERN) in Switzerland. It introduced a new way to connect the resources on the Internet to one another. The Web is based on the technology of **hypertext** and **hypermedia,** which link computer-based documents in nonlinear fashion. Unlike a traditional document, which is read sequentially from top to bottom, a hypertext document includes links to other documents, which can be viewed (or not) at the reader's discretion. A **link** is a line of text in a hypertext document that contains an embedded Internet address and other information.

When you select a link, it directs a program called a **browser** to connect to the site specified by the link and retrieve the document identified in the link. The first browsers were restricted to text that followed the links from one document to another, even if the documents were on different computers. As users began to create other document types (images, sound, and video), the text browsers evolved naturally into a more powerful GUI tool. These browsers run on your PC, and request services from an Internet host on your campus network. The host is known as the **Web server;** the program that runs on your PC is called the **client.**

Assume, for example, that you are reading a hypertext document about the federal budget deficit. You come to a reference to the Concord Coalition, a nonpartisan organization dedicated to eliminating the deficit. Rather than finishing the original text, you select a link and jump to the Concord Coalition **home page,** or starting point on the Web, shown in Figure 3.1a. From there you tour the site by clicking on any interesting link you see. We clicked on the **Information** link, then followed a few more links to the page shown in Figure 3.1b. You can click the **Back button** at any time to go back to previous pages to follow other links.

Hypermedia is similar in concept to hypertext except that it provides links to graphic, sound, and video files in addition to text files. Hypertext and hypermedia links may be to documents on the same computer or to files stored on another computer somewhere else on the World Wide Web. As the user, you don't need to know or care where the documents are physically located.

Mosaic was the first Windows-based Web browser. Developed at the National Center for Supercomputing Applications at the University of Illinois at Urbana-Champaign, NCSA, it introduced point-and-click navigation to the Web. Today there are many different browsers from which to choose, but all offer the

Links —

Click to go back to previous page —

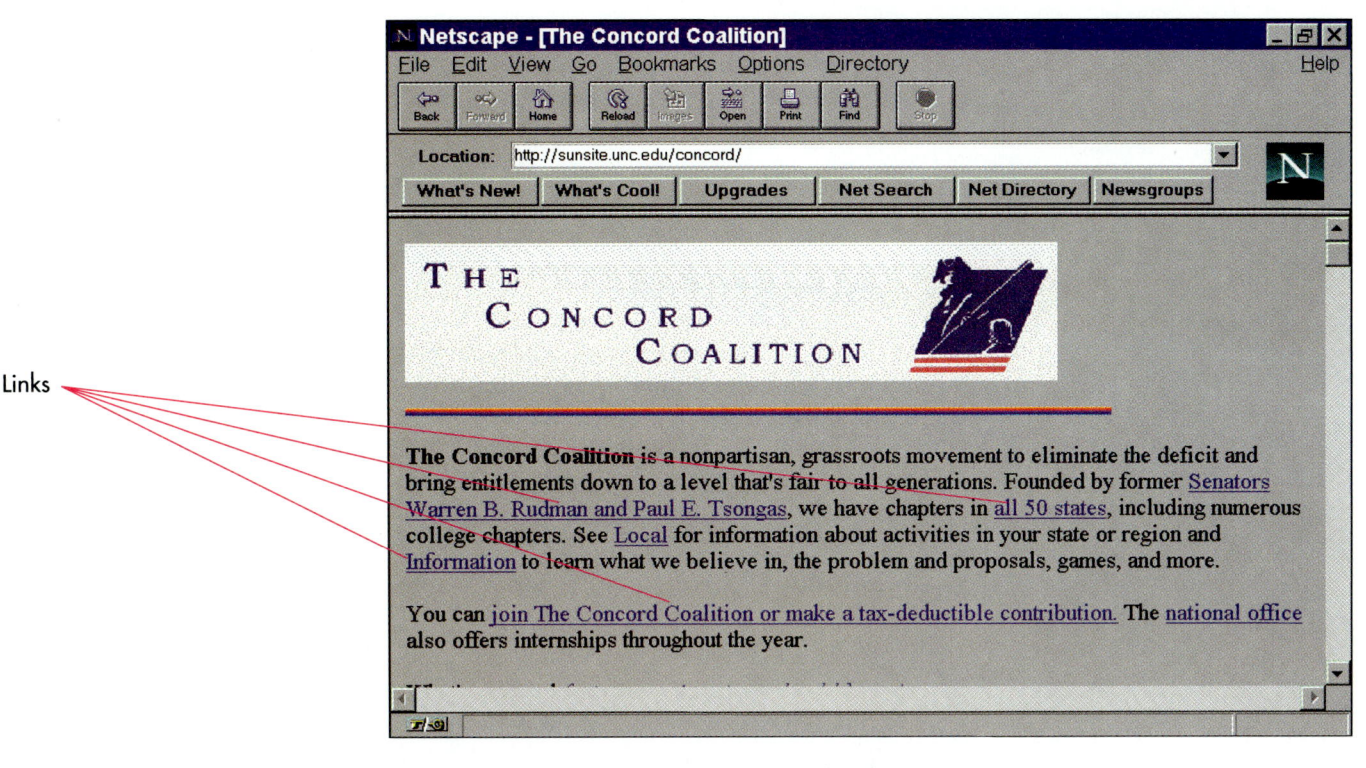

(a) Concord Coalition Home Page

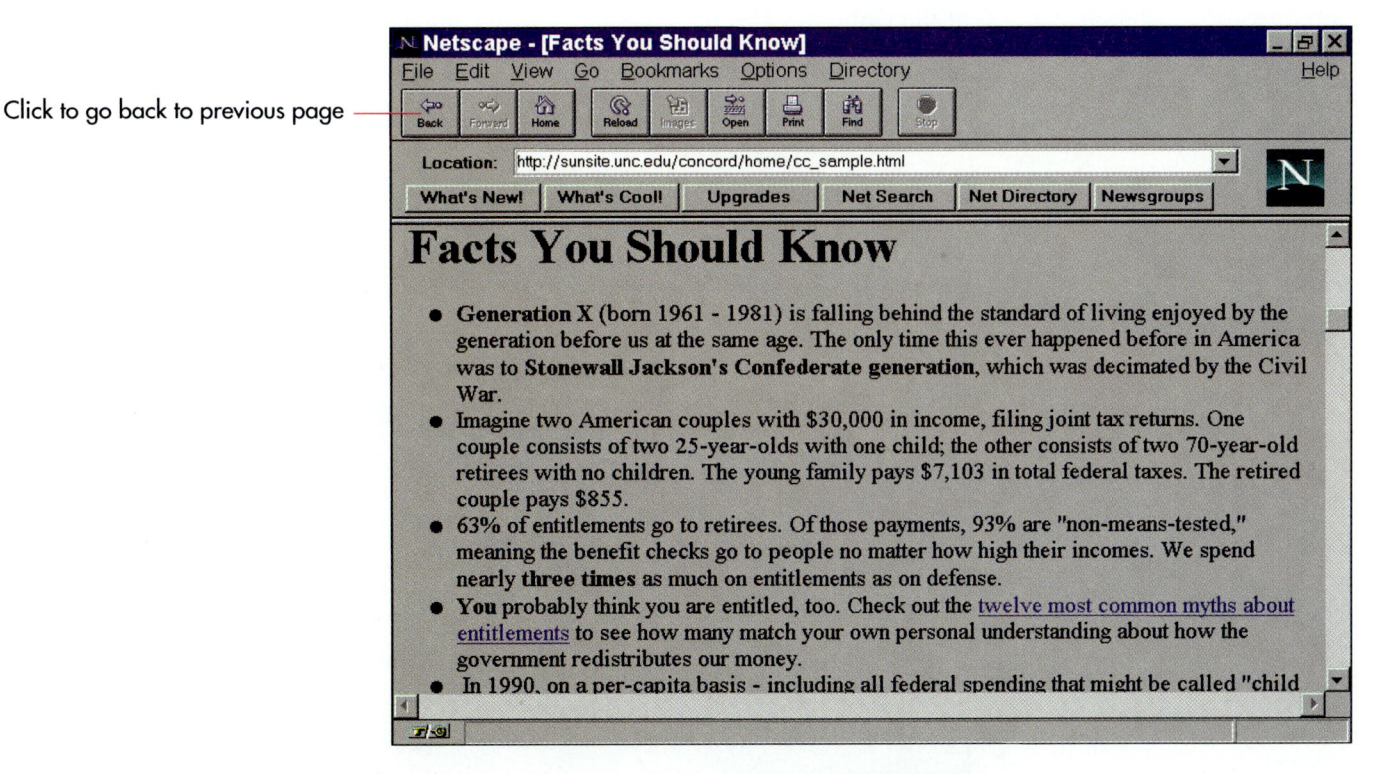

(b) Concord Coalition Fact Page

FIGURE 3.1 The Concord Coalition

FINDING THINGS ON THE WORLD WIDE WEB

same basic capabilities. We have chosen to focus on **Netscape Navigator**, commonly called **Netscape,** a newer and more powerful client than Mosaic and currently the market leader in browser programs. The discussion, however, is sufficiently general to apply to other programs.

NETSCAPE

A Windows-based browser is easy to use because it shares the common user interface and consistent command structure present in every Windows application. Figure 3.2 displays a **Netscape** screen, which contains several familiar elements. These include the title bar, Minimize, Maximize (or Restore), and Close buttons. Commands are executed from pull-down menus or from command buttons that appear under the menu bar. A vertical and/or horizontal scroll bar appears if the entire document is not visible at one time. The title bar displays the name of the document you are currently viewing.

The Uniform Resource Locator (URL)

The location (or address) of the document appears in the **location text box** and is known as a **Uniform Resource Locator** (URL). The URL is the primary means of navigating the Web, as it indicates the **Web site** (computer) from which you have requested a document. Change the URL (we describe how in the next section) and you jump to a different document.

A URL consists of several parts: the method of access, the Internet address of the computer (Web site) where the document is located, the path in the direc-

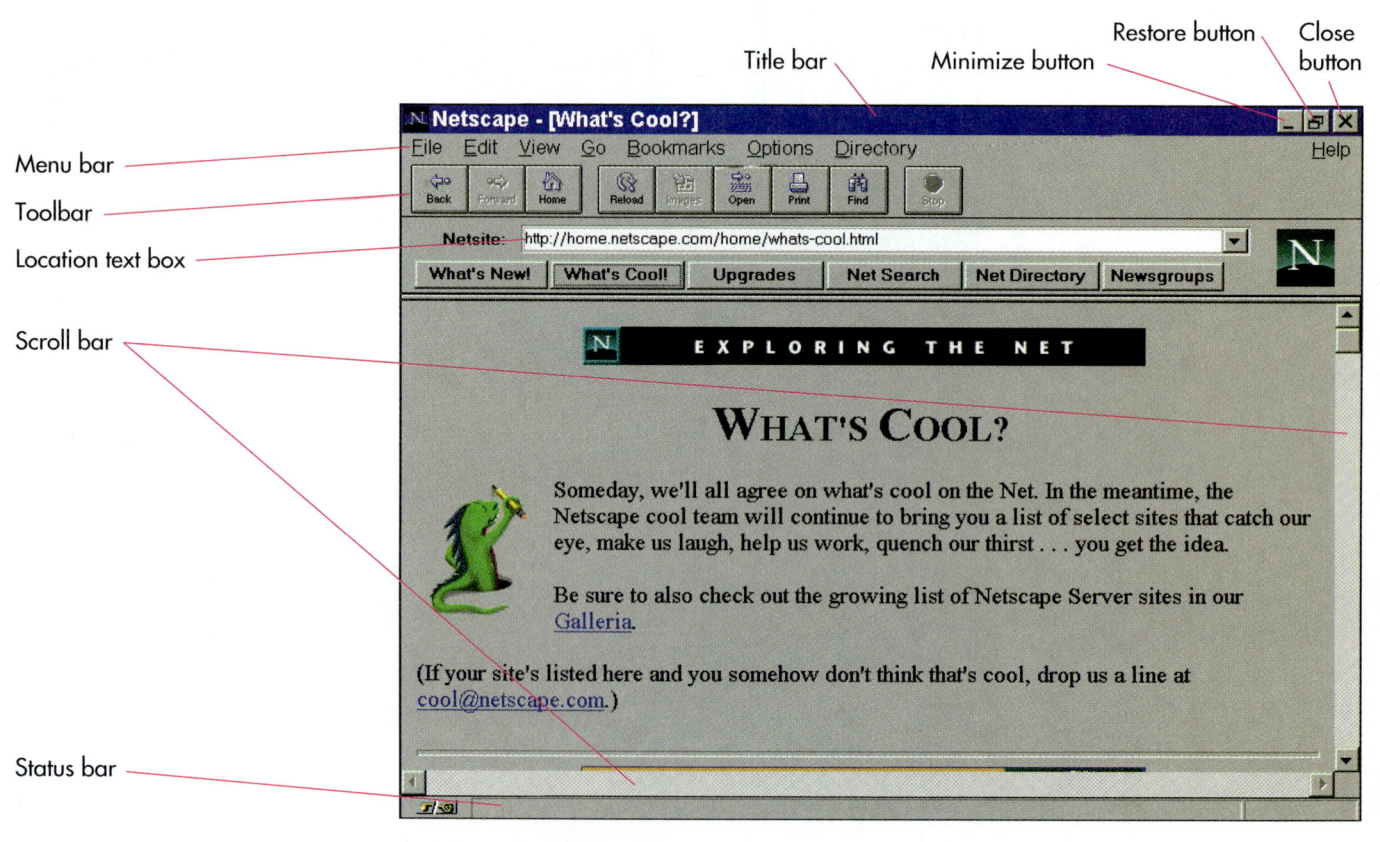

FIGURE 3.2 Netscape Screen

EXPLORING THE INTERNET

tory structure on the Web server to that document (if any), and the file name. For example:

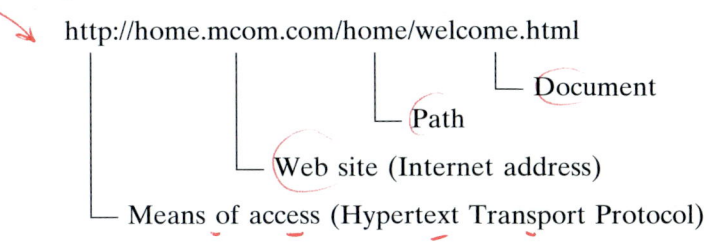

```
http://home.mcom.com/home/welcome.html
         │                │         │
         │                │         └─ Document
         │                └─ Path
         └─ Web site (Internet address)
└─ Means of access (Hypertext Transport Protocol)
```

To go to a particular site, enter its URL through the **Open Location command** in the File menu or type the URL directly in the Location text box, press Enter, and off you go. Once you arrive at a site, click the **hyperlinks** (underlined items) that interest you, which in turn will take you to other documents at that site (or even at a different site). The resources on the Web are connected in such a way that you need not be concerned with where (on which computer) the linked document is located.

Hypertext Transport Protocol (HTTP)

Consider, for example, the hypermedia document in Figure 3.3. We began by choosing a Web site and entering its URL (http://www.yahoo.com), shown in Figure 3.3a. Most of the time, however, you don't even have to enter the URL, because Netscape is constantly suggesting sites to explore. (And those sites may suggest other sites. Yes, it helps to know various sites on the Web, and we suggest several in Appendix D.). The Yahoo site consists of a searchable index of Web resources and is a good starting point for any Web exploration.

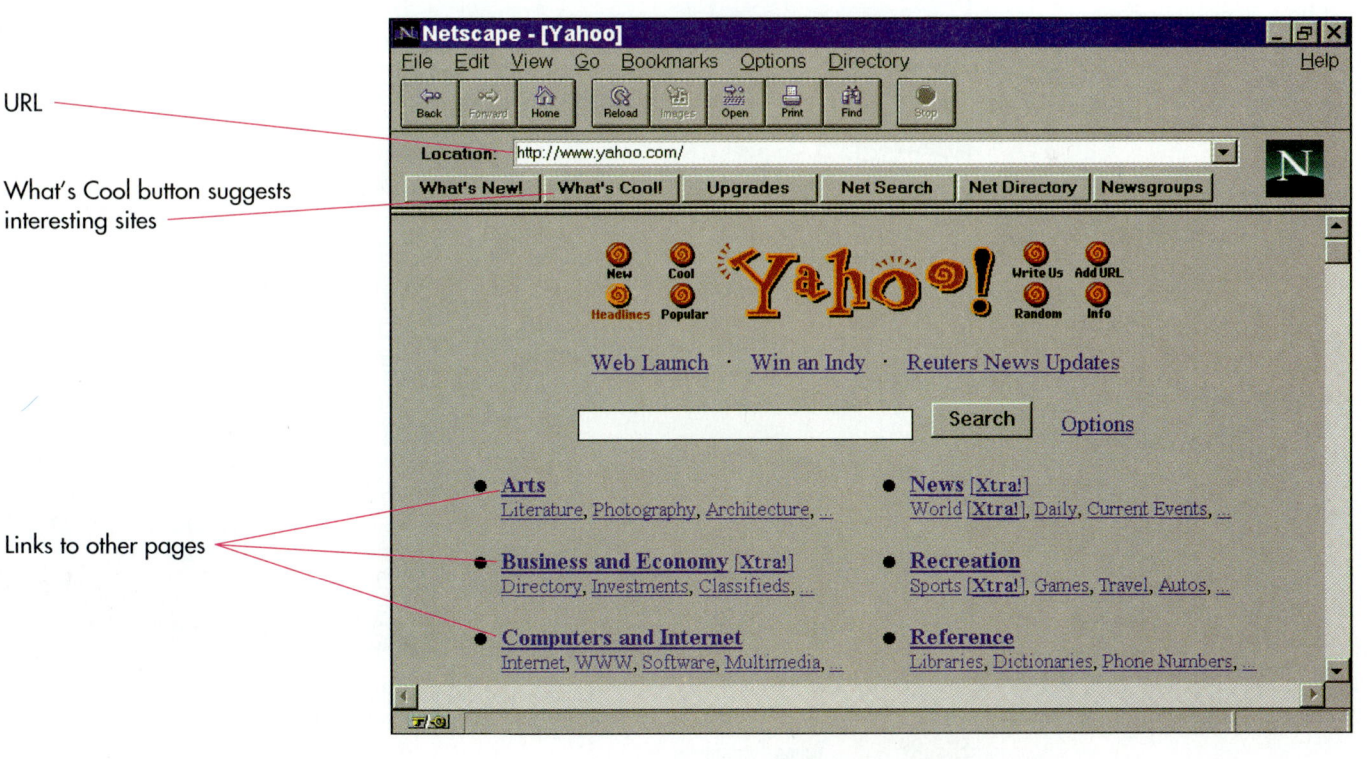

(a) The Yahoo Home Page

FIGURE 3.3   Yahoo

FINDING THINGS ON THE WORLD WIDE WEB   **89**

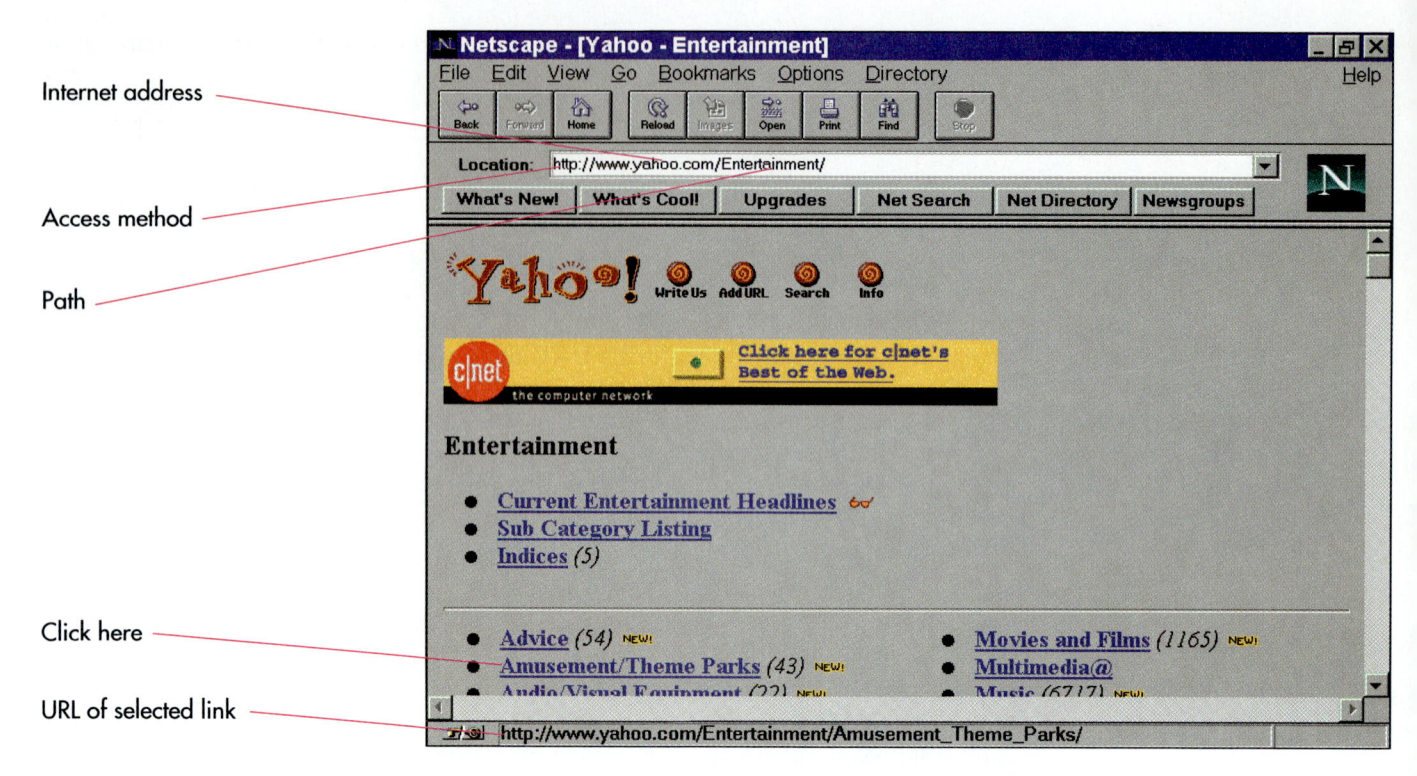

Internet address

Access method

Path

Click here

URL of selected link

(b) The Yahoo Entertainment Page

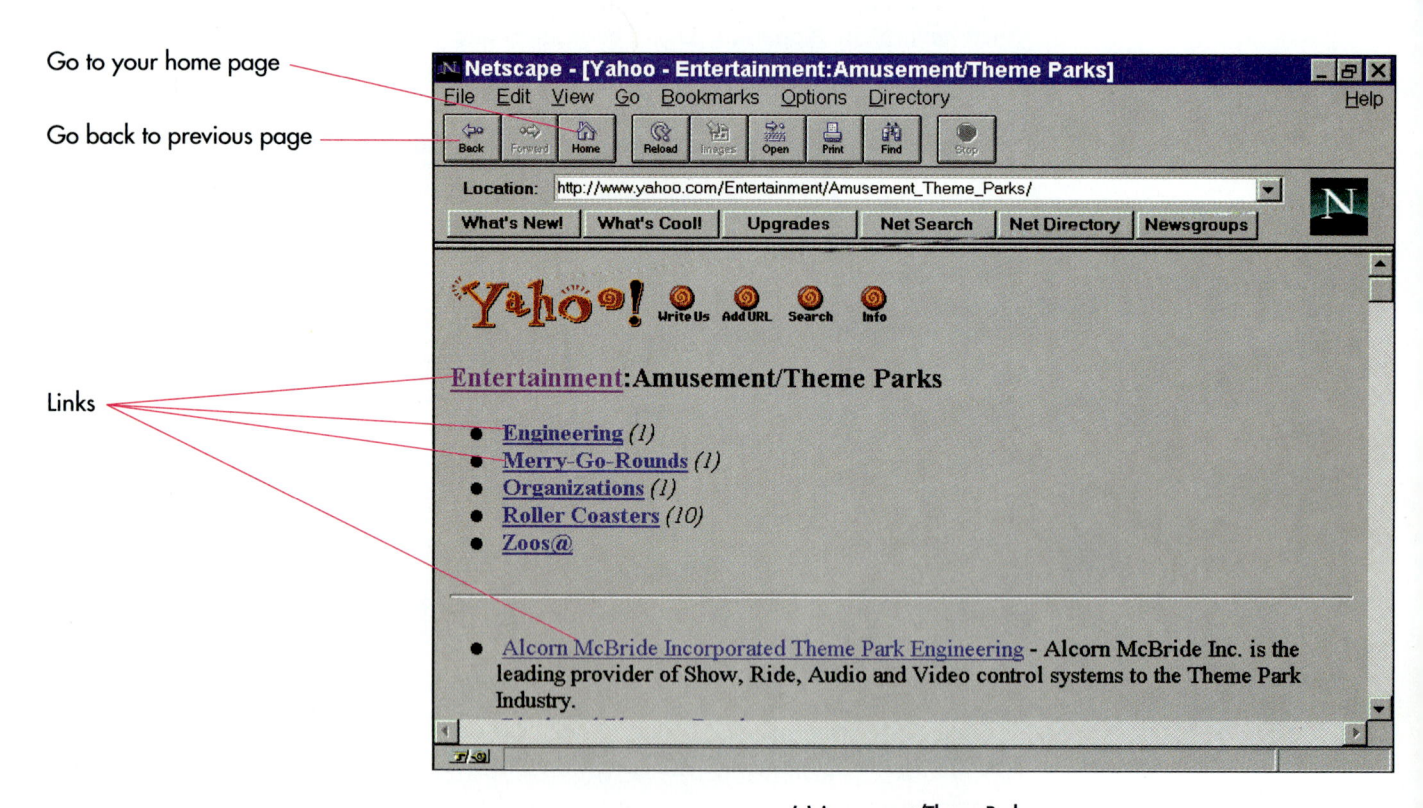

Go to your home page

Go back to previous page

Links

(c) Amusement/Theme Parks

FIGURE 3.3 Yahoo (continued)

90 EXPLORING THE INTERNET

The method of access to retrieve hypertext and hypermedia documents is called **HTTP (Hypertext Transport Protocol).** Therefore the http:// delimiter precedes the Internet address in the URL of all hypertext documents. (Not all documents cataloged on the Web are retrieved using HTTP. You will learn more about other types of Web documents in Chapter 4.)

Once you arrive at a home page (e.g., Figure 3.3a), click any link that interests you. We scrolled down and clicked on **Entertainment,** which took us to the document in Figure 3.3b. (The URL in the location text box changes automatically to reflect the location of the new document.) From there we clicked **Amusement/Theme Parks,** which took us to the document in Figure 3.3c. There is no beginning (other than the starting point or home page) and no end. You simply read a hypermedia document in any way that makes sense to you, jumping to explore whatever topic you want to see next.

The World Wide Web is a "living document" that is constantly changing. The information at many sites is updated daily, and you never know just what you will find. We doubt, for example, that you will see the same list of links if you access the Entertainment home page shown in Figure 3.3b, because new information is always being added.

Your exploration of the World Wide Web is limited only by your imagination. The Netscape What's Cool button suggests several interesting sites and is an excellent place to begin your exploration. Alternatively, you may begin with any of the sites listed in Appendix D.

IT'S STILL UNDER DEVELOPMENT

The World Wide Web is under constant development, so you shouldn't be surprised if it doesn't always work as you expect. There will be times when you will be unable to connect to a specific site because its developer has temporarily taken it offline, or because there are too many other users already at the site. Be patient and try again, or try another site. It is worth the wait!

Hypertext Markup Language (HTML)

Web documents containing hyperlinks are written using **HTML (Hypertext Markup Language),** an easy-to-learn language that controls the formatting of Web documents. An HTML document contains *tags* that describe how to display the text, hyperlinks, and multimedia elements within the document. The letters HTML appear at the end of many URL addresses to indicate that the link points to this type of document.

Figure 3.4 shows the Entertainment home page (found in Figure 3.3b) as it looks in HTML. The various tags, the commands between the angled brackets (< >), determine how the document will be displayed. Heading styles, bulleted and numbered lists, graphics, and many other features that give Web documents their look and feel can be defined by HTML tags.

You will want to learn about HTML to create your own home page if the capability to link one to your college or university's home page is offered at your school. The Web contains many online references to learn more about creating documents using HTML. An end-of-chapter exercise points you in the right direction in cyberspace to find these sites. In addition, Chapter 7 presents an overview of frequently used commands and guides you in setting up a simple home page.

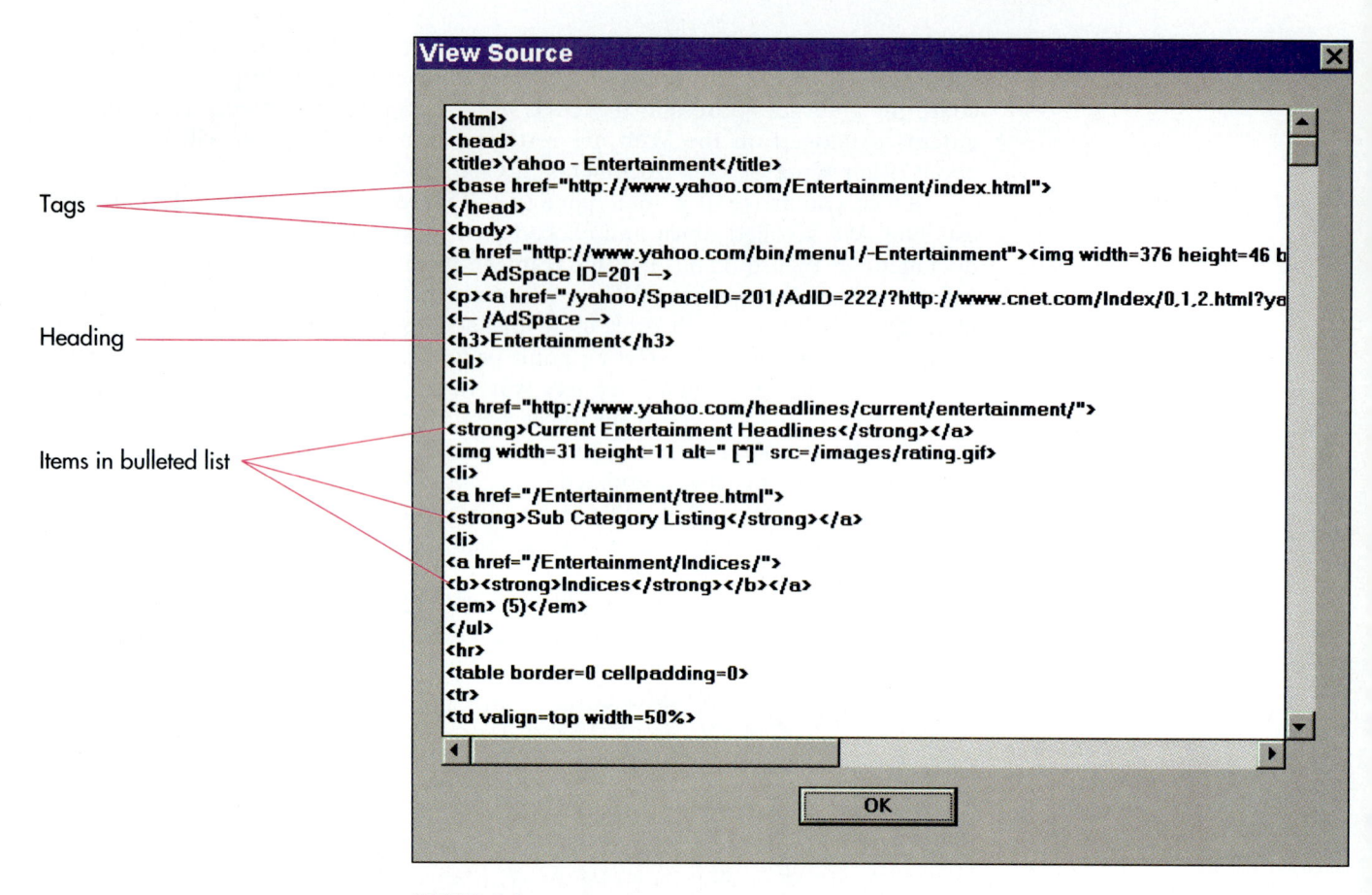

```
<html>
<head>
<title>Yahoo - Entertainment</title>
<base href="http://www.yahoo.com/Entertainment/index.html">
</head>
<body>
<a href="http://www.yahoo.com/bin/menu1/-Entertainment"><img width=376 height=46 b
<!-- AdSpace ID=201 -->
<p><a href="/yahoo/SpaceID=201/AdID=222/?http://www.cnet.com/Index/0,1,2.html?ya
<!-- /AdSpace -->
<h3>Entertainment</h3>
<ul>
<li>
<a href="http://www.yahoo.com/headlines/current/entertainment/">
<strong>Current Entertainment Headlines</strong></a>
<img width=31 height=11 alt=" [*]" src=/images/rating.gif>
<li>
<a href="/Entertainment/tree.html">
<strong>Sub Category Listing</strong></a>
<li>
<a href="/Entertainment/Indices/">
<b><strong>Indices</strong></b></a>
<em> (5)</em>
</ul>
<hr>
<table border=0 cellpadding=0>
<tr>
<td valign=top width=50%>
```

FIGURE 3.4 The Entertainment Page in HTML

Saving and Printing Web Documents

Any document you retrieve from the Web may be printed and/or saved for use at a later time. Printing simply requires you to select the Print command from the File menu as you would in any other Windows application. The Save command is generally the same as in any other Windows application. You can specify the destination drive and directory for the file you are retrieving. However, you may occasionally find documents that are in a format with which Netscape is unfamiliar or cannot display. Netscape will display a message similar to the one shown in Figure 3.5 if you try to save a document that it cannot, for some reason, automatically download to your computer.

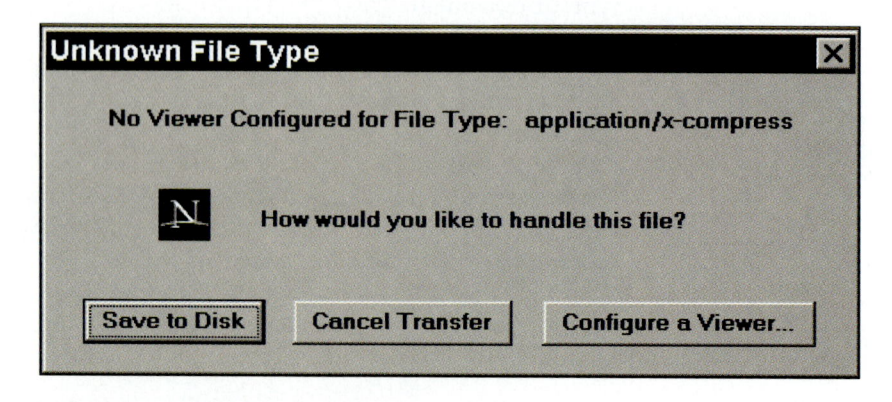

FIGURE 3.5 A Netscape Error Message

Bookmarks

Suppose you are browsing through a magazine at the library and find an interesting article you don't have time to read. You put the magazine down, then head off to class, intending to come back and finish it later. By the time you really return to the library, you've forgotten where you saw the article. Similarly, while surfing the Net you will find many interesting sites you will want to visit again, but because your travels are done with hyperlinks, it is often difficult to retrace your steps to a specific URL. A *bookmark* lets you store a URL so you can recall it at a later time. Figure 3.6 shows the bookmarks set up on the author's PC. Clicking on a bookmark links you directly to the document. Adding bookmarks, as you will discover in the following hands-on exercise, simply requires a few clicks with the mouse.

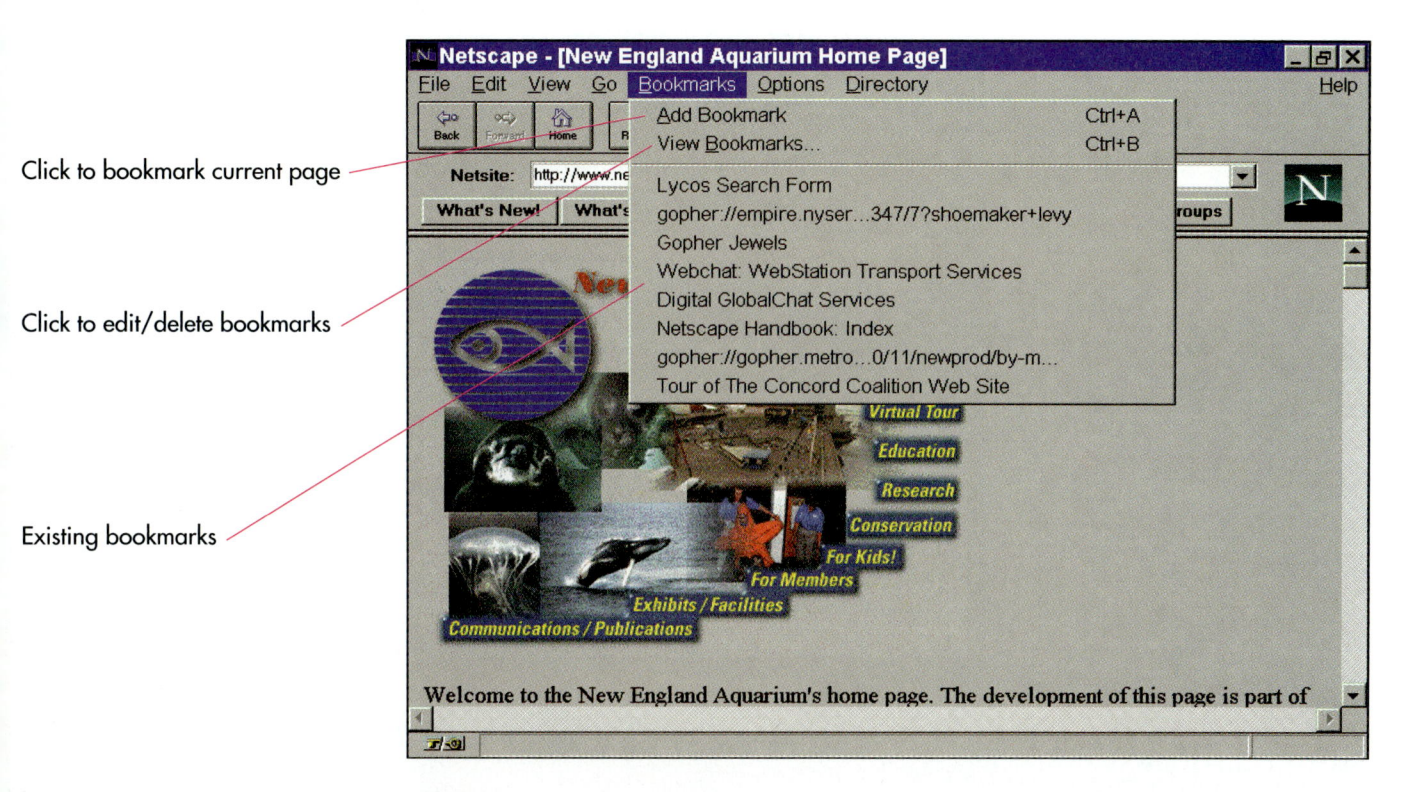

Click to bookmark current page

Click to edit/delete bookmarks

Existing bookmarks

FIGURE 3.6 Netscape Bookmarks

THE NEW NETSCAPE: ALL THIS AND JAVA TOO

By the time you read this book, a new version of Netscape Navigator will be available (but possibly not yet installed at your site). It is projected to have in-line viewers that will allow you to load and run movie, sound, and audio files without requiring additional software (if your PC has suitable hardware). It is also expected to have more sophisticated and powerful HTML capabilities. In addition, the new version will allow you to use Java applets, small applications using Sun Microsystems' new programming language for animated home pages, Java. Visit Netscape's home page, at http://home.netscape.com, for the most current information about the new release.

FINDING THINGS ON THE WORLD WIDE WEB   93

http://www.vcn.com/server/help.html

Visionary Communications, located in Wyoming, has put up a very complete site with all sorts of introductory information about the Internet and its resources. Spend some time here if you can.

LEARNING BY DOING

The World Wide Web cannot really be appreciated until you experience it yourself. The following exercise will take you to Washington, DC, to explore Congress and learn more about its workings. The exercise is written for Netscape, but it can be applied to Mosaic or any other Windows-based browser. It is the document (and associated URL) that is important rather than the particular browser. We suggest a specific starting point (Thomas, the Congressional home page, named after Thomas Jefferson, the third President of the United States), and a progression through that document. You can, however, start with any other home page, and choose any links you want. Going from one document or link to the next is what "surfing the Net" is all about. Bon voyage!

GETTING READY TO SURF THE NET

Using PC-based clients such as Mosaic and Netscape requires that the browser software be loaded on the PC you are using. Often the software must be customized specifically for your use—to save your bookmarks, for instance. Ask your instructor, lab assistant, or system administrator for the instructions to set up your browser in your campus computing environment.

HANDS-ON EXERCISE 1

Surfing the Net

Objective: To use Netscape Navigator (or another GUI browser) to surf the Net. Use Figure 3.7 as a guide in the exercise.

STEP 1: Load Netscape
- Find the appropriate program group or list that allows you to access your Internet software. (See your instructor or lab assistant for help.)
- Double click the **Netscape icon.** Most computing centers configure Netscape to display the college or university home page at start-up. If this is not the case, you will probably see the Netscape Corporation home page shown in Figure 3.7a when you start Netscape.

94 EXPLORING THE INTERNET

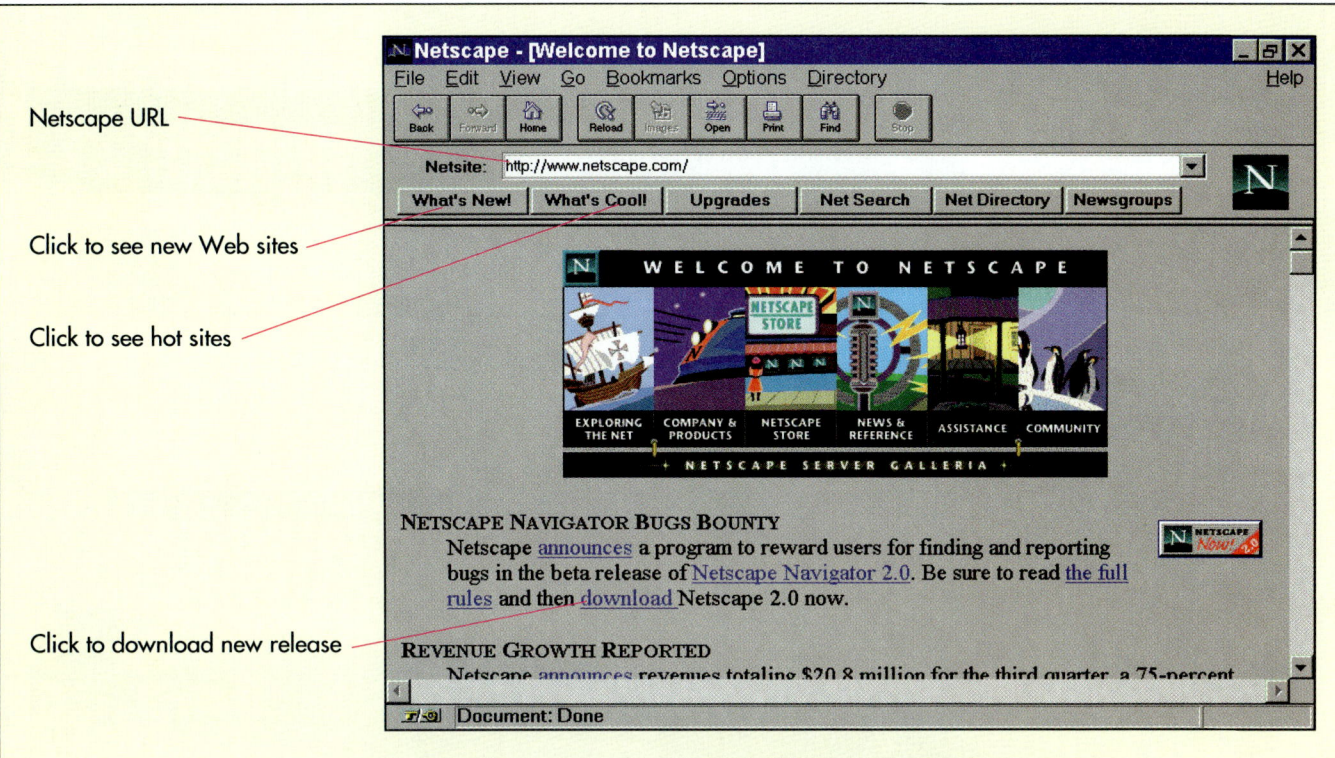

Netscape URL

Click to see new Web sites

Click to see hot sites

Click to download new release

(a) The Netscape Corporation Home Page

FIGURE 3.7 Hands-on Exercise 1

WHAT'S COOL

The What's Cool button is an excellent place to begin. The list of suggested sites changes every day, and you never know what you will find, but the results are always interesting. Click the button and see for yourself.

STEP 2: Visit Congress

➤ Pull down the **File menu.** Click the **Open button.** Type the name of the Web site you want to explore—for example, **http://thomas.loc.gov** as shown in the dialog box in Figure 3.7b. Press **Enter.**

➤ You should see the home page in Figure 3.7c (assuming that it hasn't changed since we did the exercise). If you are unable to get to this site:

- Pull down the **File menu,** click **Open URL,** and re-enter the URL shown in Figure 3.7b. You must type the address exactly as it appears in the figure (case matters). Press **Enter.**

- If you are still unable to get to the site, it may be because it is not available due to technical problems or because there are too many visitors already at the site. Click the **What's Cool button** and select a different site to explore.

➤ Scroll down and click the **hyperlink** to the **hot bills under Congressional consideration this week.**

FINDING THINGS ON THE WORLD WIDE WEB   **95**

Click to open URL

Thomas URL

Open Location

Open Location:

http://thomas.loc.gov/

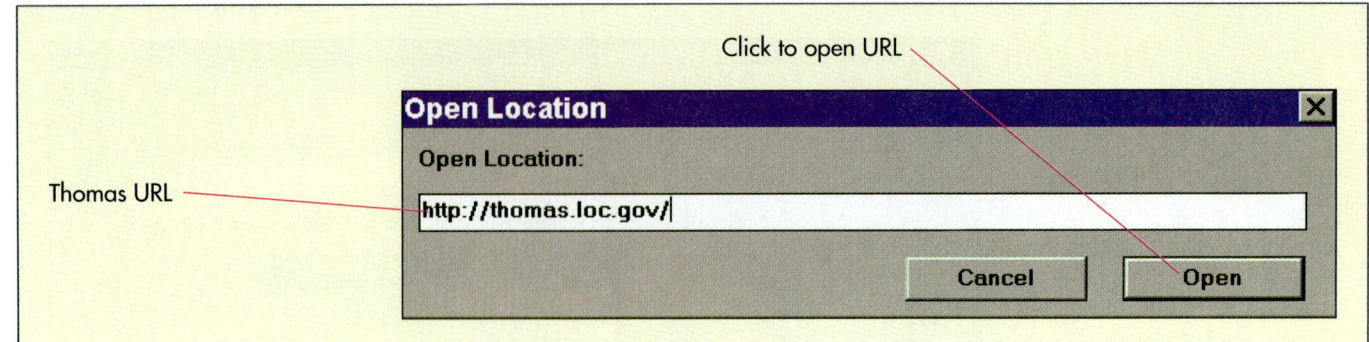

Cancel   Open

(b) The Open Location Dialog Box

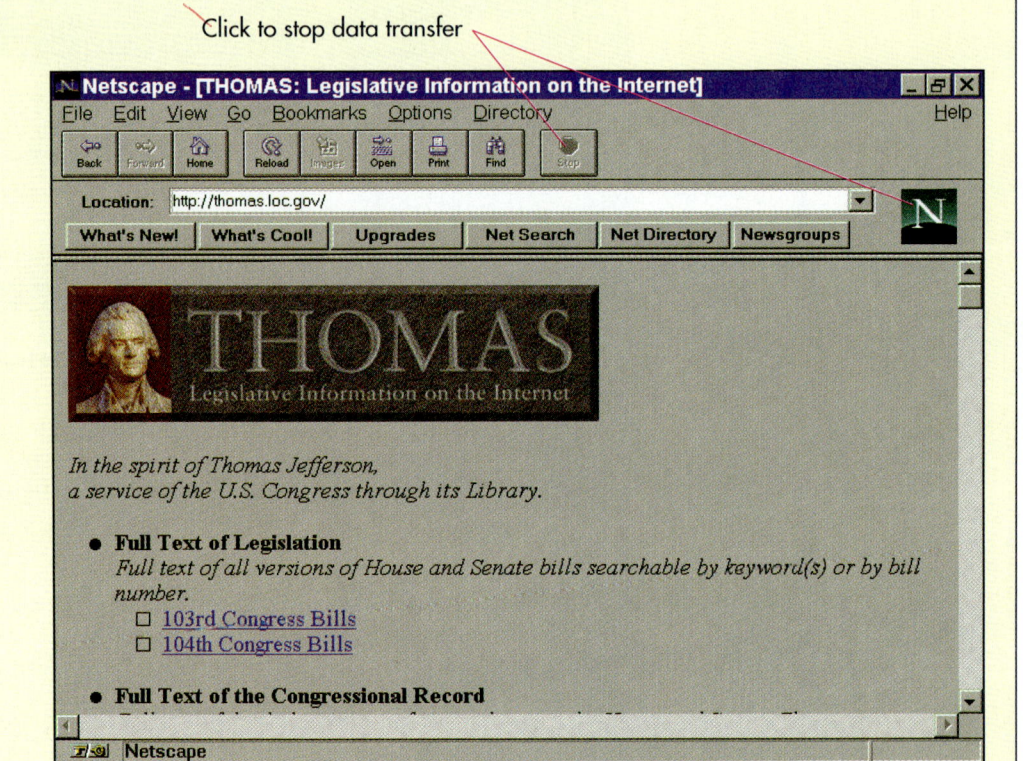

Click to stop data transfer

(c) Thomas Jefferson Home Page

FIGURE 3.7   Hands-on Exercise 1 (continued)

THE FLASHING LOGO

The Netscape logo (the capital N) in the upper-right-hand corner of the Netscape window indicates the status of a Netscape search. The icon will be animated when Netscape is connecting to a URL, searching for a document, or otherwise involved in data transfer. The icon will be still otherwise. You can click the logo at any time to cancel a search or data transfer; that is, just click the flashing "N" (or the Stop button), and the data transfer will be terminated.

96   EXPLORING THE INTERNET

STEP 3: Navigate through Thomas

➤ You should see the screen in Figure 3.7d. Continue to browse through the Congressional Web pages by clicking on hyperlinks of interest to you to get a feeling for the information contained at this site. You can get immediate information about what's happening in Washington in a way never before possible by periodically exploring the Congressional site. (Now, what will you do with the information?)

➤ Click the **Back button** to return to the previous screen. Notice that when you go back to a previous site, the links you have already visited are displayed in a different color, to indicate you have visited the site before.

THE SAVE COMMAND

You can save many Web documents as files on your local PC or network drive. Simply click the File Save command, and save as you would any Windows file. (Some files, such as those written for Macs, cannot be saved on a Windows-based PC. Others, particularly compressed files, can be saved, but you cannot use them unless you have the software necessary to uncompress them.)

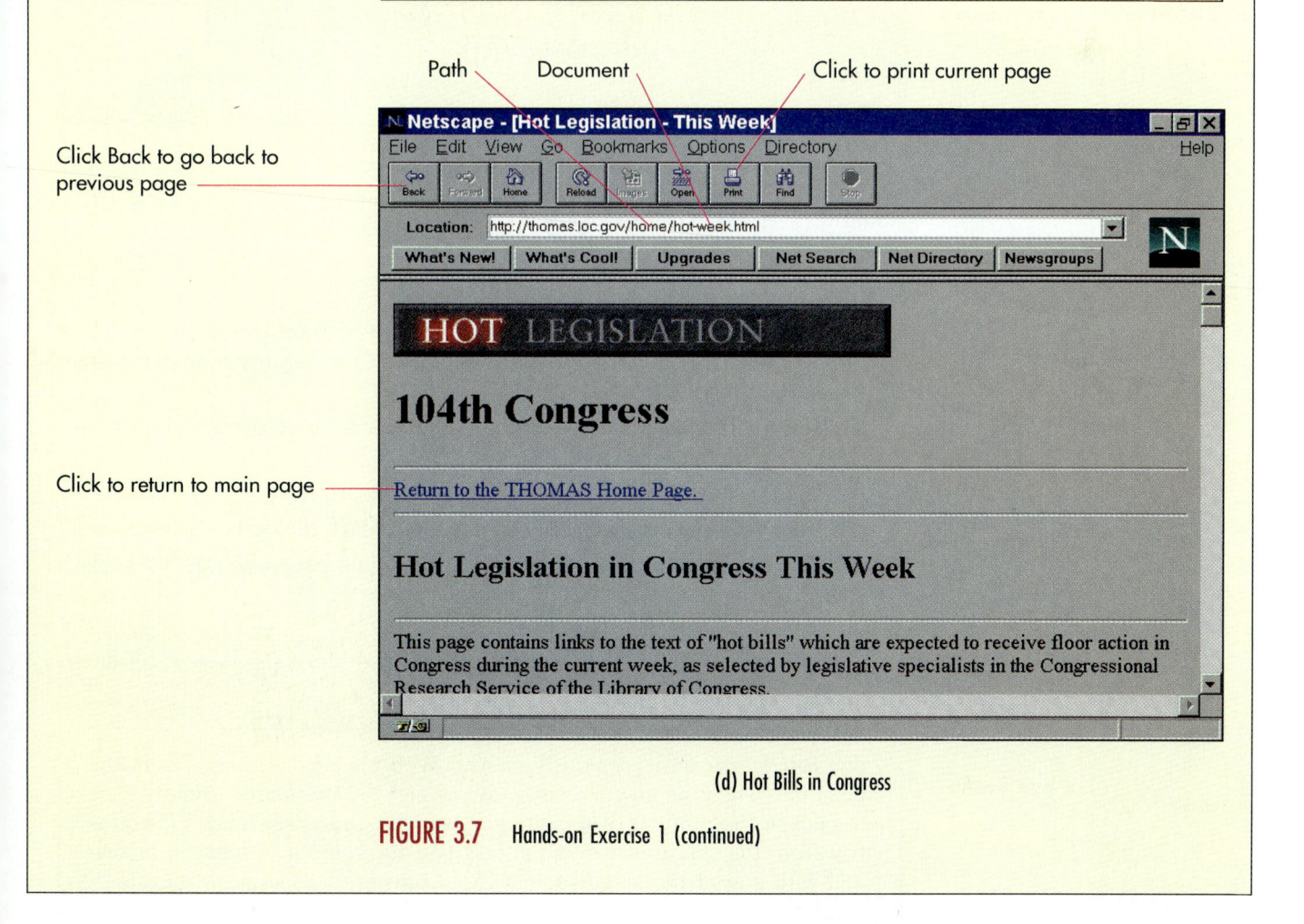

(d) Hot Bills in Congress

FIGURE 3.7 Hands-on Exercise 1 (continued)

STEP 4: Print a Web Page

➤ At any point in your journey through Thomas, pull down the **File menu.** Click **Print** to display the dialog box in Figure 3.7e.

➤ You may select the print range and number of copies, then click **OK.**

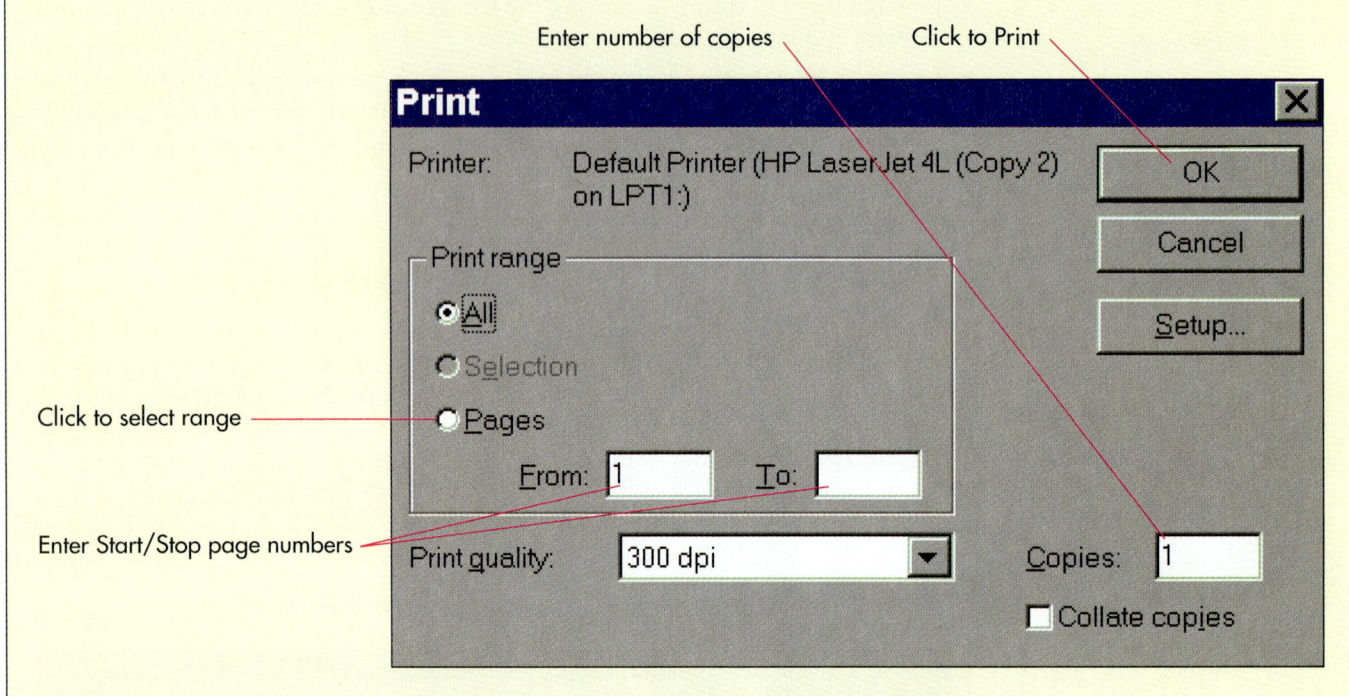

(e) The Print Dialog Box

FIGURE 3.7   Hands-on Exercise 1 (continued)

STEP 5: Link to a Web Site Using a Bookmark

➤ You will find many sites on the Web to which you want to return to explore again and again. You can do so without having to remember how to get there by creating a bookmark for the site.

- Pull down the **Go menu.** A list of sites you have recently visited is displayed, as shown in Figure 3.7f.
- Click the Thomas **Hot Legislation page** to return to it.
- Pull down the **Bookmarks menu.** The Bookmark dialog box is displayed.
- Click **Add Bookmark.** The Congressional home page will now be accessible from the bookmark list by a simple click.

THE GO AND VIEW HISTORY COMMANDS

You can return to a previously viewed Web page by clicking Go in the menu bar. The nine most recently visited sites are numbered. Simply click on or type the number of the site you want to go to. Selecting View History from the pull-down menu allows you to create a bookmark associated with one of the listed sites, without having to go back to the site.

Click for URL list

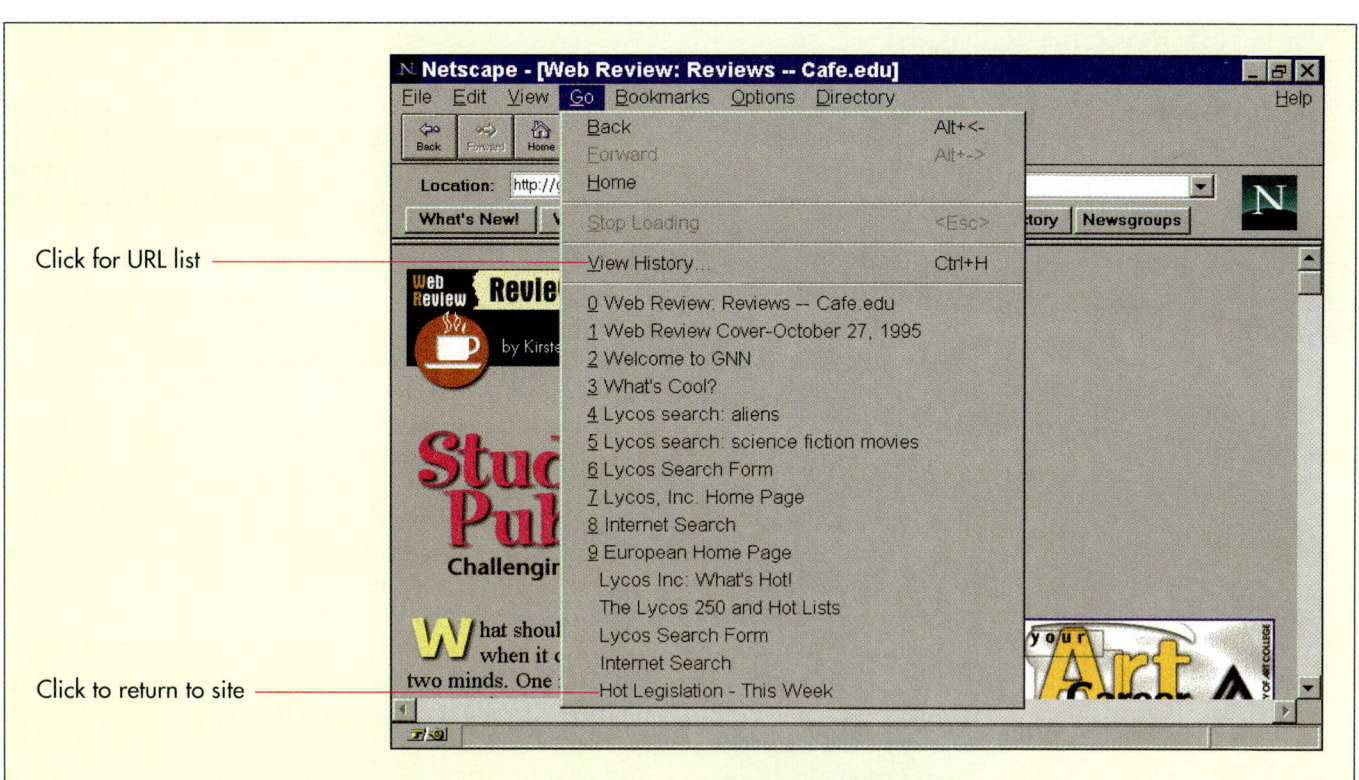

Click to return to site

(f) The Go Pull-Down Menu

FIGURE 3.7   Hands-on Exercise 1 (continued)

- Click **Home** to return to your college's home page.
- Select the **View Bookmarks** on the **Bookmarks menu,** then click the Thomas URL, which you should now see in the bookmark list. You should link directly to the Thomas page you just bookmarked.

STEP 6: Surf the Net

➤ Choose different sites to explore:
   - Click the **What's Cool button** to explore the current cool sites. We don't know what you will find, but you can expect something interesting.
   - Choose a specific site and enter its URL.
➤ Click the hyperlinks that interest you, which in turn will take you to other documents at that site (or even at a different site). Save or print the documents that you find as you see fit.

SET A TIME LIMIT

We warn you that it's addictive, and that once you start "surfing the Net," it is difficult to stop. We suggest, therefore, that you set a time limit before you begin, and that you stick to it when the time has expired. Tomorrow is another day with new places to explore.

FINDING THINGS ON THE WORLD WIDE WEB   99

WEB SEARCH ENGINES

Browsing is fun, but as we warned you in the previous tip, it can be addictive and quite time consuming. Fortunately, a more productive way to search for specific topics on the Web is available. You can use one of many Web *search engines,* programs that handle queries, to enter search criteria and locate Web resources. The easiest way to access Web search engines is directly from your browser, or use one of the URLs shown in Table 3.1, which contains a list of some of the best search engines available at time of publication.

Clicking the Net Search button on the Netscape window brings up the screen shown in Figure 3.8a. This document contains links to several search engines but only the InfoSeek engine is visible in Figure 3.8a. Click the text box to enter the topic you are searching for (e.g., rock music hall of fame), click the Search button, then wait as the search takes place. Figure 3.8b displays the results of the search, which returns 100 documents. Click on any of the links and you move to the associated page. Research was never this easy!

If you scroll farther down in the Net Search window, you will see the **Lycos** search engine link, which you will use in the following hands-on exercise. The Lycos *search form,* shown in Figure 3.8c, allows you to specify the number of terms in your query, and how many *hits,* or documents, you want to see out of the total found. (Web queries can return thousands of documents, so it is a good idea to limit the number of hits you request.) Figure 3.8d shows the search results, which will vary if a different search engine is used.

Originally developed and operated by Carnegie-Mellon University, Lycos is now a commercial venture supported by advertising revenue generated by its site and licensing fees from its software. It maintains a catalog of Web sites; as of November 1995 it contained references to 7.98 million documents. Special programs called *spiders* automatically crawl the Web each day searching for new pages to add to the catalog, which indexes more than 91% of the Web. (The name Lycos comes from the first five letters of the Latin name for Wolf Spider.)

WHO IS PAYING THE PHONE BILL?

New users on the Web are frequently concerned about running up a huge phone charge on their Internet account as they link to all these far-off sites. Your college or university is indeed paying line charges. However, they are billed at a straight monthly rate, regardless of how many times you surf the Net, or where you link to. So relax, fasten your seat belt, and go!

TABLE 3.1 Web Search Engines

Site	URL
Yahoo	http://www.yahoo.com
Lycos	http://www.lycos.com
WebCrawler	http://webcrawler.com
World Wide Web Worm	http://wwww.cs.colorado.edu/wwww
InfoSeek	http://www.infoseek.com
OpenText	http://www.opentext.com

Search text

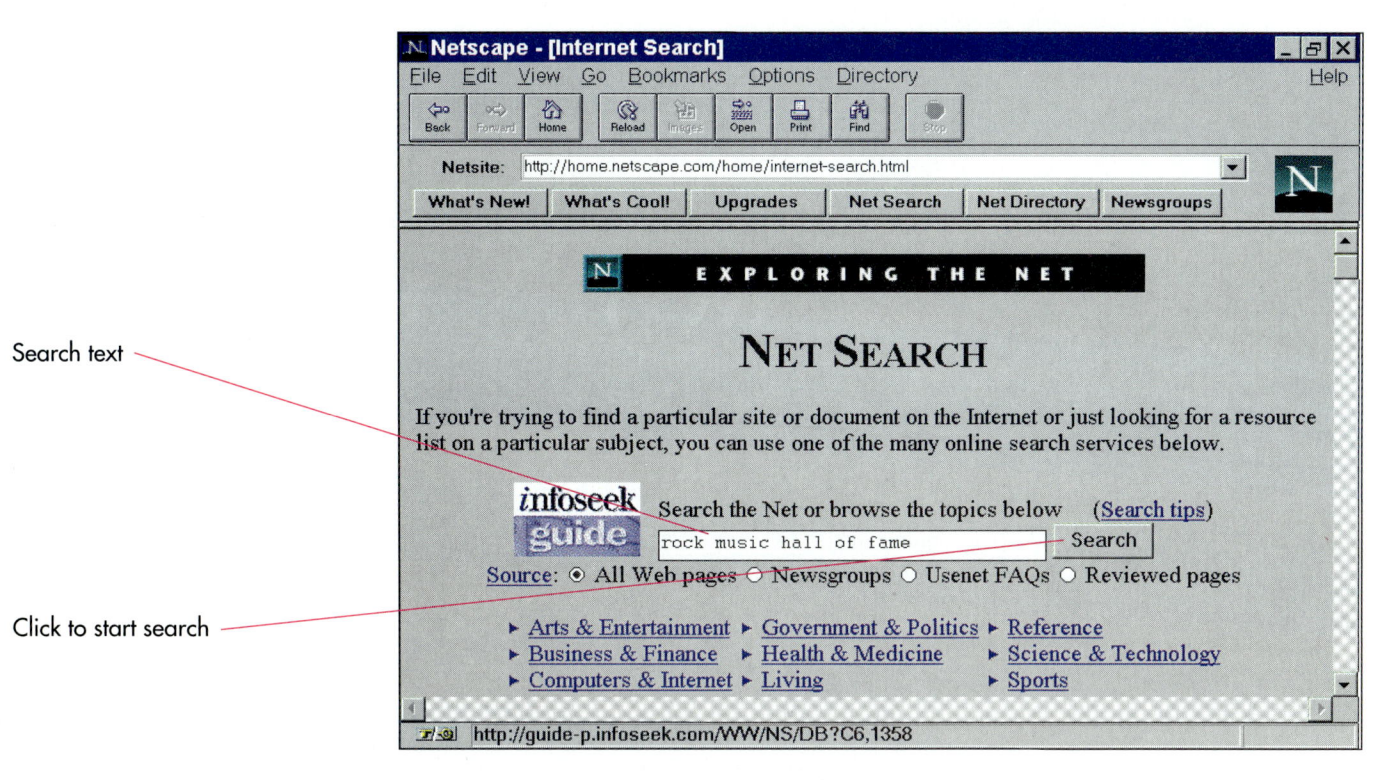

Click to start search

(a) InfoSeek Search Engine

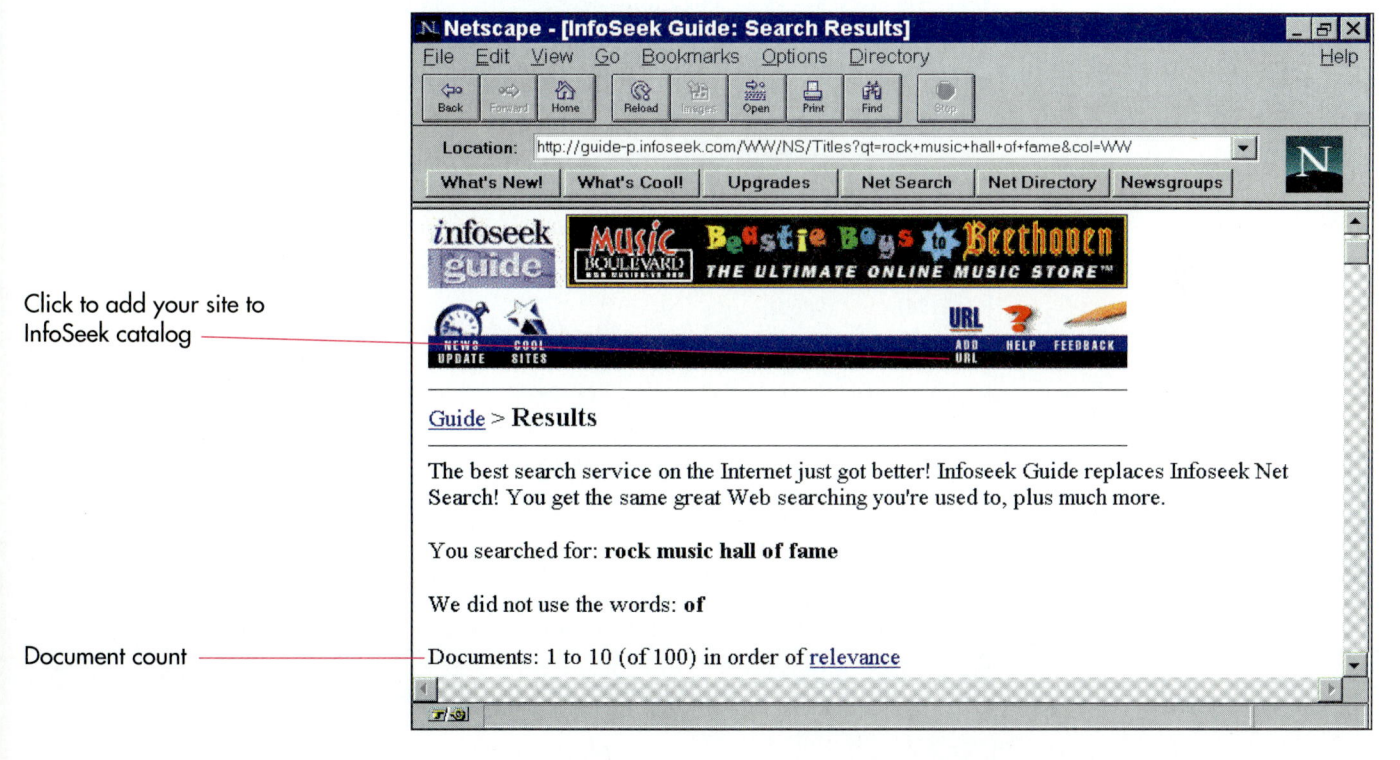

Click to add your site to InfoSeek catalog

Document count

(b) InfoSeek Search Results

FIGURE 3.8 Internet Search Engines

FINDING THINGS ON THE WORLD WIDE WEB

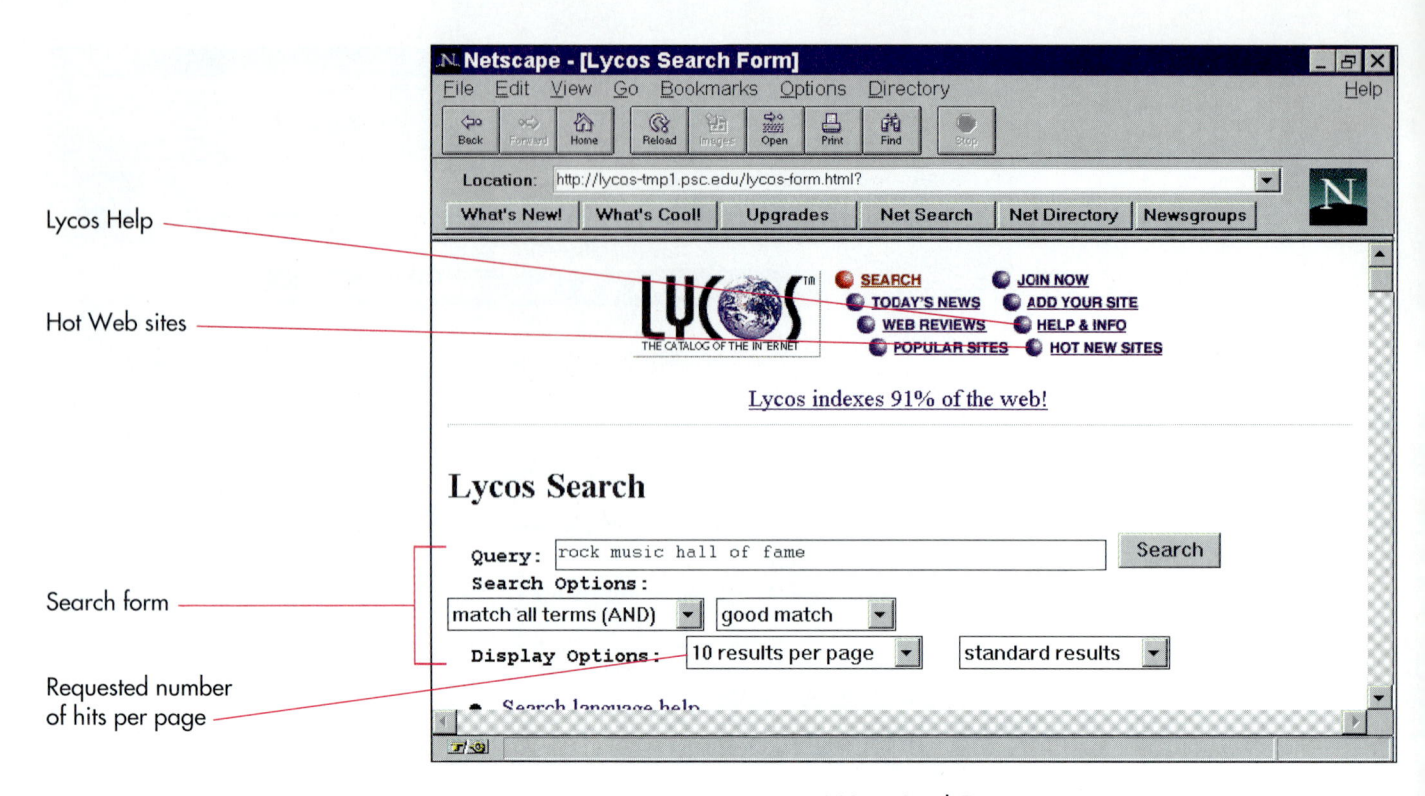

(c) Lycos Search Form

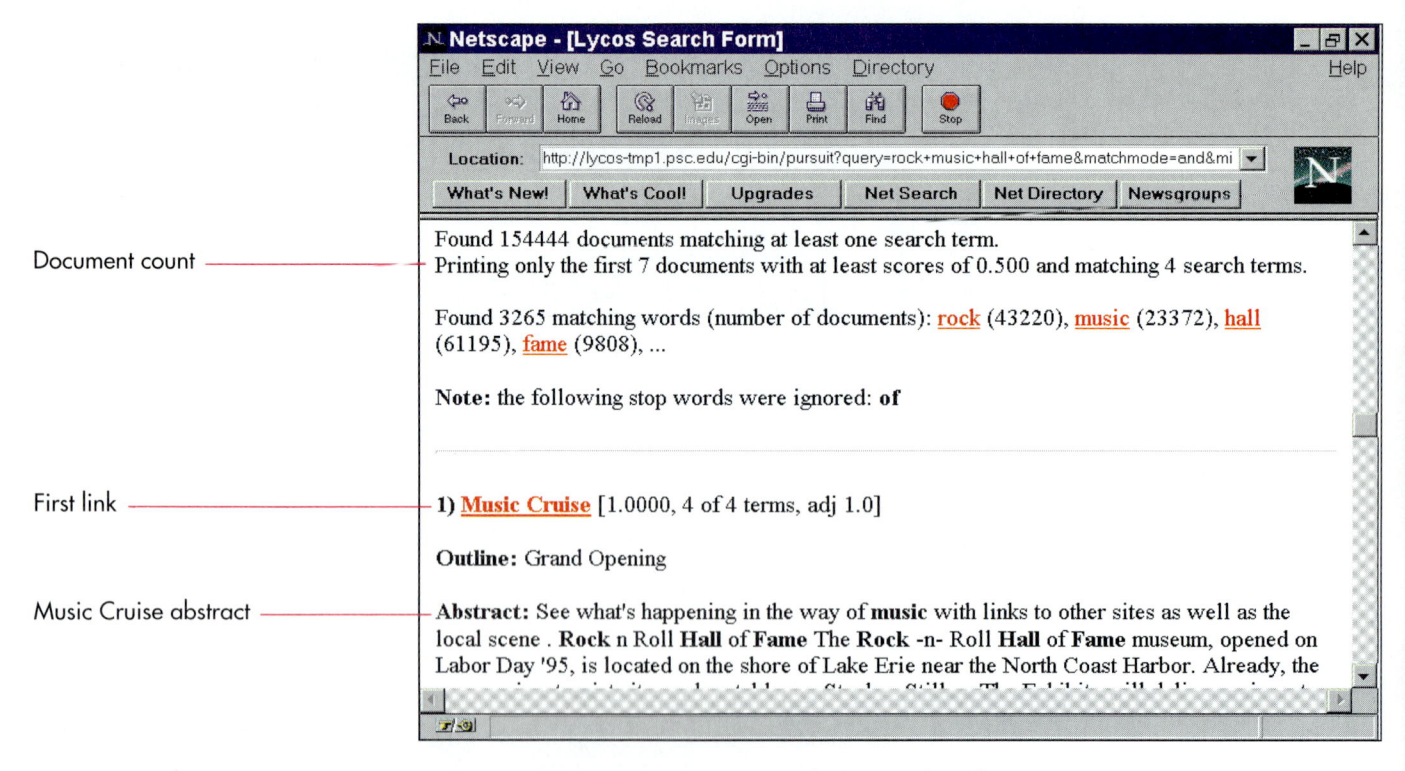

(d) Lycos Search Results

FIGURE 3.8　Internet Search Engines (continued)

102　EXPLORING THE INTERNET

These spiders also measure the popularity of the Web sites in the catalog. Lycos has developed the Lycos 250 (hot spots on the Web grouped by category) based on its data. The lists are available from the Lycos home page, so after you have finished your search, you might want to return to browse!

The WebCrawler, developed at the University of Washington, is also available from the Net Search home page. It, too, uses programs to search the Web and periodically update its URL database.

ADD YOUR HOME PAGE TO THE LYCOS CATALOG

You can add your own home page to the Lycos catalog. Go to the URL http://lycos.cs.cmu.edu/register.html#add and fill out the form. Wait a week to 10 days, then try a search on your name. You should be cataloged on the Web!

Search Rules and Techniques

The Internet, as you are by now aware, is huge and expanding exponentially. (Lycos estimates 300,000 new pages are added each week to the Web.) Each search engine has rules to help you narrow your search so you are not inundated with thousands of documents you don't want. Generally, these rules are published and available in a link from the search engine home page.

In general, the more specific your query, the better. For instance, a search on "movies" would be very broad; better to request "science fiction movies" if that is your interest. Using the WebCrawler search engine, for example, a search on "movies" yielded 4,783 documents. Searching on "science fiction movies" resulted in 391 documents, a more manageable number. The "movie" search in Lycos yielded 28,253 hits, while "science fiction movies" returned 4 hits. These discrepancies reveal another guideline for Web searches: You may want to conduct a search with more than one search engine to get the best results.

It is important that you structure any query properly. When searching on multiple terms, Netscape's default is to use OR to concatenate the terms. In the previous example this would be the same as asking the question, "Can you find any documents with the word *science,* any with the word *fiction,* or any with the word *movies*?" Obviously that would not narrow the search at all, but rather increase it threefold! Instead you will request that Netscape use AND when combining terms. The query then becomes, "Find all documents containing the three words *science, fiction,* and *movies.* All three words must be present in each document found."

Figure 3.9 illustrates the results of a search for information on "President Thomas Jefferson." Figure 3.9a shows the query as it would be entered in the WebCrawler search engine. Figure 3.9b displays the results of the search in January 1996 that found a total of 126 documents ("hits"). Note, however, that only the first 25 documents were returned according to the query in Figure 3.9a. (Your results may be different, since the Web will change between the time we conducted our search and the time you do your research.)

Figures 3.9c and 3.9d show the same query and results for the Yahoo engine, which returns only four hits. The difference is due to the search techniques that are used by the various engines. It is important, therefore, to become familiar with multiple search engines if you intend to do serious research on the Web.

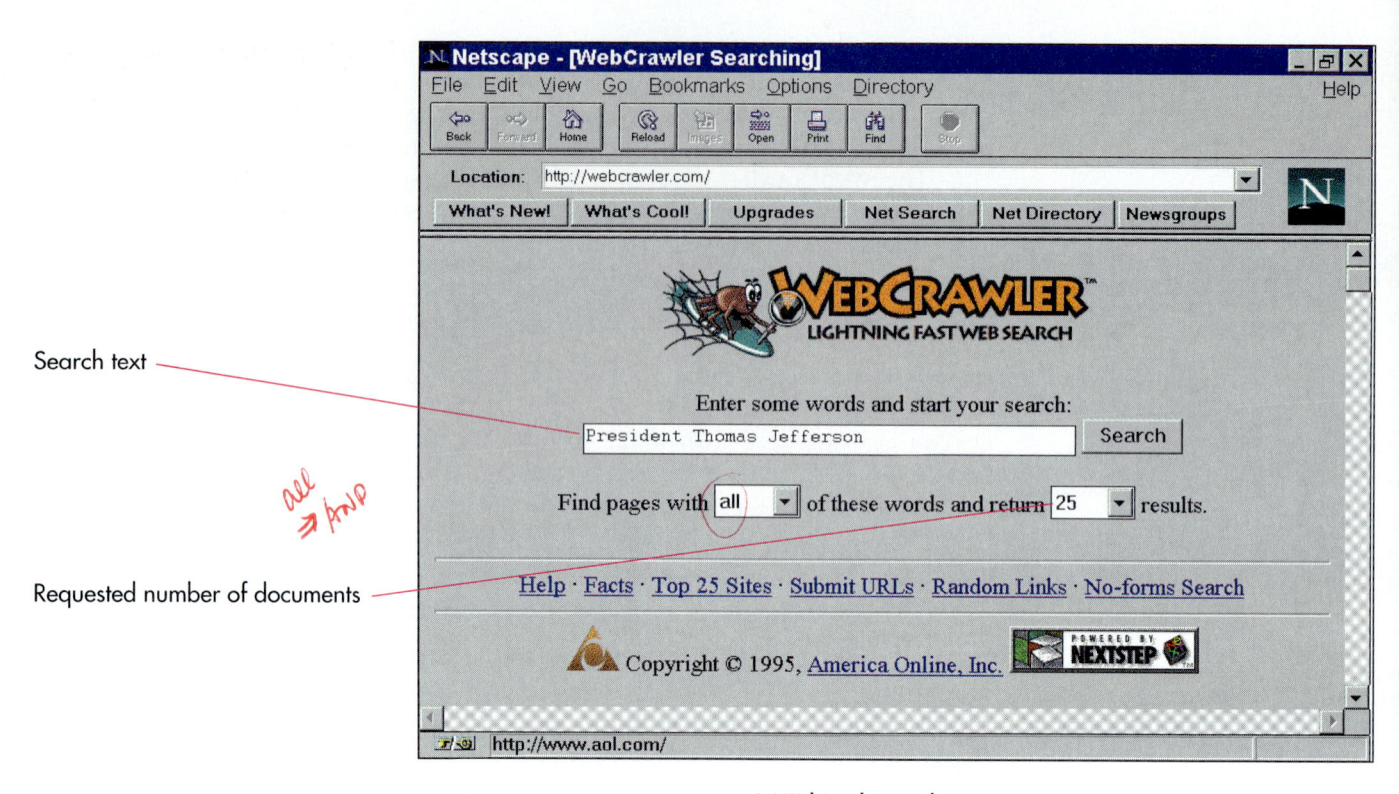

(a) WebCrawler Search Parameters

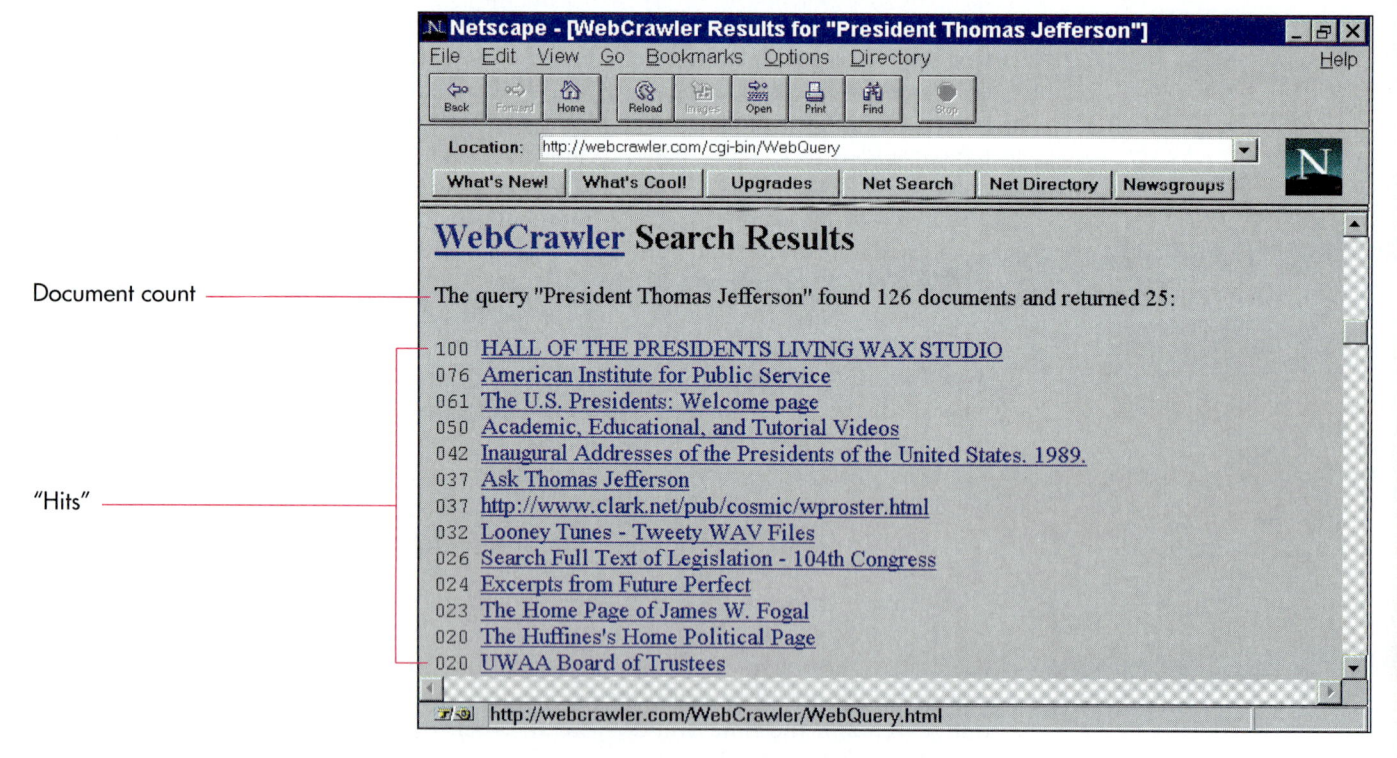

(b) WebCrawler Search Results

FIGURE 3.9   Search Engines (WebCrawler and Yahoo)

104 EXPLORING THE INTERNET

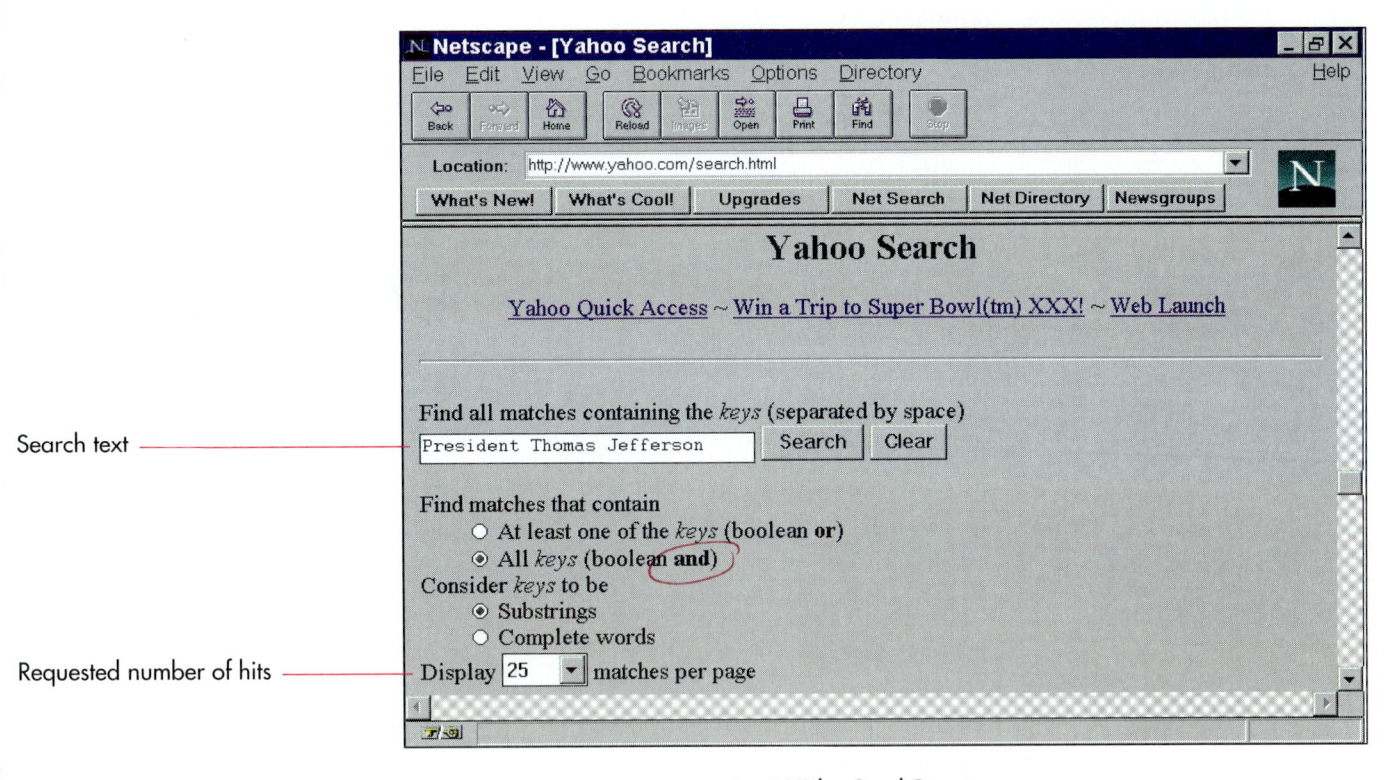

(c) Yahoo Search Parameters

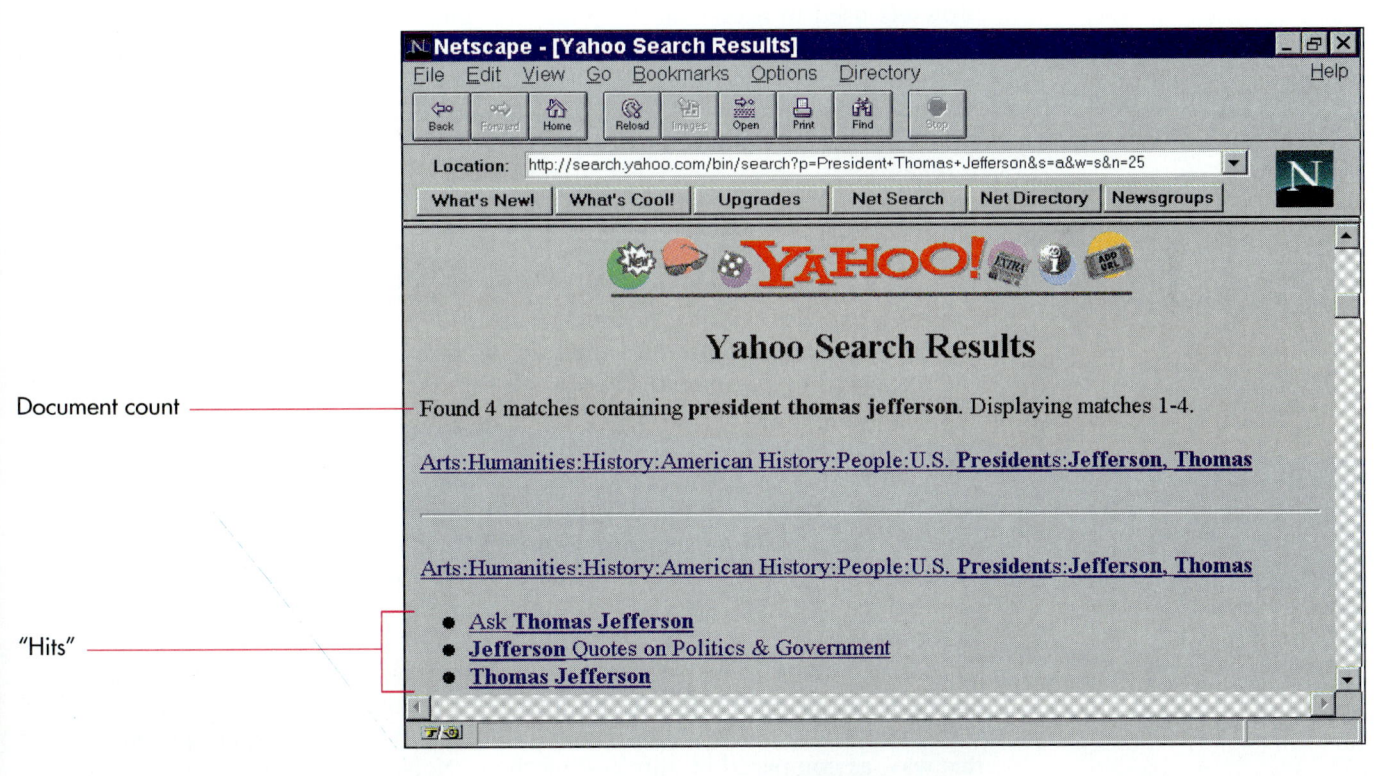

Search text — President Thomas Jefferson

Requested number of hits — Display 25 matches per page

Find all matches containing the *keys* (separated by space)

Find matches that contain
- At least one of the *keys* (boolean **or**)
- All *keys* (boolean **and**)

Consider *keys* to be
- Substrings
- Complete words

(d) Yahoo Search Results

Document count — Found 4 matches containing **president thomas jefferson**. Displaying matches 1-4.

Arts:Humanities:History:American History:People:U.S. **Presidents:Jefferson, Thomas**

Arts:Humanities:History:American History:People:U.S. **Presidents:Jefferson, Thomas**

"Hits"
- Ask **Thomas Jefferson**
- **Jefferson** Quotes on Politics & Government
- **Thomas Jefferson**

FIGURE 3.9 Search Engines (WebCrawler and Yahoo) (continued)

And, Or, and Not

Each search engine has its specific syntax, which varies from one engine to the next. All engines, however, have the same basic capabilities that enable you to restrict a search in order to return relevant documents. All search queries are in essence combinations of the logical operations, And, Or, and Not. Using the And operation for "President Thomas Jefferson," for example, will return documents about Jefferson's presidency. Using Or, however, will return documents about presidents (any president) or Jefferson. The Not operation is useful to exclude certain documents; for example, searching on "Thomas Jefferson" but specifying Not "president" will return documents about other aspects of Jefferson's life.

> http://www.superbowl.com
>
> We don't know if this site will be around next year, but we truly enjoyed it for Super Bowl XXX.

OTHER BROWSER CAPABILITIES

As we mentioned several times above, the Web is changing continuously. The browsers used to access the Web are also undergoing constant revision, and it is probable that by the time you read this book, a new version of Netscape Navigator with new features will be available. Of the features in the current version as this book goes to press, the ones we think you will find most useful are Find, Autoload Images, and Mail.

To Load or Not to Load Images

Many of the graphics you have seen in the figures throughout this chapter and the hands-on exercise you just completed are called *in-line images.* This means that the data necessary to produce the graphic image on your screen is downloaded and displayed by the browser when you request the document. Because graphics add significantly to the file size, pages with in-line images may take considerable time to load.

If you don't want to experience this time lag, you can set Netscape to load only the text portion of the document. In-line images will be represented on the page by a small icon, as shown in Figure 3.10. If the image is set up as a link, you can click it even if you haven't loaded the graphic. In this case clicking the icon placeholder that Netscape displays in place of the graphic will let you jump to the linked page.

If, after retrieving a document, you decide you want to see the images after all, simply click the Images button and the document will be reloaded, this time with the graphics. (A word of warning, though: When loading images on demand this way, as compared to autoloading them, Netscape waits until the entire document is transferred before displaying it. It can seem like a very long wait, particularly if you are accustomed to Netscape's normal mode of operation, which is to overlay parts of a document received on top of earlier portions until the entire document is loaded.)

Click to reload current page with images

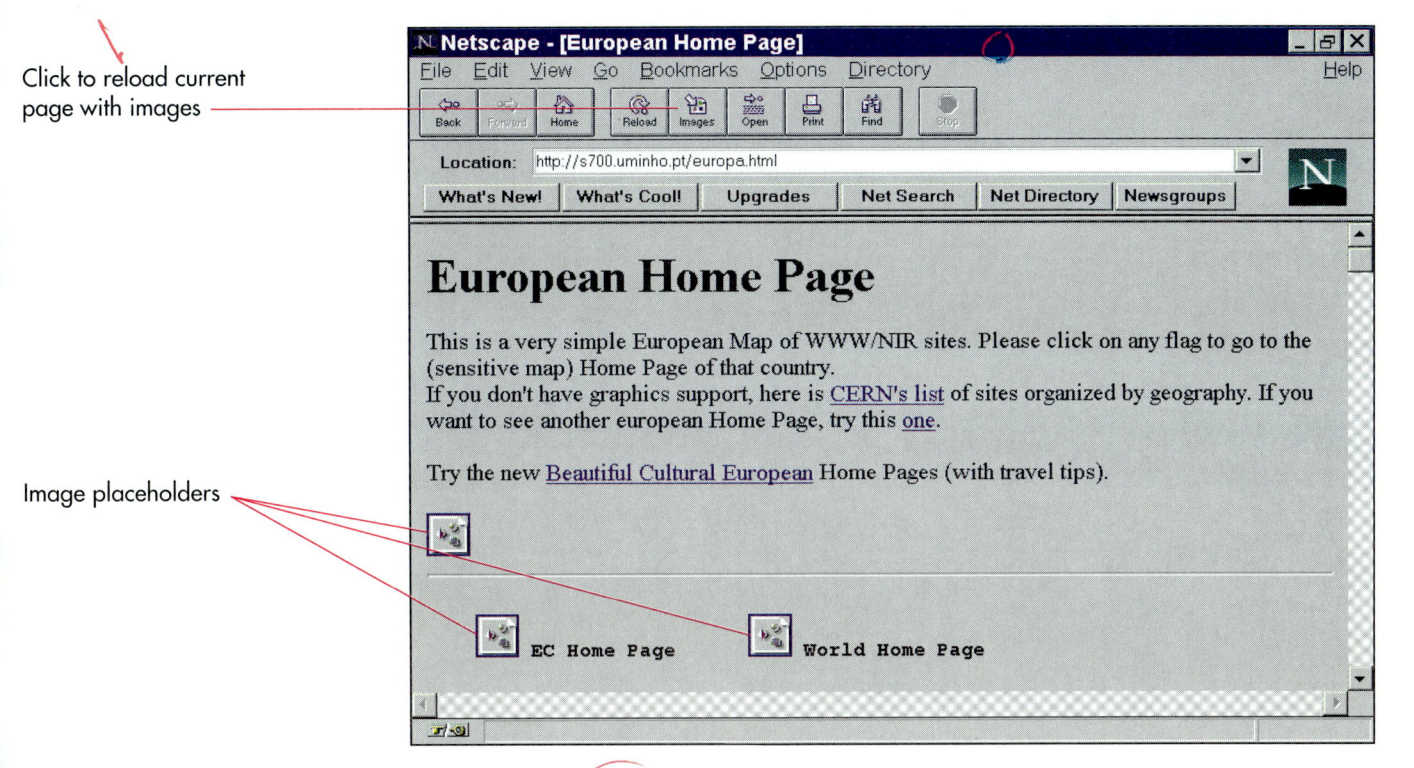

Image placeholders

FIGURE 3.10 A Web Page with Images Off

RETRIEVING IMAGES THAT ARE NOT EMBEDDED

A home page developer may want to include a large picture in a Web document, but not want visitors to have to wait for it to load each time they retrieve the page. Rather than include the entire image, he or she can reduce it significantly or choose a representative icon and enter this ***thumbnail sketch*** as a link in the document. Only those visitors who click on the thumbnail link will bring up the entire graphic. However, viewing the entire image when it is not embedded as an in-line image requires that the user have the appropriate software, or ***viewer,*** configured on his or her system to view the image.

Small version of the large picture

Using E-mail in Netscape

Assume you have found a Web document describing a great ski location in Wyoming. You want to share the information with a friend at another campus. You could print the page and mail it, but you decide that is not the way to communicate on the Information Highway. You could write down the URL of the Web document, then log onto your e-mail server and send your friend a mail message containing the URL. But what if you copied it down wrong, or misspelled it? This method seems a bit cumbersome, too.

A better way uses a preference setting you may find helpful. Netscape can be configured to allow you to send e-mail. Netscape is certainly not a substitute for Eudora, Pine, or any other mail program. But it does provide a convenient way to e-mail a page you find of interest on the Web to someone else.

FINDING THINGS ON THE WORLD WIDE WEB **107**

SETTING NETSCAPE PREFERENCES

You can set some of the Netscape preferences on your own, such as whether images will load with the document. For others, such as e-mail, you may need the assistance of your LAN administrator. It may be that in your environment some of the preferences and features in Netscape are not available. Check with your instructor and/or help desk to determine which features you can use.

HANDS-ON EXERCISE 2

Searching the Web

Objective: To use a Web search engine to find a specific resource on the Net, then locate a character string within it. To change Netscape settings and preferences, and to send e-mail using Netscape. Use Figure 3.11 as a guide in the exercise.

STEP 1: Choose a Search Engine
- Start Netscape or the browser you use in your campus computing environment.
- Click the **Net Search button** on the Netscape screen.
- Scroll or press **PageDown** until you see the InfoSeek and Lycos links.

THE RELOAD COMMAND

There are times when the requested document or resource is not returned, or is loaded incorrectly, particularly when graphics are included. You can request that Netscape reload the document simply by clicking the Reload button at the top of the screen.

STEP 2: Enter the Query Text
- Type **movies** in the Query text box under the InfoSeek link as shown in Figure 3.11a, then click the **Search button.** A short list of movie resources is displayed. (The version of InfoSeek you are using is a small version of a commercial search engine, to which you can subscribe if you wish to pay the fee.)
- Once the Netscape icon is still and the results are completed—downloaded to your PC (check the bottom line of the screen, the progress bar, for the *Document Done* message)—scroll down in the Query Results window to see more information.
- Click any of the listed movie links to browse the listed home pages.

108 EXPLORING THE INTERNET

Click to start InfoSeek Net Search

Query text

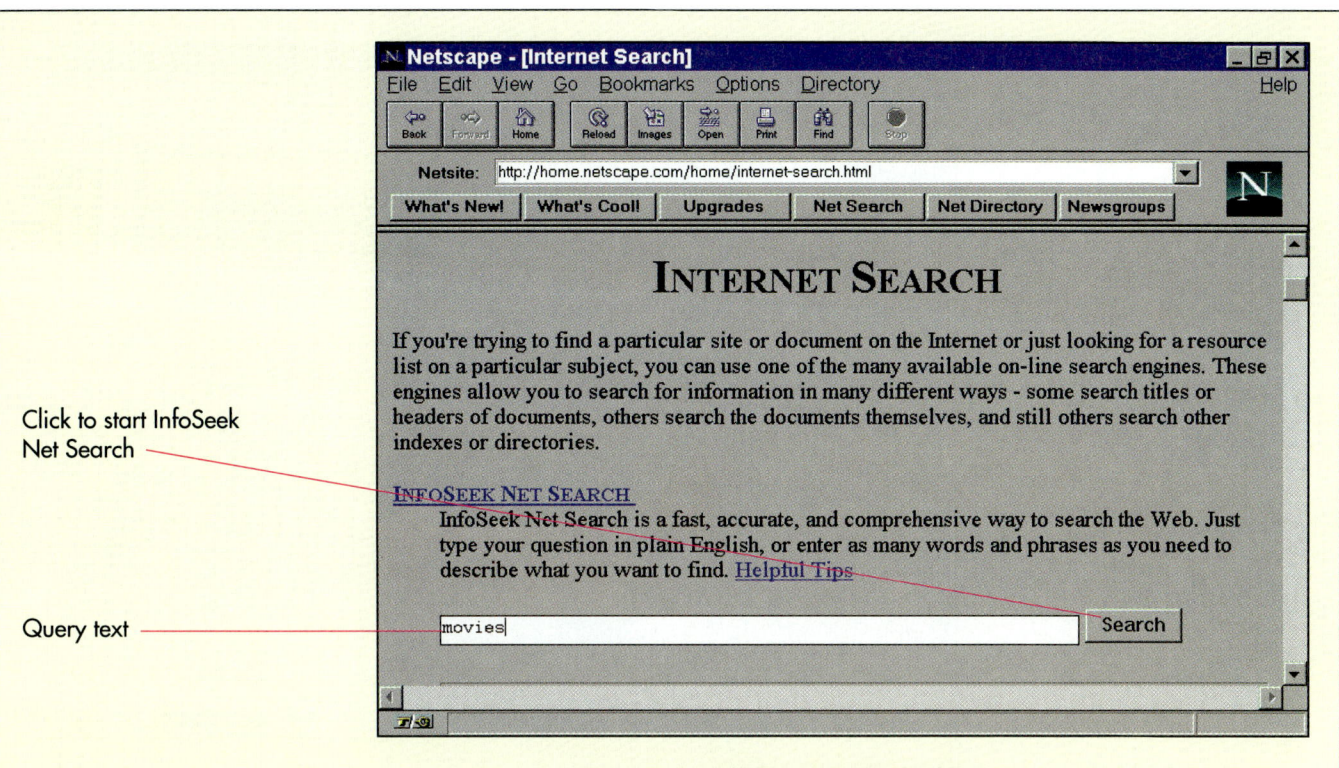

(a) The Query Text Box in InfoSeek

FIGURE 3.11 Hands-on Exercise 2

BOOKMARKING A QUERY

Running a query using a Web search engine actually creates a customized HTML page identified by the URL returned as a result of the search. You can return to the same query at a later time if you create a bookmark when the search is finished. However, be aware that the Web changes continuously, so the next time you visit the bookmarked query, the search results may be different.

STEP 3: Perform a Search on Multiple Terms

➤ Click the **Back button** until you return to the Net Search home page (or alternatively, click **Net Search**).

➤ Click on the **Lycos Home Page: Hunting WWW Information** link. You will see a screen similar to that shown in Figure 3.11b. However, the graphic will be different, as each time a browser accesses the Web server at Lycos, the server inserts a new advertisement in the graphics box.

- Type **movies** in the Query text box and click the **Search button.** The search finds a large number of documents containing the word *movies,* but displays only 10.

- Scroll or press **PageDown** to see abstracts of the 10 documents. The link for each document precedes the abstract.

- Click on any link in the list.

FINDING THINGS ON THE WORLD WIDE WEB **109**

Click to change Search Options

Enter query text here

Advertisement

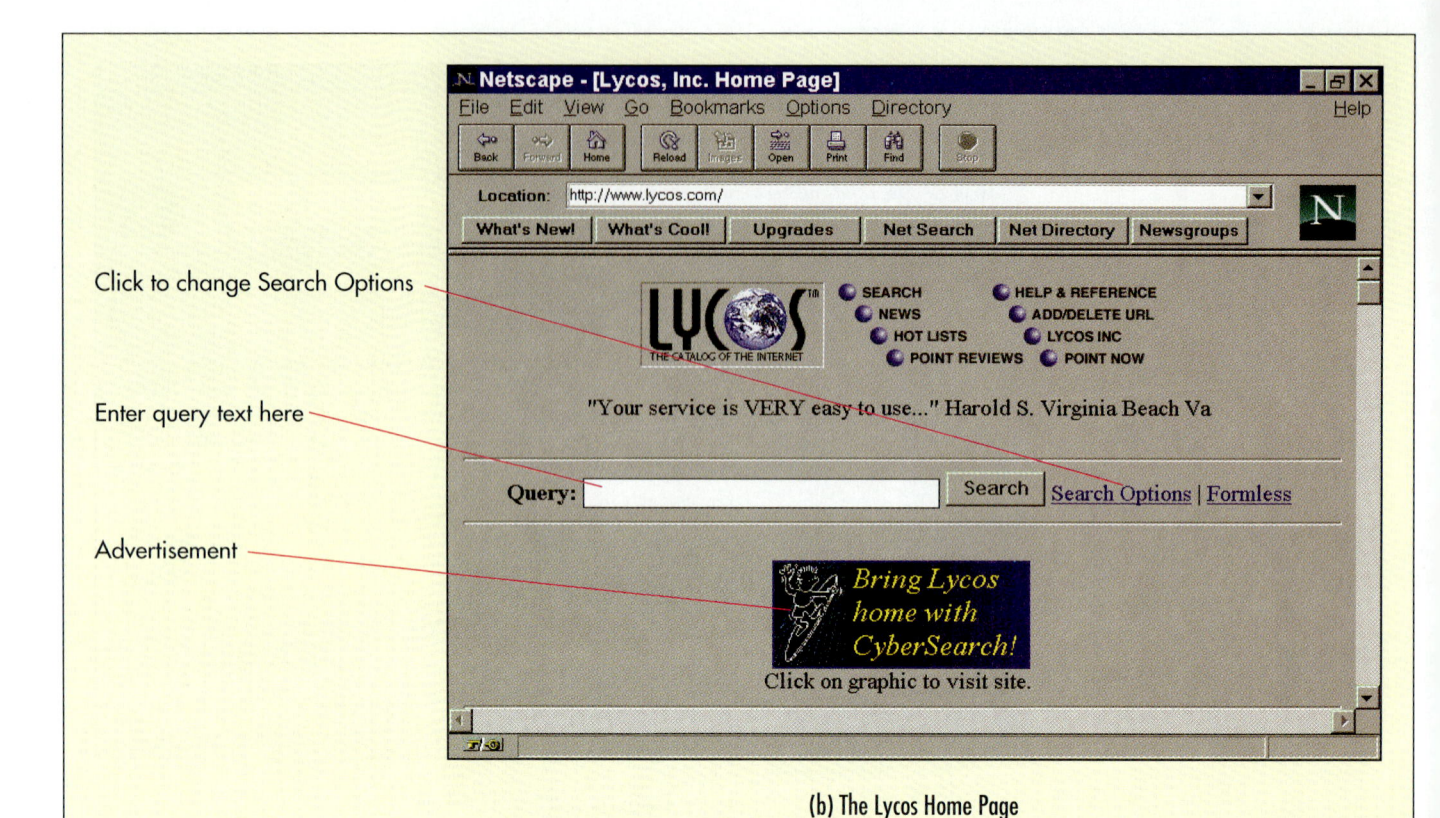

(b) The Lycos Home Page

FIGURE 3.11 Hands-on Exercise 2 (continued)

> Click **Back** until you return to the Lycos home page. Click on the **Search Options** link to display the search form shown in Figure 3.11c. A search form is a special feature of this and other search engines that will allow you to set the number of hits (the number of documents you want returned), and specify that you want to search on a phrase, such as *action movies,* instead of on a single word.

- Click in the **Query text box** and type **action movies.**
- Click on the **Down Arrow button** next to the Display Options text box that shows the number of results per page. Change the maximum number of hits to display to 20.
- The Lycos search engine as currently set will search for any documents containing the word *action* or the word *movies,* resulting in too many unrelated hits. You want to change the default search option from (OR) to (AND). Click the **Down Arrow button** next to the first Search Options text box, and select **match all terms (AND)** from the drop-down list.
- Lycos' default is to display a link followed by a short abstract from the document. You can change the form of the display of "hits" to show just a list of links, without the abstracts. Click the **Down Arrow** next to the Display Options text box that currently says **standard results**. Select **summary results** from the list. Your search form should look like the one shown in Figure 3.11c.
- Click on the **Search button** to display the results shown in Figure 3.11d. (Your results may vary.)

110   EXPLORING THE INTERNET

Annotations (left column, top screenshot):
- Click to start search
- Enter search text
- Match all terms
- Display 20 hits
- Display hits as bulleted list

Screenshot (c) content:

Netscape - [Lycos Search Form]

Location: http://twelve.srv.lycos.com/lycos-form.html?

LYCOS — THE CATALOG OF THE INTERNET
- SEARCH
- NEWS
- HOT LISTS
- POINT REVIEWS
- HELP & REFERENCE
- ADD/DELETE URL
- LYCOS INC
- POINT NOW

Lycos indexes 91% of the web!

Lycos Search

Query: action movies [Search]

Search Options: match all terms (AND) | loose match
Display Options: 20 results per page | summary results

- Search language help

(c) The Completed Lycos Search Form

Annotations (left column, bottom screenshot):
- Document count
- Summary list

Screenshot (d) content:

Netscape - [Lycos search: action movies]

Location: http://lycos-tmp1.psc.edu/cgi-bin/pursuit?query=action+movies&matchmode=and&minscore=.1&

Lycos search: action movies

Lycos Jan 5, 1996 catalog, 18053764 unique URLs

Found 118638 documents matching at least one search term.
Printing only the first 15 documents with at least scores of 0.100 and matching 2 search terms.

Found 249 matching words (number of documents): action (53102), movies (38560), ...

1) What's On Tonite! Category Summary (1/6) [1.0000, 2 of 2 terms, adj 1.0]
2) Spider-Man Live Action Series and Movies 1977-1979 [0.8745, 2 of 2 terms, adj 0.8]
3) Yahoo - Entertainment:Movies and Films:Genres:Action/Adventure [0.8178, 2 of 2 terms, adj 0.7]
4) Yahoo - Entertainment:Movies and Films:Genres:Action/Adventure:James Bond [0.7994, 2 of 2 terms, adj 0.7]
5) IPL Movies [0.6283, 2 of 2 terms, adj 0.3]

http://lycos-tmp1.psc.edu/sow/TrueCounting.html

(d) Lycos Search Results

FIGURE 3.11 Hands-on Exercise 2 (continued)

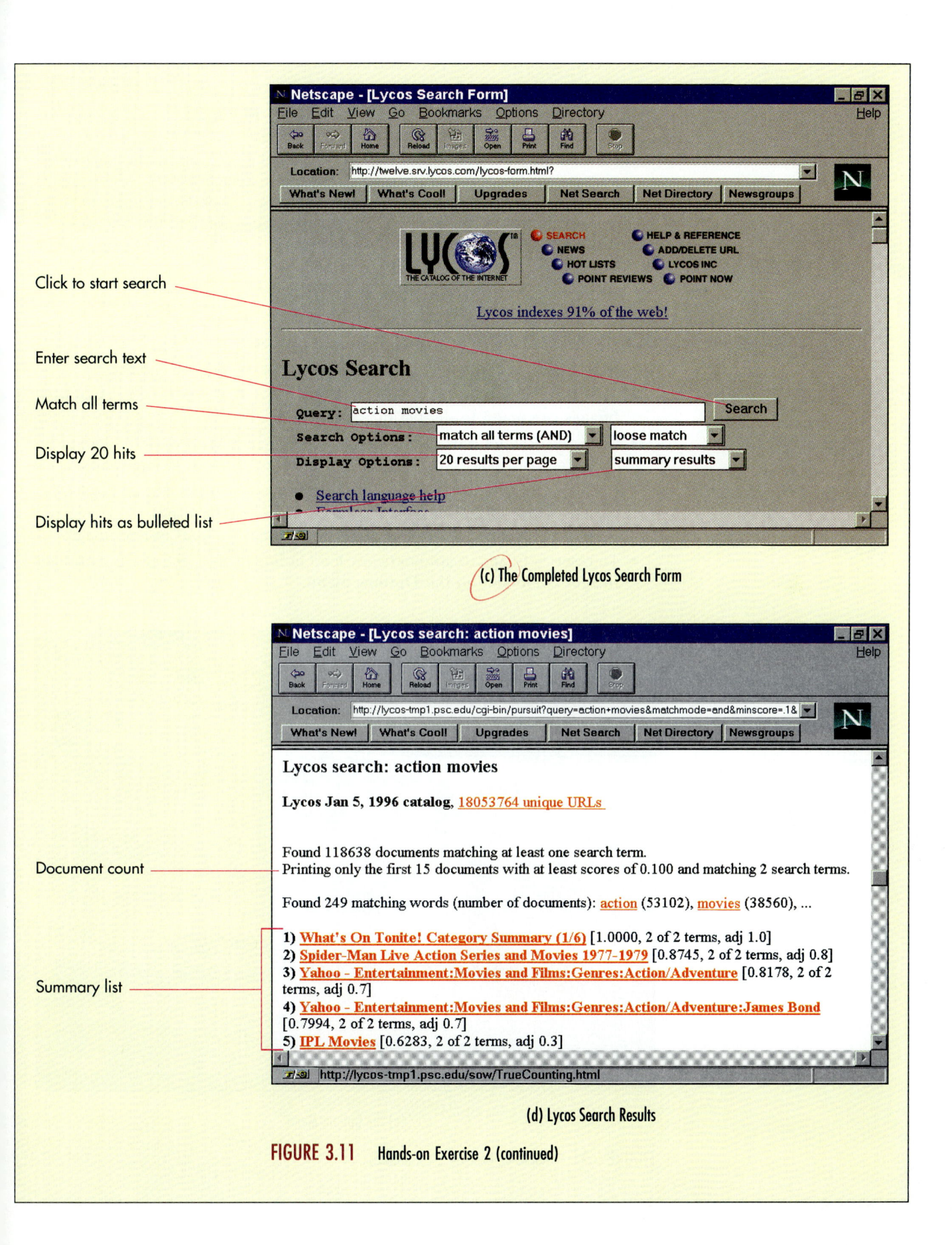

FINDING THINGS ON THE WORLD WIDE WEB

JUMP DIRECTLY TO LYCOS WHEN YOU START NETSCAPE

If you frequently search the Web, you can set Lycos up as the page to which Netscape automatically opens at start-up. Select Preferences on the Options menu. From there choose the Styles tab. Click Home Page location and enter the Lycos URL, http://www.lycos.com, in the text box. Select Save Options on the Options menu. The next time you start Netscape, you will link directly to Lycos.

STEP 4: Load a Web Page without In-line Images

➤ Select **Options** on the menu bar to pull down the menu shown in Figure 3.11e.

- The Autoload Images command is on by default. Click the **Autoload Images command** to disable it.
- Click the **Reload button** to redisplay the current Web page. It should be displayed with placeholder icons substituting for the in-line graphics.
- Click the **Images button.** Netscape will reconnect to the site and redisplay the page with in-line images. However, since you have not yet reselected Autoload Images, subsequent pages will display without in-line images.
- To reset Netscape to automatically load in-line images, select the **Autoload Images command** on the **Options menu.**

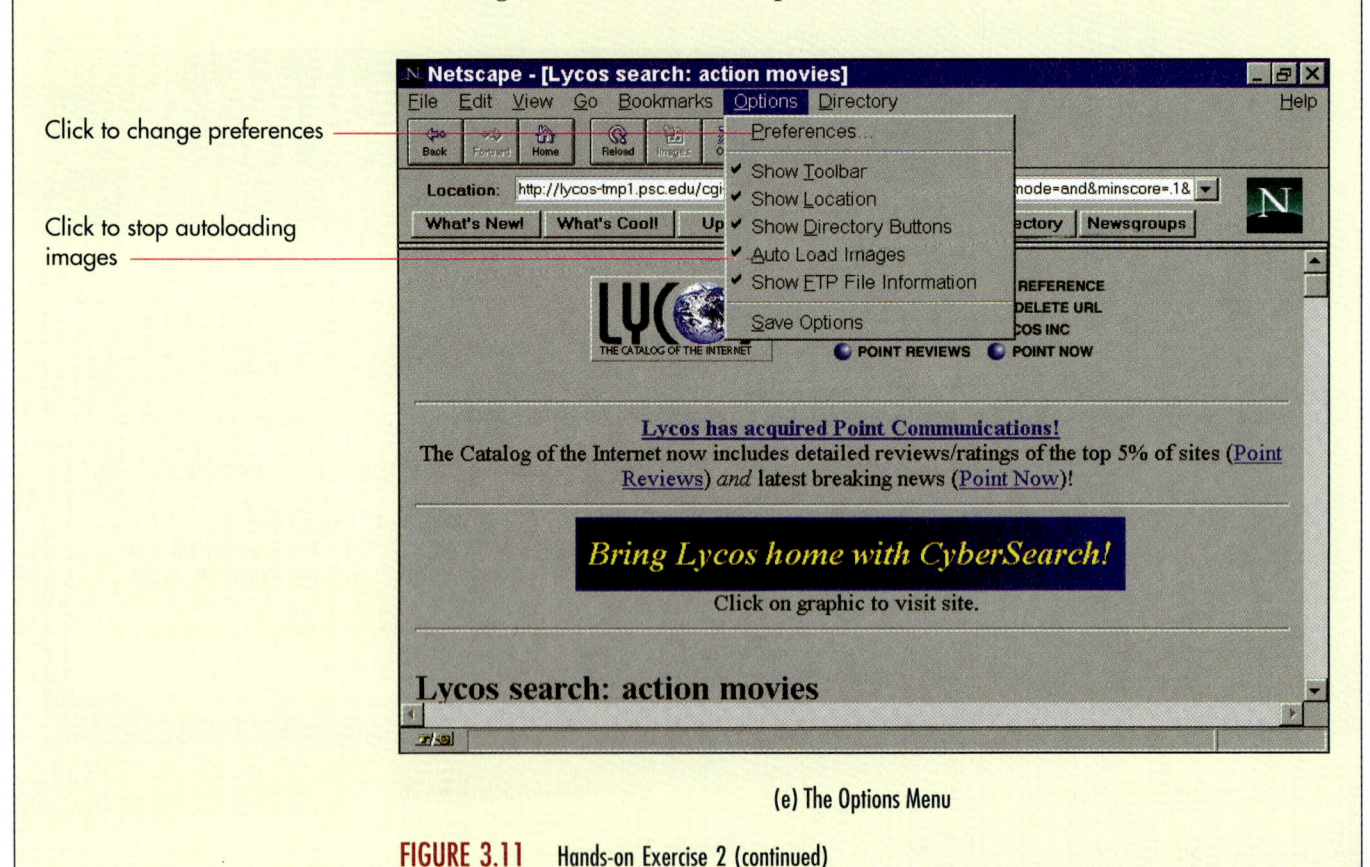

Click to change preferences

Click to stop autoloading images

(e) The Options Menu

FIGURE 3.11 Hands-on Exercise 2 (continued)

112 EXPLORING THE INTERNET

STEP 5: Send E-mail with Netscape

➤ To send e-mail with Netscape, you must change settings in the Preferences dialog box. Select **Preferences** from the **Options menu.** Select the **Mail and News tab.** You will see a dialog box similar to Figure 3.11f.

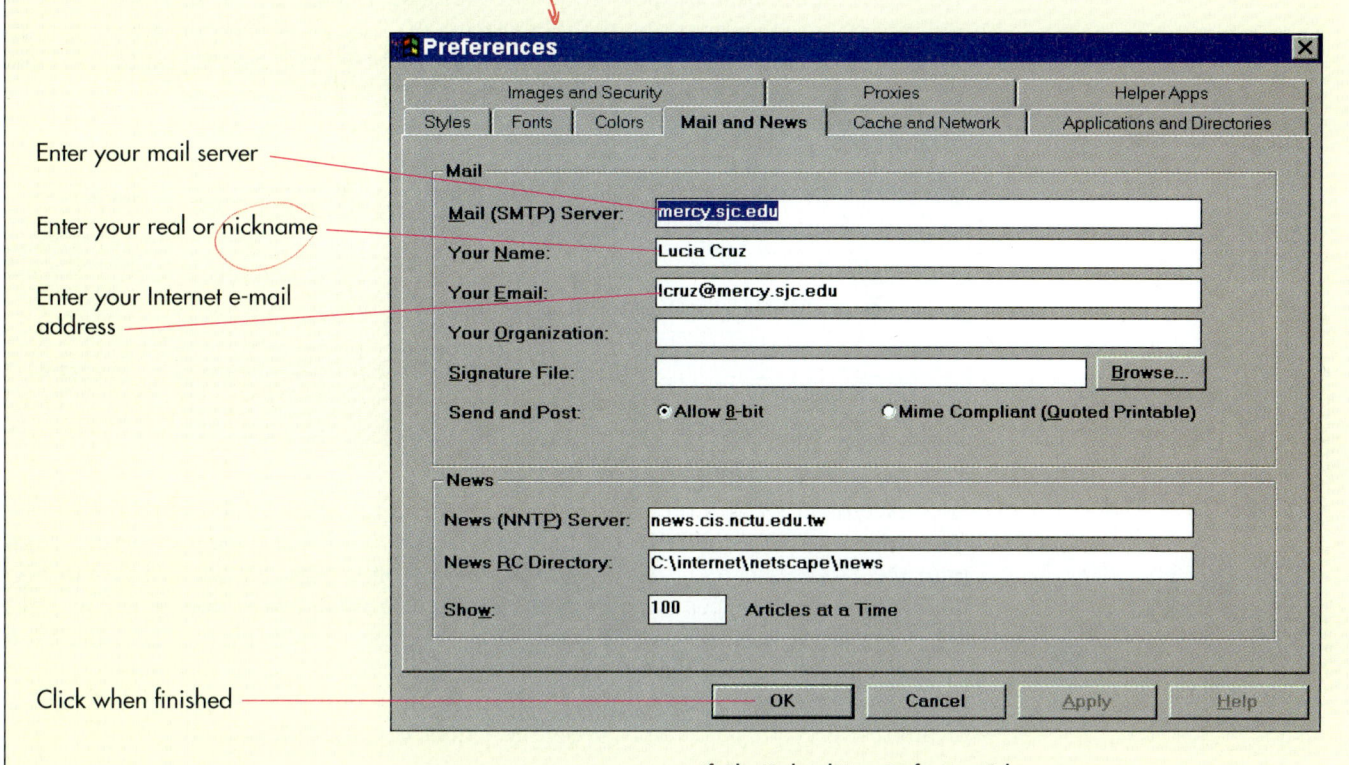

[Screenshot of Preferences dialog — Mail and News tab]

Annotations:
- Enter your mail server
- Enter your real or nickname
- Enter your Internet e-mail address
- Click when finished

Mail (SMTP) Server: mercy.sjc.edu
Your Name: Lucia Cruz
Your Email: lcruz@mercy.sjc.edu
Your Organization:
Signature File: [Browse...]
Send and Post: ⦿ Allow 8-bit   ○ Mime Compliant (Quoted Printable)

News (NNTP) Server: news.cis.nctu.edu.tw
News RC Directory: C:\internet\netscape\news
Show: 100 Articles at a Time

[OK] [Cancel] [Apply] [Help]

(f) The Mail and News Preferences Tab

FIGURE 3.11   Hands-on Exercise 2 (continued)

- Enter the name of your mail server, your real name, and your Internet e-mail address, as shown in the example in Figure 3.11f. (See your instructor or help desk for specific information and instructions.) Click **OK.**
- Select **Save Options** on the **Options menu** to save your mail setup.
- Select **Mail Document** on the **File menu** to compose your e-mail message.
  - Enter the name of the person to whom you wish to send the current page. We suggest that you send the page to yourself to test whether it works.
  - Click to position the insertion point at the end of the URL in the message area and press **Enter** three times to insert three blank lines below the URL.
  - Type some explanatory text to add to the information you are sending.
  - Click the **Quote Document button** at the bottom of the screen to include the text of the current document in the message.
  - Click **Send.** Your message is on its way.

FINDING THINGS ON THE WORLD WIDE WEB

LYNX

Netscape is a fun and exciting way to browse and search the Web, but not everyone has access to it. You must have a PC with lots of memory running Windows and TCP/IP, and a very fast connection to your Internet host, to be able to retrieve Web documents that include graphics. Because not all users have this type of equipment, programmers at the University of Kansas developed **Lynx,** a text-based Web browser that runs on a Unix Internet host. You can log on to the Unix machine with a telnet session, type Lynx at the Unix prompt, and use the arrow keys on your keyboard to scroll through the links in a Web document.

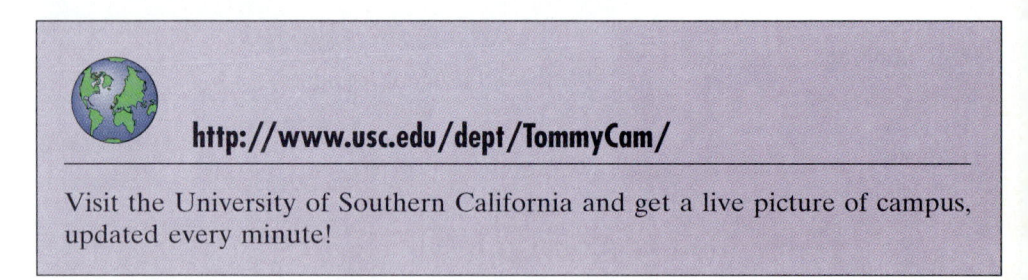

> http://www.usc.edu/dept/TommyCam/
>
> Visit the University of Southern California and get a live picture of campus, updated every minute!

A typical Lynx screen is shown in Figure 3.12a. It does not have the graphics or the formatted HTML text that is available with a graphical browser. Compare the "look and feel" of the White House home page, shown in Lynx in Figure 3.12b, with the types of pages you saw when browsing with Netscape. The links are there; what is missing are the graphics and text formatting that give the Web its visual appeal and impact. However, Lynx provides the same easy navigation of the Web as Netscape and other browsers. When you find and select a link that is of interest to you, you simply press the Enter key, and off you go.

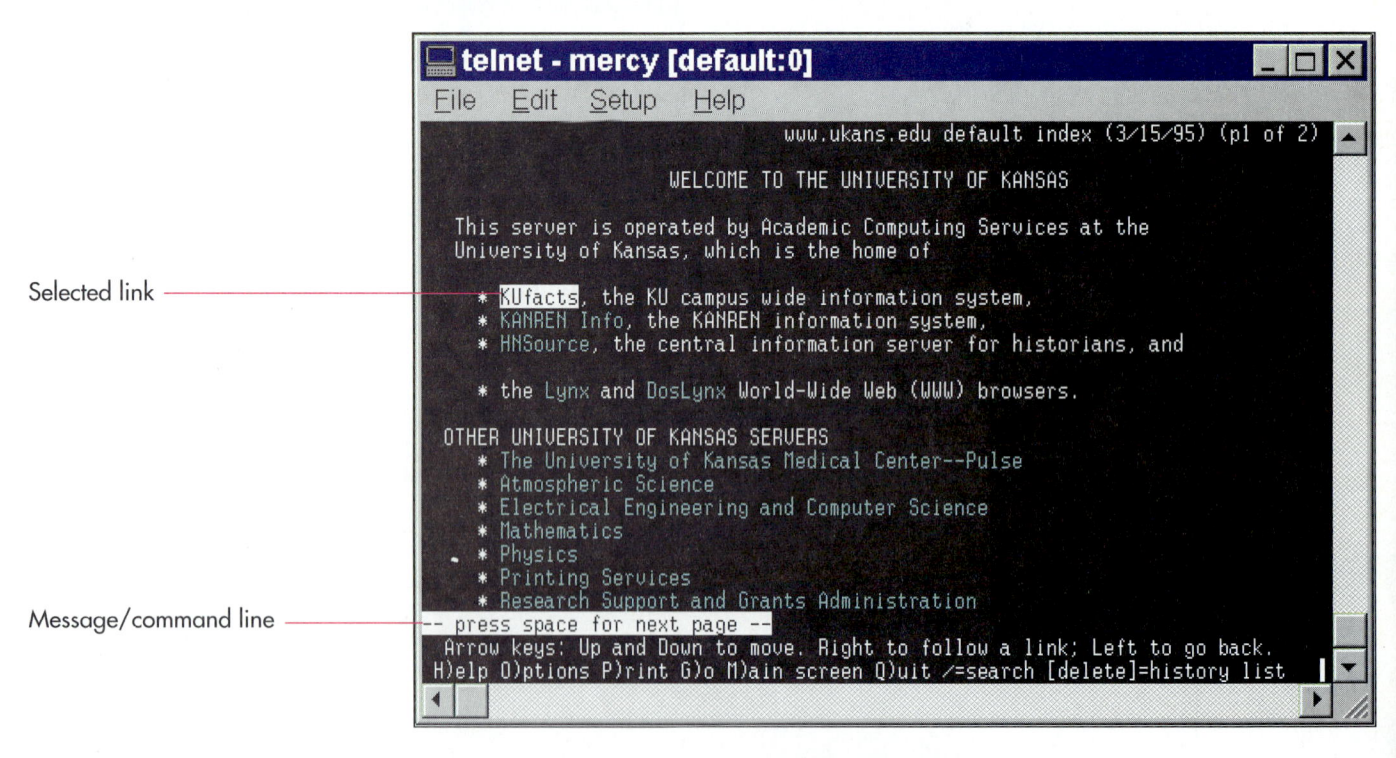

(a) The Lynx Main Page

FIGURE 3.12 Lynx

114 EXPLORING THE INTERNET

Press Enter to jump to selected link

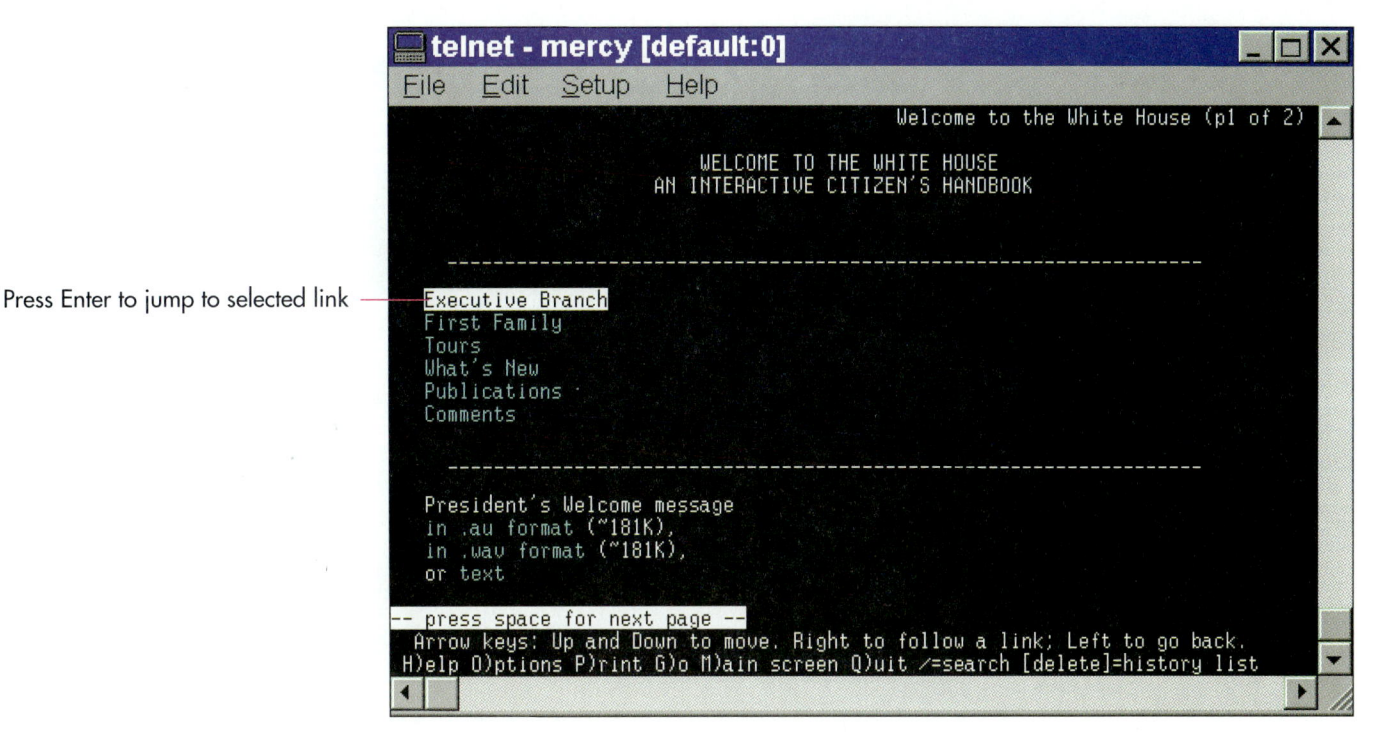

(b) The White House Home Page in Lynx

FIGURE 3.12   Lynx (continued)

HANDS-ON EXERCISE 3

Using Lynx on the World Wide Web

Objective: To use a text-based Web browser such as Lynx to surf the Net and search for documents. Use Figures 3.12 and 3.13 as guides in the exercise.

STEP 1: Log On and Start Lynx

➤ Log on to your network and telnet to your Unix system. (You did this in the hands-on exercise in Chapter 1. If you don't remember how, review those instructions; if you need help, see your instructor or help desk.)

➤ At the Unix prompt, type **lynx.** You will see a screen similar to Figure 3.12a. The hyperlinks are shown in blue or other contrasting color, while the static text is in white, and the background is black.

STEP 2: Navigate in Lynx and Select a Link

➤ Press the **Up/Down arrow keys** to move up and down the page to a desired link. Once you have selected a link, press **Enter** or **Right Arrow.** You will jump to the selected document. (If you go past the desired link, press the **PageUp key;** the cursor will jump back to the top of the previous page.)

➤ Press the **space bar** to display the next page of text; press **b** to display the previous page.

➤ Press the **Left Arrow** to go back to the most recent link.

FINDING THINGS ON THE WORLD WIDE WEB   **115**

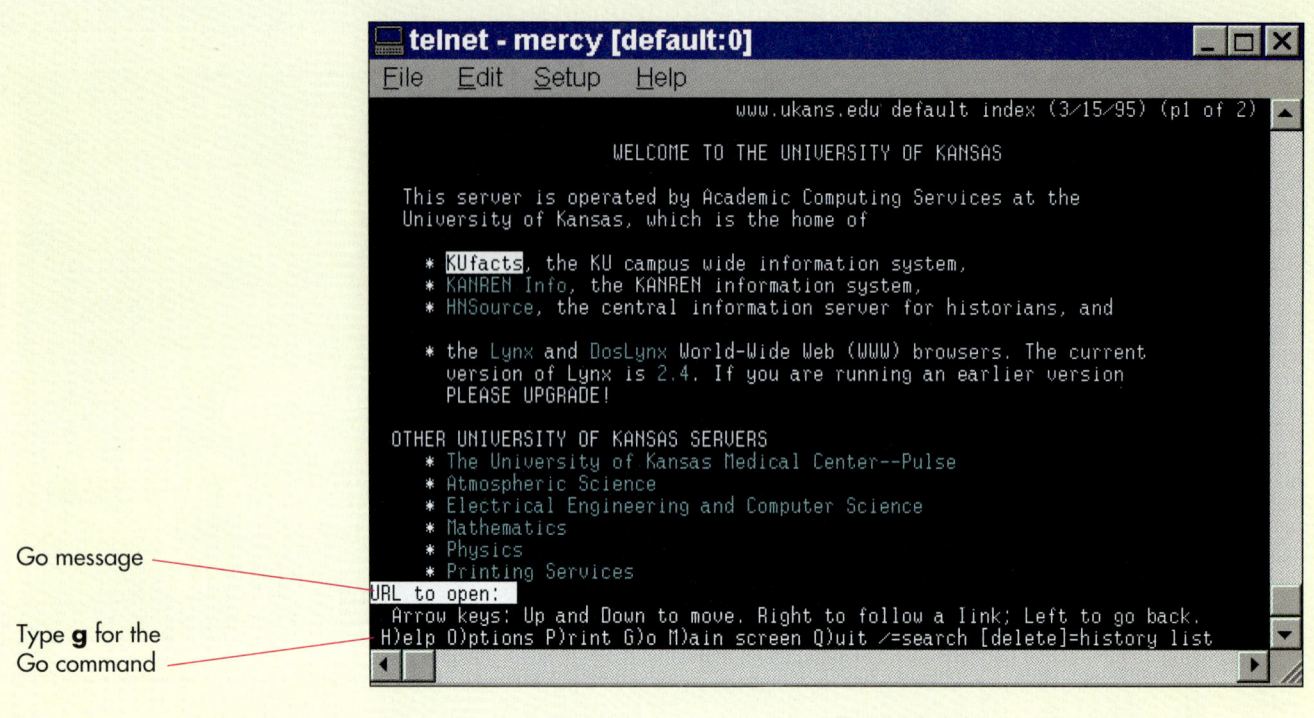

(a) The Lynx Go Command

FIGURE 3.13 Hands-on Exercise 3

STEP 3: Linking to a Specific URL

➤ You can link to a specific home page using Lynx. The menu at the bottom of the screen shows frequently used commands, one of which is Go.

- Type the letter **g**; the command line shown in Figure 3.13a is displayed.
- Fill in the URL of the site you want to visit: **http://www.whitehouse.gov**
- When finished, press **Enter.** You will immediately link to the site.

YOUR KEYBOARD MAY ACT IN STRANGE WAYS IN LYNX

Because you get to Lynx by telnetting, the Unix system thinks it is communicating with a terminal. The keys on your PC keyboard may be sending signals that Unix interprets differently than does the PC. If you have problems with the arrow keys, backspace keys, and so on, check first to be certain the NumLock key is off. Then experiment to see if any other keys substitute for the ones that are not working properly. Finally, see your instructor or help desk for assistance.

STEP 4: Searching with Lynx

➤ You can jump to the Lycos search engine with Lynx just as you would with Netscape.

- Type the letter **g** to invoke the Go command.

- Delete the existing URL, if any, by pressing **Backspace** or the **Left Arrow key.** (If neither key works properly, check with your instructor or help desk to find out which key will delete left when using telnet.)
- Enter the URL of the Lycos search engine, **http://www.lycos.com,** at the prompt.
- Press **Enter.**

➤ At the Lycos home page, shown in Figure 3.13b, press the **Down Arrow key** once to select the Query text field. There may be a short delay when selecting fields in Lynx. Pause before continuing so you will be sure the Query field is selected. The cursor will be blinking at the left edge of the text entry line.

- Type **movies.**
- Press the **Down Arrow key** once to select **Search.** Your screen should look like Figure 3.13c.
- With Search selected, press the **Right Arrow key** or **Enter.** Lycos performs the search and returns the results shown in Figure 3.13d.
- Press the **space bar** to see the second page. Press **b** to go back a page.
- The links to the documents shown in the abstracts are displayed in blue. Select any link using the **Up/Down Arrow keys.**
- Press **Enter** to jump to the document.

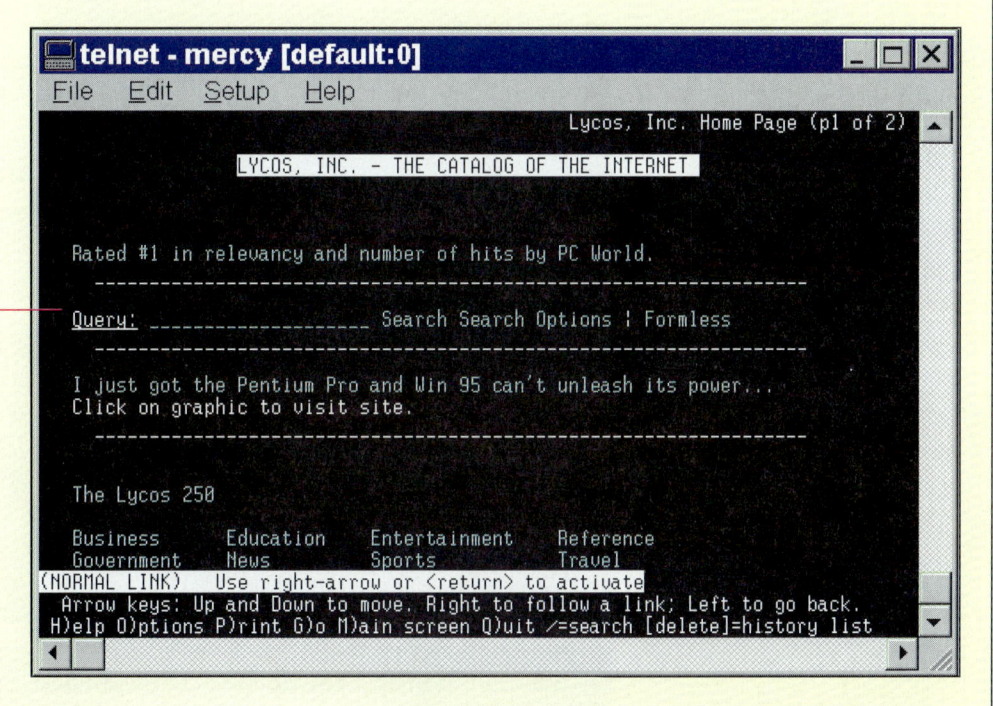

Query text field →

```
telnet - mercy [default:0]
File  Edit  Setup  Help
                                           Lycos, Inc. Home Page (p1 of 2)
              LYCOS, INC. - THE CATALOG OF THE INTERNET

   Rated #1 in relevancy and number of hits by PC World.
   ----------------------------------------------------------------
   Query: _____ Search Search Options | Formless
   ----------------------------------------------------------------

   I just got the Pentium Pro and Win 95 can't unleash its power...
   Click on graphic to visit site.
   ----------------------------------------------------------------

   The Lycos 250

   Business       Education      Entertainment     Reference
   Government     News           Sports            Travel
(NORMAL LINK)    Use right-arrow or <return> to activate
 Arrow keys: Up and Down to move. Right to follow a link; Left to go back.
 H)elp O)ptions P)rint G)o M)ain screen Q)uit /=search [delete]=history list
```

(b) The Lycos Home Page

FIGURE 3.13   Hands-on Exercise 3 (continued)

STEP 5: Perform a Search Using Multiple Terms

➤ Go back to the Lycos home page by pressing the **Left Arrow key** until you are there (or press **g** and enter the Lycos URL).

- Press the **Down Arrow key** until you select the **Search Options link.**

Query text ⟶

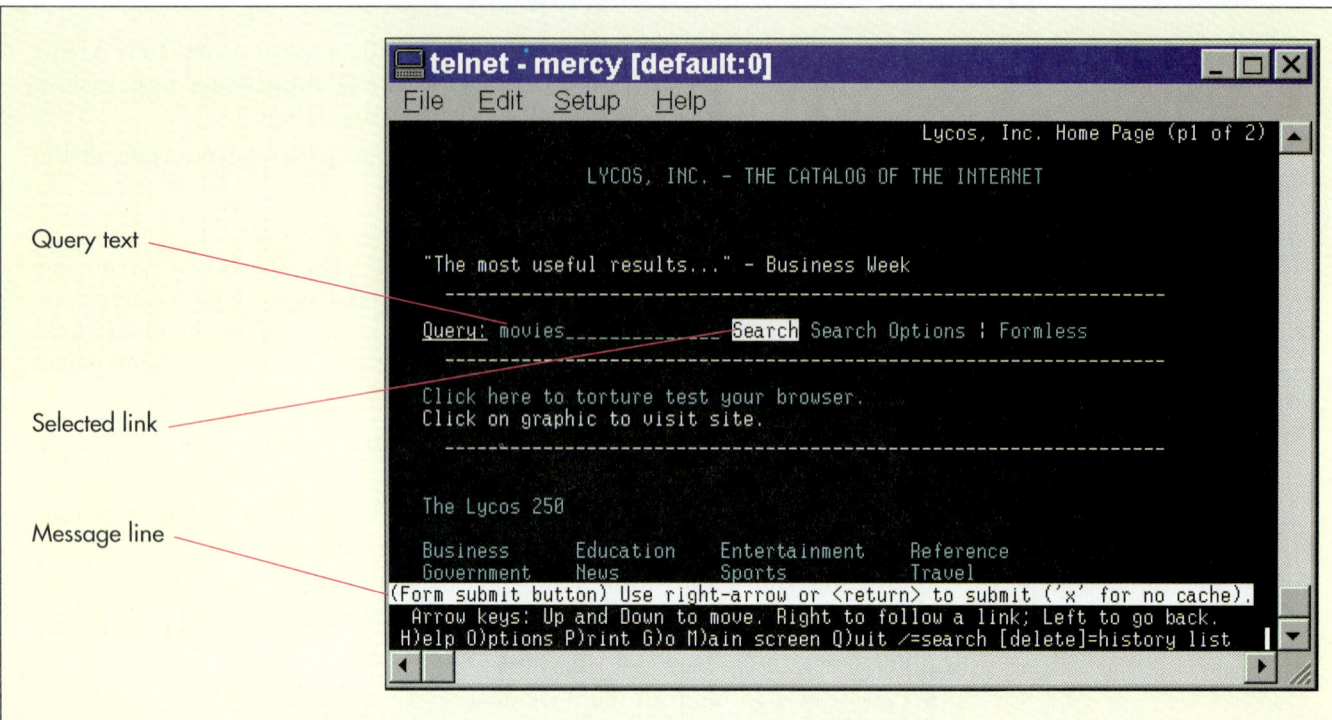

Selected link ⟶

Message line ⟶

(c) The Search Link

(d) Movie Search Results

FIGURE 3.13   Hands-on Exercise 3 (continued)

- Press **Enter.** The search options page shown in Figure 3.13e is displayed.
- Press the **Down Arrow key** until the cursor is in the **Query** text field. Enter the text of your query, **action movies.**

118   EXPLORING THE INTERNET

- Press the **Down Arrow key** until you select the **match any term (OR)** Search Options link below the query text. Your screen should match Figure 3.13f.

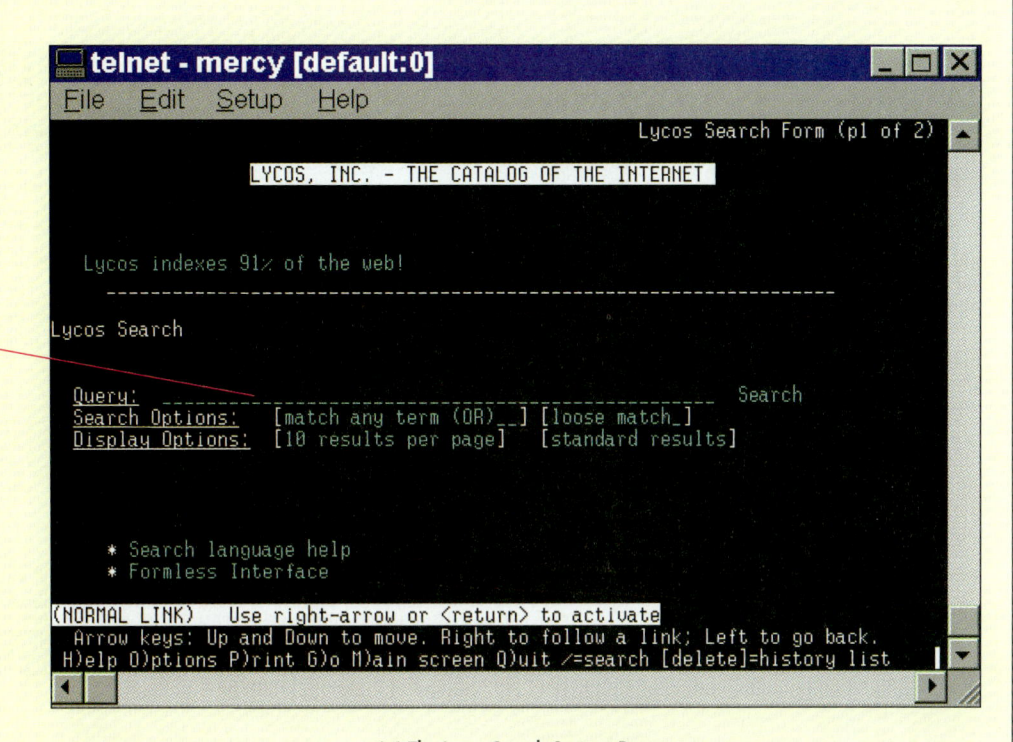

(e) The Lycos Search Options Page

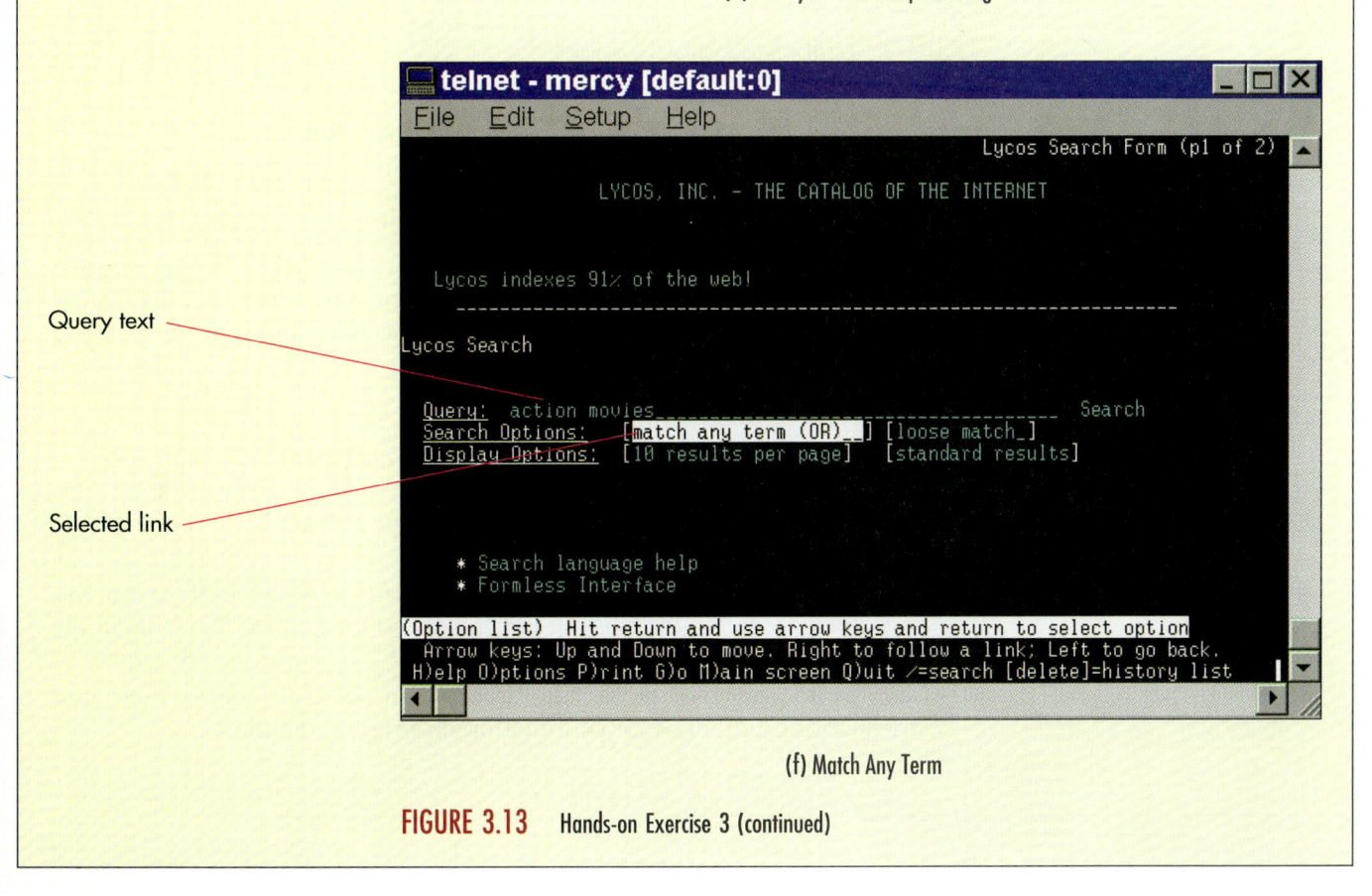

(f) Match Any Term

FIGURE 3.13 Hands-on Exercise 3 (continued)

- Press **Enter**. The menu shown in Figure 3.13g is displayed. Use the **Up/Down Arrow keys** to select the option you want. In this case select **match all terms (AND)**. Press **Enter**.

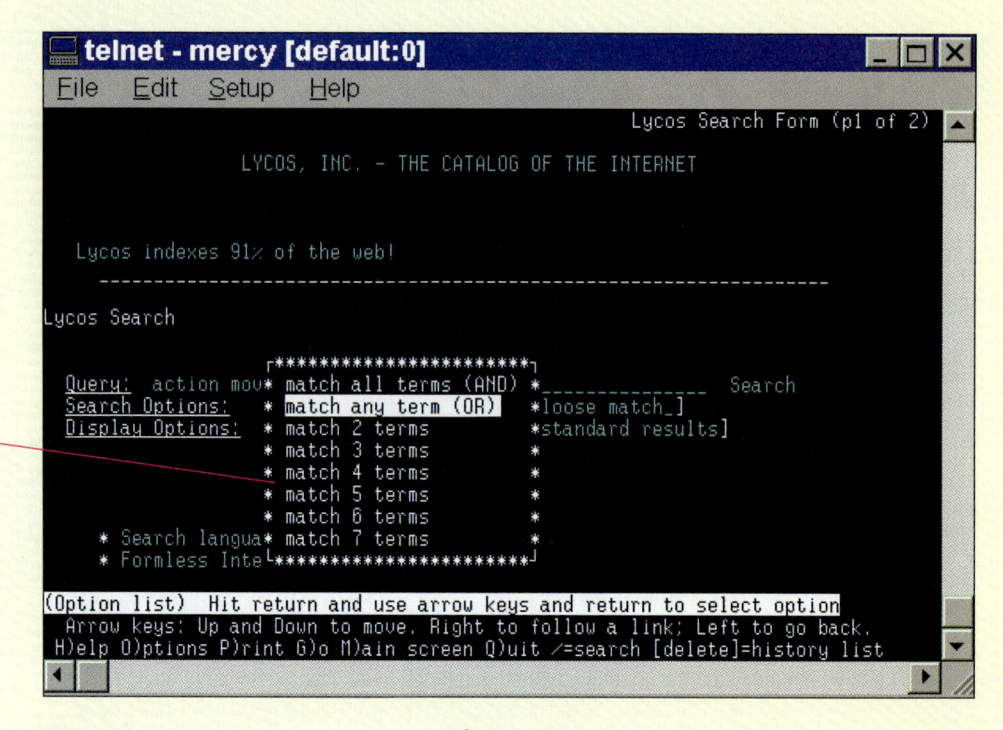

Match terms menu

(g) The Terms Menu

FIGURE 3.13 Hands-on Exercise 3 (continued)

- Since you have already gone past the Search link on this page, press **PageUp** to return to the top of the page, then press **Down Arrow** until **Search** is selected.
- Press **Enter**. Your query results will be displayed as a text-only document. You can see the search results by pressing the space bar to display the next page, shown in Figure 3.13h. Using the **Down Arrow key** you may select any hyperlink in the document. Press **Enter** to jump to the selected URL.

STEP 6: Download a File

➤ You can use Lynx to download a Web page or file.

- Use the arrow keys to select the URL of the document you want to download and press **d** (for download). A message shown in Figure 13.3i is displayed, indicating that the file will be downloaded to disk. Press **Enter** to save the file to disk.
- Press **Enter** to accept the existing file name or press the **Left Arrow key** repeatedly to delete the existing file name, and type a new file name in the command line.
- The file is copied to your home directory on the Unix server. (See your instructor or help desk for information on printing the file.)

First hit —

(h) The Query Results

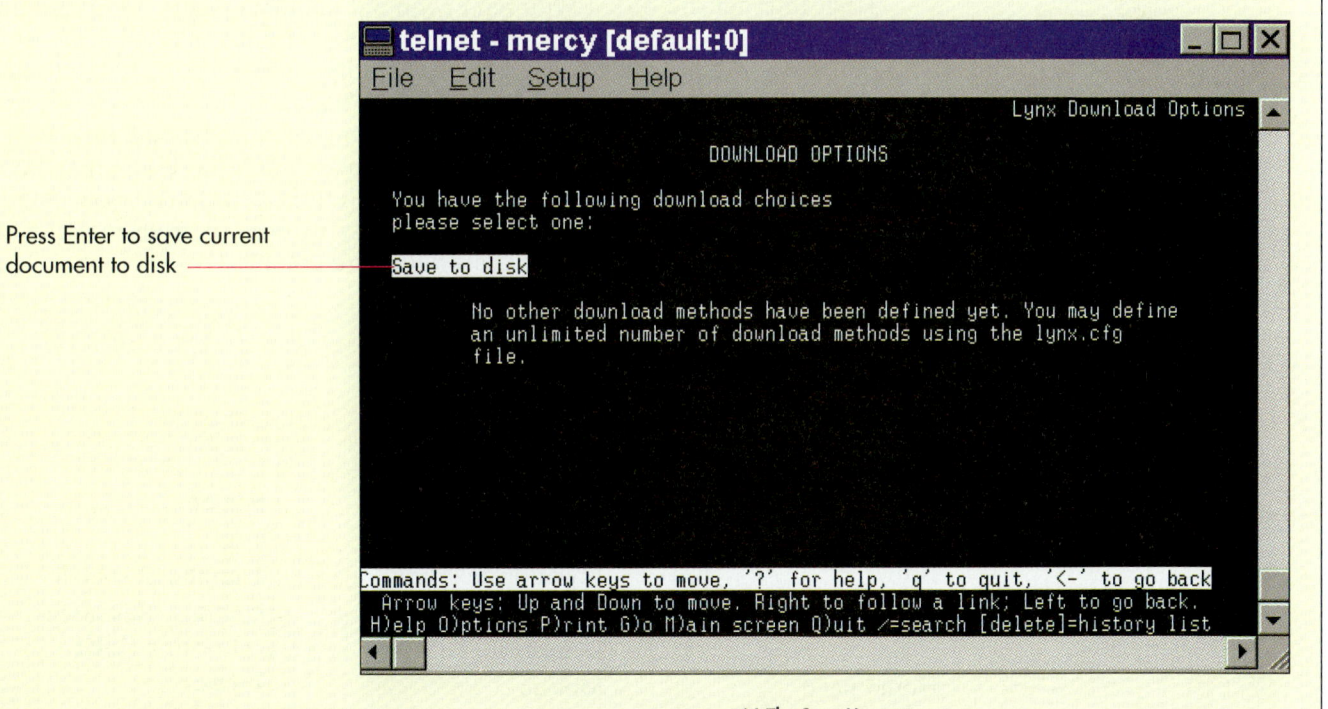

Press Enter to save current document to disk —

(i) The Save Message

FIGURE 3.13   Hands-on Exercise 3 (continued)

STEP 7: Exit Lynx and Log Off

- Press **q** to quit Lynx. At the prompt press **Enter** to confirm. (You can do a quick exit, without the confirmation, by typing an uppercase **Q**.)
- Type **exit** or whatever command you usually use to exit the Unix system. Press **Enter.** You are logged off.

FINDING THINGS ON THE WORLD WIDE WEB   **121**

http://www.ajb.dni.us

America's Job Bank is one of the largest job listings on the Net. Using this resource, thousands of Internet users find employment opportunities all over the United States.

SUMMARY

In the past, Internet resources could be obtained only by using difficult-to-master Unix-based commands and text-based retrieval systems. Today these resources are easily accessible through the World Wide Web using a Web browser such as Netscape. Netscape provides a Windows-based graphical user interface that allows users point-and-click access to millions of Web documents and files via hyperlinks. The documents are created using a word processor and HTML, which provides the tags that define each hypertext link to other documents. HTML also provides formatting tags used to define the appearance of Web documents. The files on the Web may contain text, graphics, sound, and/or video links.

Each Internet site with a Web server can put up home pages, which can then be accessed using a Web browser. Since the number of home pages on the Internet is currently in the millions and growing rapidly, browsing is a fun but inefficient way to search for information on the Web. Search engines provide a simple means of entering a query, to which the search engine will respond with a number of "hits," or Web documents that meet the search criteria. Users may bookmark the query or any frequently visited site to return to the same document at a later time. Browsers also provide the capability to print Web documents and save them to a local disk. For those users without a graphical Web browser, Lynx provides text-based browsing capability.

KEY WORDS AND CONCEPTS

Back button
Bookmark
Browser
Client
Hit
Home page
Hyperlink
Hypermedia
Hypertext
Hypertext Markup
  Language (HTML)
Hypertext Transport
  Protocol (HTTP)

In-line image
Link
Location text box
Lycos
Lynx
Mosaic
Netscape Navigator
Open Location
  command
Reload button
Search engine
Search form

Spider
Tag
Thumbnail sketch
Uniform Resource
  Locator (URL)
Viewer
Web server
Web site
World Wide Web
  (WWW)

Multiple Choice

1. Which of the following statements about the World Wide Web is true?
   (a) It has been in existence since the beginning of the Internet
   (b) Both graphics and text-based resources are linked on the Web
   (c) It can be accessed only by using a GUI-based browser
   (d) All of the above

2. When linking to a Web resource:
   (a) Your request must be routed through the Web server at the European Particle Physics Lab (the WWW developers)
   (b) You may link to a Web resource on the same computer or anywhere else on the Web
   (c) You must know the URL for the hyperlink to work
   (d) All of the above

3. Which of the following standard Windows elements are found in Netscape?
   (a) The Maximize button
   (b) A File menu
   (c) The title bar
   (d) All of the above

4. Which of the following defines the address of the current Web resource?
   (a) The title bar
   (b) The URL in the Location text box
   (c) Both (a) and (b)
   (d) Neither (a) nor (b)

5. Which part of the URL **http://www.microsoft.com/Windows/www.html** identifies the Internet address of the Web site?
   (a) http://
   (b) www.microsoft.com
   (c) Windows
   (d) www.html

6. Which of the following Netscape menus or buttons allows you to access a previously visited Web site without entering the URL?
   (a) File
   (b) Open
   (c) Go
   (d) None of the above

7. Which of the following is generally the first link at a Web site?
   (a) The home page
   (b) The root
   (c) The search form
   (d) The gopher server

8. When using Netscape, clicking on a link:
   (a) Brings up the Open URL dialog box so you can edit the link
   (b) Brings up a text-based menu for the site
   (c) Requires you to enter your username and password
   (d) None of the above

9. How does Netscape indicate it is in the process of transferring a Web document?
   - (a) The Netscape logo flashes
   - (b) A message is displayed in the URL text box
   - (c) Both (a) and (b)
   - (d) Neither (a) nor (b)

10. Which Netscape command allows you to create a bookmark for a previously visited site without returning to it?
    - (a) View History
    - (b) Bookmarks
    - (c) Both (a) and (b)
    - (d) Neither (a) nor (b)

11. If you are trying to limit the number of "hits" in a search on *space shuttle*, which of the following logical operations would you use?
    - (a) And
    - (b) Or
    - (c) Both (a) and (b)
    - (d) Neither (a) nor (b)

12. Which of the following is a text-based Web browser?
    - (a) HTML
    - (b) HTTP
    - (c) Lynx
    - (d) Netscape

13. Which of the following allows you to use hyperlinks to access World Wide Web resources?
    - (a) Lynx
    - (b) Netscape
    - (c) Both (a) and (b)
    - (d) Neither (a) nor (b)

14. A URL may be entered in:
    - (a) The Location box on the Netscape screen
    - (b) The Go dialog box
    - (c) Both (a) and (b)
    - (d) Neither (a) nor (b)

15. A hyperlink may point to:
    - (a) A sound file
    - (b) A text file
    - (c) A video file
    - (d) Any of the above

ANSWERS

1. b	6. c	11. a
2. b	7. a	12. c
3. d	8. d	13. c
4. b	9. a	14. c
5. b	10. a	15. d

Exploring the Internet

1. Using Figure 3.14, match each action with its result; a given action may be used more than once or not at all.

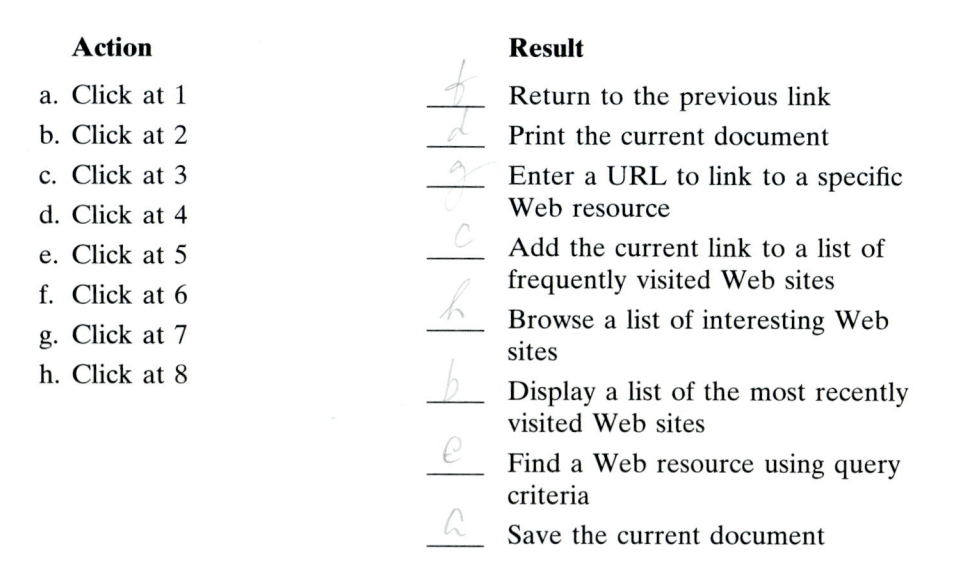

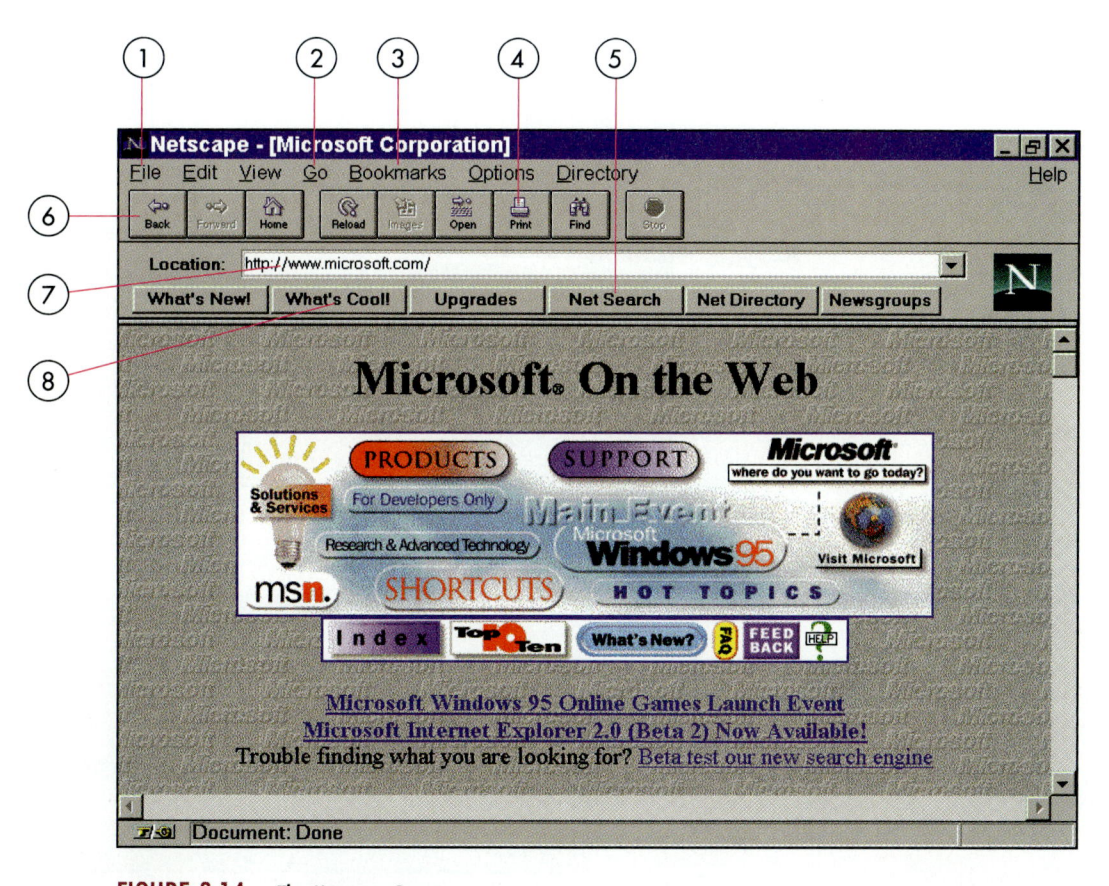

   Action
   a. Click at 1
   b. Click at 2
   c. Click at 3
   d. Click at 4
   e. Click at 5
   f. Click at 6
   g. Click at 7
   h. Click at 8

   Result
   __f__ Return to the previous link
   __d__ Print the current document
   __g__ Enter a URL to link to a specific Web resource
   __c__ Add the current link to a list of frequently visited Web sites
   __h__ Browse a list of interesting Web sites
   __b__ Display a list of the most recently visited Web sites
   __e__ Find a Web resource using query criteria
   __a__ Save the current document

FIGURE 3.14   The Netscape Screen

2. Answer the following with respect to Web access at your college or university:
   a. What Web browser are you using?
   b. Does it provide a Windows GUI (graphical user interface)?
   c. What is the easiest way to access a search engine using your browser?
   d. Do you have Lynx or another text-based Web browser for access from the Unix prompt?
   e. What is your college or university's URL?
   f. Can you set up your own bookmarks on the system?
   g. Where do you go to get help?

3. The messages shown in Figure 3.15 appeared (or could have appeared) in conjunction with one of the hands-on exercises in this chapter. Explain the nature of each message and indicate the necessary corrective action (if any).

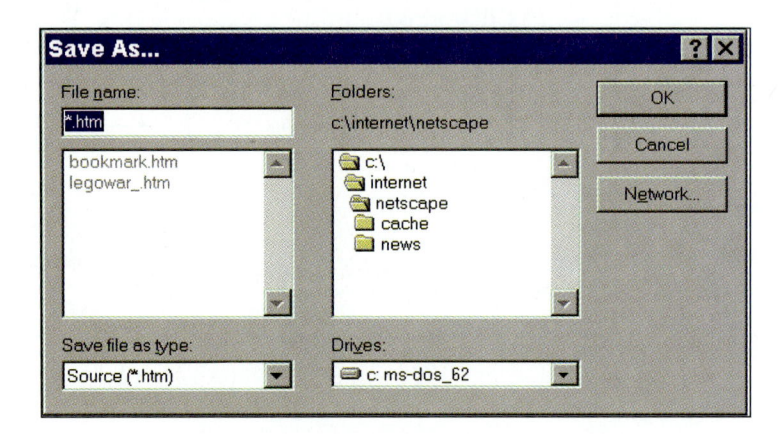

(a) Message 1

(b) Message 2

(c) Message 3

FIGURE 3.15   Messages for Problem 3

126   EXPLORING THE INTERNET

4. Describe in ordinary English what the Lycos search form shown in Figure 3.16 will search for and what results it will display when the search is completed. How could you reduce the number of "hits" found and displayed by the search?

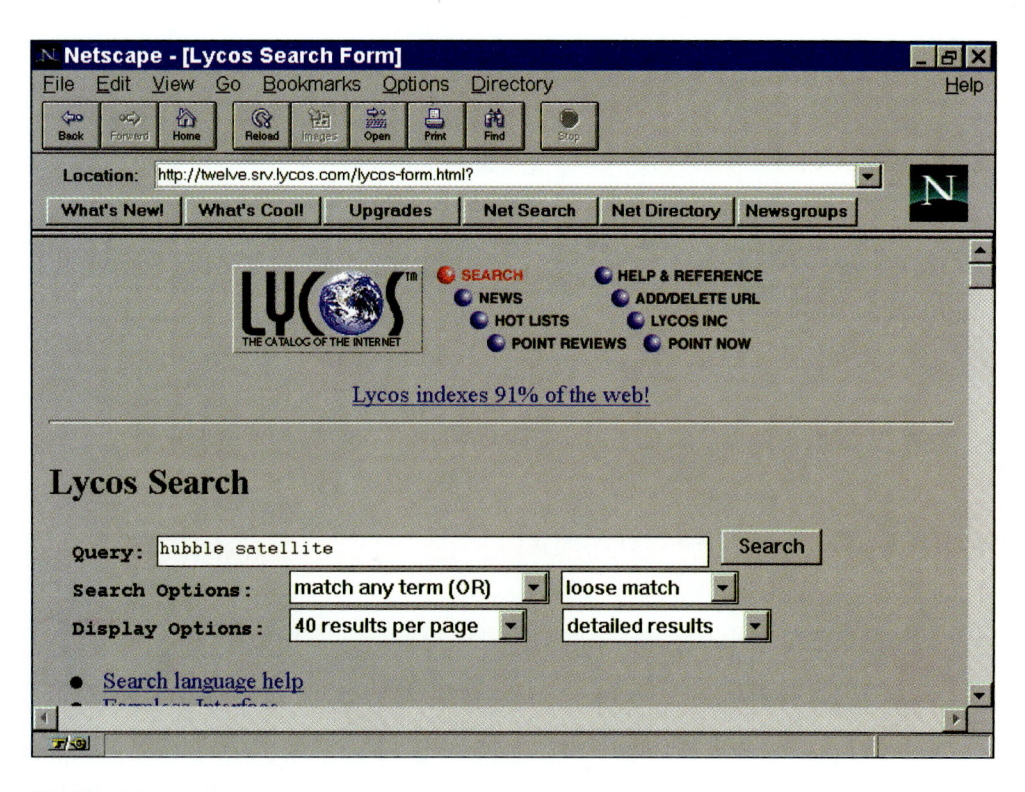

FIGURE 3.16 A Lycos Search Form

Practice with the World Wide Web

1. Get Help: Online help in Netscape has a new meaning. It is not online on your system, it's online on the Internet. Netscape Communications Corporation, the company that markets Netscape, can update its help files instantly as the product changes or problems are noted. Get a look at online help by clicking the Help menu in Netscape, and notice the URL as you do so. Spend some time exploring the various links—there's lots of good stuff there.

2. Learn about HTML: Suppose you want to learn more about using HTML to create Web documents. Why go to a bookstore and spend $29.95 when the information is available online? The trick is to find it. Using whatever search engine is available to you, construct a search on the keywords *learning HTML*. Explore the sites that are "hits."

3. Read a Zine: Online publishing is becoming a hot, and very competitive, topic on the Net. TV news services, news magazines, and newspapers have Web sites. Visit the sites shown in Table 3.2, and compare the various offerings in terms of visual appeal, graphics quality, and so on. They all provide examples of the best (or most interesting) zines (electronic magazines) of the Net.

TABLE 3.2　Web Publishing Sites

Site	URL
MTV	http://mtv.com/MTVNEWS/index.html
Time Magazine	http://www.pathfinder.com/@@BnqVKTFCdgMAQDBT/time/timehomepage.html
ESPN	http://espnet.sportszone.com
Wired Magazine	http://www.wired.com/newform.html

4. Just the FAQs, Please: The Internet and the World Wide Web can be very intimidating to the newcomer. However, it doesn't have to be for long. All the information you need to understand the Net is on the Net! General information about popular subjects is often kept in files titled Frequently Asked Questions (FAQs). Compose a search to find out more about the World Wide Web; something like *WWW FAQs* should work. Follow the hyperlinks until you feel comfortable with the terms you're reading. Set up bookmarks to return to any interesting sites.

Case Studies

Copyright Law in Cyberspace

The possibilities of electronic publishing are immense, as are the opportunities to plagiarize. How are authors' and artists' rights being protected in the online world? Research the latest information in cyberspace about cyberspace software and artistic piracy. Will the Internet be commercially viable for the publishing industry, given the ease with which anyone can retrieve and copy electronic information?

Cyberspace Education

The possible uses of online information sources are limited only by the imagination. Search the net for educational sites at all levels (K through 12th grade, university, postgraduate). What added value does the Net provide that learners cannot get from print media or from classroom instruction?

Here's to Your Health

Do you have a health-related question you've been wanting to ask? Try looking up an answer on the Internet. Using whatever search engine you have access to, enter the search words for your question and link to the sites that look promising. Keeping yourself informed about health issues can help you stay healthy!

It May Be Fun, but Is It Efficient?

You have a paper on Thomas Jefferson due on Monday. See what information you can find about Jefferson on the World Wide Web. You will discover that a search on Thomas Jefferson leads to many unrelated links (**Thomas Jefferson University,** for example). Try your search with different search parameters (*Thomas Jefferson constitution,* or *Thomas Jefferson President,* for instance. Is this an efficient way to get information?

Index

A

Advance Research Projects Agency (ARPAnet), 2
Alias. *See* Nickname
Application layer, 22
Archie, 12, 13
Archives, for mailing lists, 64

B

Back button, in Netscape, 86, 97
Blind carbon copy, 40, 50
Bookmarks, in Netscape, 93, 98, 109
Browser. *See* Web browser

C

Carbon copy, 40, 50, 57
Channel, 12
Chat program, 12, 13, 30
Client, 19, 86
Client software, 44
Command line interface, 55
Commercial service providers, 14, 15
Concord Coalition, 86–87
Cyberspace, 3, 91

D

Digest command, in mailing lists, 64
Distribution list, 60, 65–66, 71–73
Domain, 24, 25
Domain Name System (DNS), 24, 30
Domain root server, 25
Downloading
　files, 10
　with Lynx, 120
　mail messages from Internet server, 44

E

E-mail, 3–5, 30, 39–77
　addresses, 46, 48, 50
　attaching documents to, 40, 62
　composing, 42
　deleting, 54, 59
　editing messages in, 50
　forwarding, 42, 54
　mailboxes for, 40, 54, 61–62, 68, 73–74
　rejected messages, 53
　replying to, 42, 53, 59
　retrieving, 51, 58
　sending, 42, 50, 57
　structure of messages in, 40–42
　subscribing to mailing lists using, 63–64, 68, 70, 75–76
　using Netscape for, 107–108, 113
Eudora, 3, 4, 43
　configuring, 46
　deleting messages in, 51
　distribution lists, 65–66
　editing messages in, 50, 51
　mailboxes in, 43, 54–55, 68
　nicknames, 65–66
　passwords, 49
　sending e-mail with, 49–51
　signatures in, 66

F

File server, 17
File Transfer Protocol (FTP), 10–12, 30
Flaming, 63
Folder index, 44, 58
Folders, e-mail, 58, 61–62, 73–74
Fully Qualified Domain Name (FQDN), 24

G

Gopher, 7–10, 30
Gopherspace, 12
Graphical User Interface (GUI), 3, 30, 44, 86
Graphics, including in HTML documents, 106–107

H

Header, 23, 40
Hits, 100
    changing the number of, 110
Home page, 86
Hyperlink, 89, 95
Hypermedia, 86
Hypertext, 16, 86
Hypertext Markup Language (HTML), 16, 30, 91
Hypertext Transport Protocol (HTTP), 89, 91

I

In-line image, in Web pages, 106, 112
Information Superhighway, 16, 107
Internaut, 3
Internet, 1, 2, 20, 30, 103
    architecture, 22–24
    defined, 2
    evolution of 2, 3, 30
    logging on to, 26–28
    server, 17
Internet address, 24, 25, 46, 50, 88
Internet host, 12, 40
Internet layer, 22, 23, 24
Internet Protocol (IP), 21
IP address, 22, 23, 25, 30

J

Java, 93
Jumping, between Web documents, 85, 86

L

Link, 7, 86, 91
List owner, 63
Listproc, 63
Listserv, 63
Local Area Network (LAN), 17
Location text box, 88
Logging on, to a Telnet session, 28
Login ID, 19
Lurking, 63
Lycos, 100, 102, 103, 109, 112, 116–117
Lynx, 5, 6, 86, 114–121

M

Mailboxes, 40, 42, 44, 54, 61, 62, 68
Mail client, 44
Mail folder, 61, 73–74
Mailing list, 4–5, 62–64
    archives, 64
    digest option for, 64
    etiquette of, 63
    finding, 63
    moderated lists, 63
    subscribing to, 63–64, 68, 70, 75–76
    suspending mail from, 64
Mail server, 44
Majordomo, 63
Moderator, 63
Mosaic, 5, 86

N

Netscape, 5, 6, 85, 88–89
    bookmarks, 98
    e-mail in, 107, 113
    Go menu, 98
    Home button, 99

Images, 106
Preferences menu, 108, 113
Print command, 98
Query Results window, 108
Reload button, 108
Save command, 97
View History command, 98
Netscape Navigator. *See* Netscape
Network access layer, 22–23
News, 12
Newsgroup, 12, 14
Newsreader, 12
Nickname, 44, 46, 65–66
Nickname list, 60, 65–66

O

Offline, mail retrieval, 12
Open Location command, 89

P

Packet, 21, 22, 30
Password, 19, 30, 42, 55
  choosing, 42
Path, within URL, 88–89
Pine, 3, 4, 57–60
  deleting messages in, 59
  distribution lists in, 71–73
  exiting, 60
  folders in, 44, 45, 58, 73
  menus in, 57, 58
  replying to messages in, 59
  retrieving and reading mail in, 58
  subscribing to a mailing list using, 75–76
  using to send e-mail, 57–58
Posting, to newsgroups, 12
Post Office Protocol (POP), 44, 46
Progress bar, in Netscape, 108
Protocol, 10

Q

Query Results window, in Netscape, 108
Queries
  using a Web browser, 100–106, 108–111
  using Lynx, 117–119

R

Reload button, 108
Router, 21, 23, 44, 50
Routing table, 23

S

Search button, 100
Search engine, WWW, 7, 30, 86, 100–111
  search criteria, 100
Search form, 100, 110
Shell account, 55
Signature, 60, 66–68
Simple Mail Transfer Protocol (SMTP), 44, 46
Spider, 100
Stack, 22, 23, 30
Stop button, 96
Subscribing. *See* Mailing list, subscribing to
Sun Microsystems, 93
Surfing, 3, 94, 99
Suspend, 62, 64

T

TCP/IP protocol, 21–22, 23, 30
Telnet, 20, 115
Terminal, 19
Terminal session, 19
Thomas, U.S. Congress home page, 94–97
Thumbnail sketch, 107
Transmission Control Protocol (TCP), 21
Transport layer, 22, 24

U

Uniform Resource Locator (URL), 88–89, 91
Unix, 17, 19, 55
Upload, 44
Usenet, 12, 30
UserID, 42, 57
Username, 30, 31

V

Veronica, 12
Viewer, 107
Virtual, 14

W

Web browser, 5, 30, 86
WebCrawler, 103
Web documents, saving and printing, 92

Web server, 86
Web site, 7, 88
What's Cool, in Netscape, 95
Workstation, 17
World Wide Web (WWW), 5, 30, 85–122

Y

Yahoo, 89–92